The SEARCH *for*
SOCIAL
ENTREPRENEURSHIP

The SEARCH *for* SOCIAL ENTREPRENEURSHIP

PAUL C. LIGHT

BROOKINGS INSTITUTION PRESS
Washington, D.C.

ABOUT BROOKINGS

The Brookings Institution is a private nonprofit organization devoted to research, education, and publication on important issues of domestic and foreign policy. Its principal purpose is to bring the highest quality independent research and analysis to bear on current and emerging policy problems. Interpretations or conclusions in Brookings publications should be understood to be solely those of the authors.

Copyright © 2008
THE BROOKINGS INSTITUTION
1775 Massachusetts Avenue, N.W., Washington, D.C. 20036
www.brookings.edu

Library of Congress Cataloging-in-Publication data
Light, Paul Charles.
    The search for social entrepreneurship / Paul C. Light.
        p.   cm.
    Includes bibliographical references and index.
    Summary: "Outlines the debate on how to define social entrepreneurship, examining the four main components of social entrepreneurship: ideas, opportunities, organizations, and the entrepreneurs. Presents research on high-performing nonprofits, exploring how they differ across the four key components. Offers recommendations for future action and research in this burgeoning field"—Provided by publisher.
    ISBN 978-0-8157-5210-3 (cloth : alk. paper) — ISBN 978-0-8157-5211-0 (pbk. : alk. paper)
    1. Social entrepreneurship. 2. Nonprofit organizations—Management. I. Title.
HD60.L544 2008
658'.048—dc22   2008025541

9 8 7 6 5 4 3 2 1

The paper used in this publication meets minimum requirements of the American National Standard for Information Sciences—Permanence of Paper for Printed Library Materials: ANSI Z39.48-1992.

Typeset in Sabon with Myriad display

Composition by Cynthia Stock
Silver Spring, Maryland

Printed by R. R. Donnelley
Harrisonburg, Virginia

CONTENTS

Appendixes

PREFACE

Research on social entrepreneurship is finally catching up to its potential for supporting socially entrepreneurial activity in society as a whole. Drawn by increasing financial support and public interest, researchers are laying the foundation for a distinctive field of inquiry.

The increased research activity can be seen in a number of indicators, including the number of recent articles cited in the references at the end of this book. Many schools of business and public affairs have launched new training programs for nascent social entrepreneurs, which in turn have created demand for teaching cases and curriculum and which in turn again have created demand for rigorous research.

This demand curve is already producing results. Major journals have started to feature occasional articles and special issues on social entrepreneurship, the *Stanford Social Innovation Review* remains a faithful outlet for applied research, and three new volumes of research studies and cases have been released in the past year, one edited by Alex Nicholls of Oxford University's Saïd Business School; a second by Jane Wei-Skillern, James E. Austin, Herman Leonard, and Howard Stevenson of the Harvard Business School; and a third by Johanna Mair, Jeffrey Robinson, and Kai Hockerts of the IESE Business School at the University of Navarra.

The demand curve is also creating long needed dialogue about research opportunities and assumptions, some at star-studded conferences, some on interactive Internet platforms, and some in more intimate venues as researchers and entrepreneurs meet one on one. The curve is also driving the expansion of traditional research outlets, for example, the Social Science Research Network, which is now organizing and searching the growing inventory of social entrepreneurship research using a new taxonomy designed by Susan Davis of Ashoka.

This momentum is creating a fertile environment for attracting faculty to the study of social entrepreneurship, which Johanna Mair and Ignasi Martí described in 2006 as a "source of explanation, prediction, and delight." As the infrastructure of social entrepreneurship grows, so does the demand for applied research. It is a magnetic effect that often shapes a field of research—if you pick a compelling question and provide reasonable support, the researchers will come.

There are other reasons for the recent spike in research, not the least of which is the remarkable publicity surrounding Muhammad Yunus, who won the 2007 Nobel Peace Prize for his work with the Grameen Bank, one of the most studied and admired socially entrepreneurial efforts in the world. The spike is also driven by the exponential growth in the number of cases for study and the basic excitement surrounding the notion that intractable problems such as poverty, hunger, and disease can actually be solved. "On the most basic level," Roger Martin and Sally Osberg wrote in 2007, "there's something inherently interesting and appealing about entrepreneurs and the stories of why and how they do what they do."

Yet, as Martin and Osberg continue, "interest in social entrepreneurship transcends the phenomenon of popularity and fascination with people. Social entrepreneurship signals the imperative to drive social change, and it is that potential payoff, with its lasting, transformative benefit to society, that sets the field and its practitioners apart." The same might be said for researchers who study *social benefit organizations,* the term I use in this book as a substitute for *nonprofits* out of respect for Bill Drayton's plea that researchers stop using "non" terms in the field. As he wrote in 2007, "You cannot describe half of the world's operations by what they are not."[1]

The rest of this book will explore the recent spike in more detail, starting with what I believe to be a healthy debate about the definition of social entrepreneurship and ending with a discussion of a research project

1. Drayton (2007, p. 5)

designed to compare the characteristics of high-performing social benefit organizations engaged in socially innovative activity with their less
socially innovative high-performing peers. Drawing upon lessons learned
from the literatures on business and social entrepreneurship as well as a
survey of 131 highly, moderately, and not-too entrepreneurial social benefit organizations, this book is divided into seven chapters. (I use the
term *not-too entrepreneurial* throughout this book out of respect for the
high-performing organizations that focus most of their energies on delivery of basic services.)

The first chapter examines the current debate about the basic definition
of social entrepreneurship. Given the growing convergence about the goals
of socially entrepreneurial activity, this chapter discusses the need for
greater clarity about the underlying assumptions that shape the dialogues
about who becomes a social entrepreneur, what constitutes a socially
entrepreneurial idea, when socially entrepreneurial opportunities arise,
and where socially entrepreneurial activity occurs. Greater transparency
of these underlying assumptions is essential if we are to advance efforts to
distinguish social entrepreneurship from other forms of social action.

The second chapter compares new and existing organizations as
launch sites for socially entrepreneurial activity. The prevailing wisdom
in business and social entrepreneurship suggests that new, small organizations are the best location for changing the social equilibrium. However, there is also growing evidence that old, large organizations can be
just as successful in developing new ideas as their younger peers. The
growing research base on corporate entrepreneurship also suggests that
the development of new ideas need not occupy the entire organization.
The key to success is not the size or age of the organization so much as
the underlying culture needed for imagination.

The third chapter explores strategies for linking the four components
of social entrepreneurship: entrepreneurs, ideas, opportunities, and
organizations. The chapter introduces the notion that these components
can be treated as separate, yet interactive, components of social entrepreneurship. It then turns to the search for strategies that might increase
the chances that these components will succeed. As the literatures on
business and social entrepreneurship suggest, there is very little hard
research that shows a clear path through the ecosystem that surrounds
these four components.

The fourth chapter examines these two literatures in search of evidence
on the basic assumptions that should guide future research. Although the

knowledge base is relatively young, recent years have produced dozens of new insights on how entrepreneurs think and behave, why some ideas succeed when others fail, when opportunities open and close, and how organizations shape entrepreneurial success. To the extent possible, I focused my search on the period 2005 to 2008, which produced more than a third of the 230 articles and handful of books that formed the basis of my literature review, several of which involve studies of studies. All counted, this book is based on more than 500 studies. Scholars might call this a very informal meta-analysis in which a large body of research is distilled to its core findings.

The fifth chapter introduces my 2006 survey of socially entrepreneurial organizations. The first step in comparing highly, moderately, and not-too entrepreneurial organizations is to translate abstract definitions and assumptions into a usable framework for actually assigning organizations to categories. Because this process is highly subjective, readers are warned to consider the coding process as an illustrative approach for building larger samples of organizations for deeper statistical analysis. Even accepting the caveats, however, the chapter suggests that there may be more socially entrepreneurial activity in the social benefit sector than previously suggested.

The sixth chapter presents the results of my 2006 survey. In presenting the similarities and differences among the 131 highly, moderately, and not-too entrepreneurial organizations in my sample, the chapter asks how these organizations differ across the four components of social entrepreneurship. As the analysis suggests, highly entrepreneurial organizations are more alike than different from their less entrepreneurial peers—they have many of the attributes of high-performing organizations, as well as occasional vulnerabilities that perhaps are due to their lack of access to unrestricted revenue. Their great strength is their commitment to their vision, which is manifested at the very top of the organization in the continued involvement of their founders and is driven down through the organization. This strength also creates potential vulnerabilities as the highly entrepreneurial organizations occasionally ignore tools that might strengthen their organizations. Appendix C provides a comparison of the key trends, significant and suggestive, between the survey in 2006 and its predecessor in 2001.

The seventh and final chapter of this book offers an overview of this study and recommendations for future action. The chapter also asks how the study affects the underlying assumptions embedded in the definition of social entrepreneurship. Given the natural caveats regarding the depth of the available evidence, the chapter suggests that we all have considerable work ahead in sorting the true assumptions from the false. It also examines ways to improve the odds that social entrepreneurship might succeed by helping entrepreneurs survive the natural stresses of a vision-driven life, building ideas that have maximum potential impact, finding especially ripe opportunities for attacking the social equilibrium, and creating organizations that provide the kind of high performance needed for sustainable change.

Readers are cautioned that this book is designed to advance the conversation about social entrepreneurship, not present the definitive model of how to succeed. Although it contains findings that should be useful in framing future research, it is best viewed as a good faith effort to address differences across different levels of socially entrepreneurial activity. As such, readers should pay close attention to the caveats offered along the way and approach the study design as an illustration of how future research might separate what does matter from what does not to pattern-breaking change. And this is what the field appears to need most right now.

Readers should also note that the study deals more with *socially entrepreneurial activity* than with *social entrepreneurship,* a term that is sometimes reserved for social entrepreneurs who produce large-scale change in the prevailing social equilibrium. The question, of course, is what constitutes enough success to deserve accolades. Although readers can take solace in the fact that the field of business entrepreneurship also struggles with this question of success, the field of social entrepreneurship could easily collapse if it does not adopt a reasonable definition of success that might give entrepreneurs more hope that they can make a difference and researchers more opportunity to explore patterns in socially entrepreneurial activity.

At least for now, we might establish a scale of potential and actual success that allows for the kind of comparative research that can distinguish between what does and does not matter to outcomes. And we should also search for failures that offer lessons on barriers to success. If business entrepreneurship is analogous, the failures may outweigh the successes by margins of four or five to one.

Finally, readers should note that this book is built around my own research journey, which began in 2005 with a reasonably deep reading of the literature on social entrepreneurship. This reading produced my article in 2006 on the need for a more inclusive definition of terms in the *Stanford Social Innovation Review.* The journey continued in 2006 and 2007 with a much deeper reading of the business literature and the survey of 131 highly, moderately, and not-too entrepreneurial organizations. If this project is best described as a journey, this book is perhaps best taken as a kind of travel guide, and it reflects my own observations about social entrepreneurship as of early 2008. I have no doubt missed many important vistas in my journey, but I have enjoyed the trip more than I ever imagined I would.

ACKNOWLEDGMENTS

Just as social entrepreneurship cannot occur without a network of support, neither can books on social entrepreneurship. Luckily, I have been welcomed enthusiastically into the social entrepreneurship network and supported by a range of scholars, entrepreneurs, and funders who helped bring this book to fruition. Paul Brest, J. Gregory Dees, Cheryl Dorsey, Bill Drayton, Victoria Hale, Maria Otero, Russell Wheeler, and several anonymous reviewers helped make this book more sensible, while the Ewing Marion Kauffman Foundation and Jeffrey Skoll Foundation provided essential funding for the study.

I have learned a great deal in the three years I have spent on this project, much of it from my students and colleagues. My dean, Ellen Schall, has been ever protective of my time, while Carmen Rogers and Sara Wheeler-Smith have been ever available and dedicated at the helm of my research team. I must take full credit for all that I have written, but I am thankful that I have had such a warm embrace from those who share my interest in the development of a field called social entrepreneurship. I am also grateful that the Brookings Institution Press and its team have added so much to the quality of this book.

The SEARCH *for*
SOCIAL
ENTREPRENEURSHIP

CHAPTER ONE

 # DECLARING ASSUMPTIONS

Despite enormous enthusiasm for social entrepreneurship among a new generation of change makers, the field of social entrepreneurship is not yet a field per se. It does not have paths to tenure for its young professors, a growing inventory of quantitative data for its researchers, or a guaranteed source of private or government funding for its institutions. Its elder scholars are anything but elderly, or at least they or we think we are not, and its younger scholars have to balance their interest in social entrepreneurship against work in more respected fields.

Moreover, the field relies on case studies and storytelling for most of its findings, has few nationally recognized journals for its articles, and is still fighting to build a reputation for rigorous analysis. Not surprising, it is not clear that promising scholars will receive academic acclaim for their work. There are no awards for the best article or book of the year, few chaired professorships that might offer the financial protection for full-time focus, and little clamor for more research from social entrepreneurs themselves.

There are hopeful exceptions to this portrait, however. Several national foundations continue to invest heavily in research: Ashoka is creating intersections between research and practice, the Skoll Foundation continues to invite researchers to its annual world forum on social entrepreneurship, and scholars are still producing important insights for future validation. But for now, social entrepreneurship research is more a part-time commitment than a full-time pursuit.

Indeed, as a field of inquiry, the study of social entrepreneurship is barely past its infancy. As such, it resembles the early years of the study of business entrepreneurship. Despite its growth over the past three decades, one of the field's leading scholars, Murray Low, described the field in 2001 as a "catchall" for scholars who cannot agree on basic definitions. Comparing the definitions he found in major journals on business entrepreneurship, Low reported that the search for common themes nearly drove him mad.

> Our best efforts resulted in a six by twenty matrix, where one axis listed major subjects (new ventures, venture capital/angels, entrepreneurs, corporate venturing, small/family business, and "other"), and the other axis listed primary focus such as decision making, performance, gender geography, etc. . . . However, the most interesting finding was that we needed a 120-cell matrix to classify a total of 131 articles. While a more parsimonious classification scheme might have been possible, it seems clear that the boundaries of our field remain vague.[1]

This diversity has its advantages. "One can argue in favor of a field that is inclusive and eclectic," Low concluded. "In many ways, the broad range of subjects is the strength of our field. The primary criterion for becoming an entrepreneurship researcher is passion for the subject, not adherence to a paradigm. However, this inclusiveness and eclecticism is not free of cost."[2] If entrepreneurship wants to grow up into a legitimate academic field, it must be more disciplined.

Scott Shane reached the same conclusion in 2006: "Despite the high level of entrepreneurial activity in the world economy, and a corresponding focus of business schools on teaching in this area, scholarly research in entrepreneurship remains quite limited. Although the number of researchers who have investigated this phenomenon has increased in recent years, the quality of their theoretical and empirical contributions has been relatively poor, with few studies meeting the standards of leading academic journals."[3]

These frustrations reflect enduring differences across the academic disciplines. Economists tend to define entrepreneurship as a sweeping

1. Low (2001, p. 20).
2. Low (2001, p. 20).
3. Shane (2006, p. 155).

change in the prevailing economic equilibrium; political scientists tend to view it as part of the agenda-setting process that determines who gets what, when, where, and how from government; psychologists tend to look for evidence of basic motivations for achievement, autonomy, and affiliation; historians look for the seeds of broad social movements that have deep links to long-standing social and political injustice; and anthropologists search for social customs that might explain broad cultural patterns of innovation. Can geneticists be far behind in finding a DNA marker of entrepreneurial intent?

A BASIC AGREEMENT

Because the field of social entrepreneurship is so young, it is hardly surprising that many scholars might be confused about basic definitions. Writing in 2006 of the study of social entrepreneurship as that combination of "explanation, prediction, and delight," Johanna Mair and Ignasi Martí rightly concluded that the concept of social entrepreneurship is still poorly defined: "While complementary definitions, each focusing on different aspects of the phenomenon, are necessarily an impediment in the search for theory, we still do not have a comprehensive picture of the phenomenon and lack a clear understanding of how social entrepreneurship should be studied."[4]

As such, the term is very much like *leadership,* which James Phills calls "everything and nothing." Writing in 2005, he argued that this "mythical and mysterious" term is like a Rorschach test: "It can be whatever we want it to be, and that is part of its popular appeal. But at the same time, this conceptual ambiguity contributes to leadership's status as one of the most fragmented and disappointing bodies of research and knowledge in the field of management."[5]

The same holds for the study of social entrepreneurship. In 2006, for example, Jay Weerawardena and Gillian Sullivan Mort offered an inventory of at least 20 different definitions used in past research on social entrepreneurship. Noting the field's brief, fragmented history, the two authors concluded that researchers have yet to produce an evidence-based theoretical framework of what matters and does not matter to successful social entrepreneurship.

4. Mair and Martí (2006, p. 37).
5. Phills (2005, p. 47).

Notwithstanding this frustration, there is general consensus on the goal of social entrepreneurship. Having invented the term in the early 1980s, Bill Drayton has long argued that social entrepreneurship involves "large-scale systemic social change." According to Drayton, systemic change comes from individuals with a powerful, new system-changing idea; creativity in goal setting and problem solving; a driving ambition to achieve impact; total absorption in their work, "in sickness and in health"; the desire to change an entire system; and ethical fiber. As Drayton so eloquently summarized his definition in 2005, social entrepreneurs seek nothing less than a new world:

> The job of the social entrepreneur is to recognize when a part of society is not working and to solve the problem by changing the system, spreading solutions, and persuading entire societies to take new leaps. Social entrepreneurs are not content just to give a fish or to teach how to fish. They will not rest until they have revolutionized the fishing industry. Identifying and solving large-scale social problems requires social entrepreneurs because only entrepreneurs have the committed vision and inexhaustible determination to persist until they have transformed an entire system.[6]

Drayton's focus on systemic change has been echoed by leading scholars such as J. Gregory Dees. Writing in 1998, Dees defined social entrepreneurship as the production of social value by individuals with

> —a mission to create and sustain social value, as change agents in the social sector;
> —the relentless pursuit of new opportunities to serve that mission;
> —a commitment to a process of continuous innovation, adaptation, and learning;
> —the readiness to act boldly without being limited by resources currently in hand;
> —heightened accountability to the constituencies served and for the outcomes created.[7]

In turn, Dees's focus on sustaining social change underpins what Roger Martin and Sally Osberg labeled a "new, stable social equilibrium" in

6. Drayton (2002, p. 123).
7. Dees (1998, p. 4).

2007, while Dees's list of key entrepreneurial behaviors fits Martin and Osberg's inventory of the personal characteristics needed to persevere.[8]

The Drayton and Dees's definitions are strikingly similar, if only because both authors are deeply committed to describing a set of behaviors that Dees calls "exceptional." Largely through their work, most of us researchers have coalesced around the notion that social entrepreneurship must change the status quo by creating social value (Dees), systemic social change (Drayton), a new social equilibrium (Martin and Osberg), or pattern-breaking change (Light). All share the same meaning. There may still be strong disagreements about the underlying assumptions about social entrepreneurship, but not about its basic goal.

This agreement helps to distinguish social entrepreneurship from social enterprise and social capitalism. For many years, the terms were used interchangeably to describe revenue-generating activity on behalf of a social mission. But as much as social entrepreneurship might benefit from social enterprise, social entrepreneurship has an entirely different goal. Whereas social entrepreneurship seeks tipping points for innovation and change, social enterprise seeks profits for reinvestment and growth. As Dees wrote of the confusion in 2003,

> Far too many people still think of social entrepreneurship in terms of nonprofits generating earned income. This is a dangerously narrow view. It shifts attention away from the ultimate goal of any self-respecting social entrepreneur, namely social impact, and focuses it on one particular method of generating resources. Earned income is only a means to a social end, and it is not always the best means.[9]

This debate now seems settled, although Janelle Kerlin reported in 2006 that the two terms are still used interchangeably in Europe.

Many other debates remain open, however. Once again, Low's analysis is well worth reading as a cautionary tale for the future of social entrepreneurship:

> Why does entrepreneurship as an academic field receive so much attention but so little respect? Is it because entrepreneurship researchers are not smart enough? Or like the subject they study, are they too action-oriented to commit to scholarly demands? Does the

8. Martin and Osberg (2007, p. 39).
9. Dees (2003, p. 1).

problem lie with a larger academy that is parochial, conservative, and overly critical? Or is it simply that the field is still too young?

The right answer is "none of the above." I believe the correct answer lies in the nature of the phenomenon. The strong student interest in entrepreneurship is in turn driven by fundamental changes in the business environment. Mega-trends such as the development of new information technologies, genetics, globalization, and accelerated financial markets have increased the need for speed, innovation, and collaboration. As a consequence, the determinants of business success and the opportunities for start-ups have changed. In the "new" economy, there is an increased need for "entrepreneurial" thinking that is fast, flexible, opportunity-driven, and creative with respect to the acquisition of resources and the management of risk.

And herein lies the opportunity and the potential pitfall for entrepreneurship as an academic field. The opportunity is to provide models and concepts to explain and facilitate commerce in the new economy. The potential pitfall is that this task is too broad and unfocused to be achievable.[10]

It is a call that cannot be met without a much deeper inquiry about the basic definition and assumptions that propel the field of social entrepreneurship forward.

THE FOUR COMPONENTS OF SOCIAL ENTREPRENEURSHIP

My assumptions about social entrepreneurship fall into four broad components: entrepreneurs, ideas, opportunities, and organizations. These four components not only help organize the rapidly growing literatures on business entrepreneurship, they clarify the search for strategies that might help entrepreneurs develop and launch better ideas, discover opportunities, and create more creative organizations.

There is plenty of evidence that social entrepreneurship involves more than an entrepreneur and a pattern-breaking idea. The only problem, if it is a problem at all, is that the field as a whole has yet to decide which components matter most, or how individual dispositions vary with organizational context.

10. Low (2001, p. 18).

Entrepreneurs

Entrepreneurs are the first component of social entrepreneurship and can be found in every definition I read for this book. However, some definitions give entrepreneurs greater prominence than others. Although Drayton argues that there is no entrepreneur without a powerful, system-changing idea that seeks widespread impact, there is no chance of success without the talent, creativity, and entrepreneurial intent of the individual. As he wrote in 2005, "these people are compelled to change the whole society. From childhood, an entrepreneur intuitively seeks out an area of interest, for example, health, and then begins the long search for an idea that will be his or her vehicle for leaving a scratch on history."[11]

This focus on entrepreneurs inevitably leads the search for traits and characteristics that might separate these gifted individuals from the rest of society. According to Drayton, "entrepreneurs are easy to spot long before they have made their mark. They are married to their vision—and will stick with it for decades if needed. They are equally focused on the 'how to' questions. They ask themselves: How do I get from here to my goal fifteen years from now? How do the pieces fit together? How do I solve this and the next problem?"[12] Thus does the "democratic revolution" occur.

Entrepreneurs also show deeper qualities, Drayton stated:

What qualities define an effective social entrepreneur? First, the person must be creative in both goal setting and problem solving. Second—and this is the toughest screen—is entrepreneurial quality. This is not leadership, or the ability to administer, or the ability to get things done. The driving force here is the fact that such a person is emotionally, deeply committed to making change throughout the whole of society. Once one understands that this commitment itself is the driving force, then everything else follows. The final quality essential to success as a social entrepreneur is ethical fiber. People will not make significant changes in their lives if they do not trust the person asking them to do so.[13]

11. Drayton (2005, p. 2).
12. Drayton (2005, p. 2).
13. Drayton (2005, p. 3); for a more detailed description of Ashoka's fellowship selection process, see Sen (2007).

Ideas

Ideas are the second component of social entrepreneurship, and they also are found in all of the definitions I have collected. Comparing business and social entrepreneurship in 2007, Martin and Osberg argued that the critical difference between the two is the "value proposition." Unlike business entrepreneurs who focus on serving markets that can afford a new product or service, social entrepreneurs seek no profit for their investors or themselves.

> Instead, the social entrepreneur aims for value in the form of large-scale, transformational benefit that accrues either to a significant segment of society or to society at large. Unlike the entrepreneurial value proposition that assumes a market that can pay for innovation, and may even provide substantial upside for investors, the social entrepreneur's value proposition targets an under-served, neglected, or highly disadvantaged population that lacks the financial means or political clout to achieve the transformative benefit on its own.[14]

Entrepreneurs clearly play a significant role in transformational change, but only when they are absolutely committed to the idea. Indeed, writing in 2003, Martin warned the social benefit sector to avoid the "heroic leadership trap."

> Take-charge leadership misapplied not only fails to inspire and engage, it produces passivity and alienation. And this is true not only in the for-profit and government sectors. When nonprofit leaders assume "heroic" responsibility for making critical choices, when their reaction to problems is to go it alone, work harder, and do more—with no collaboration or sharing of leadership—their "heroism" is often their undoing.[15]

Opportunities

Opportunities are the third component of social entrepreneurship, and they are at the center of most, but not all, of the definitions I reviewed over the past two years. Viewed as a moment of possibility, opportunities are sometimes taken as a Peter Pan phenomenon—that is, if you believe you can fly, you will fly.

---

14. Martin and Osberg (2007, pp. 34–35).
15. Martin (2003, p. 36).

Writing in 1998, Dees offered a very different view. Like Drayton, Dees reserved a significant role for the entrepreneur as the starting point of change. However, Dees also argued that a powerful vision is not enough to create disequilibrium. Opportunities must be identified and exploited. Indeed, entrepreneurs are defined in part by their ability to recognize and "relentlessly" pursue new opportunities. "Where others see problems, social entrepreneurs see opportunity," he wrote. "They are not simply driven by the perception of a social need or by their compassion. Rather they have a vision of how to achieve improvement and they are determined to make their vision work. They are persistent."[16]

Opportunities also provide resources and the potential for collaboration, which leads to Dees's notion that social entrepreneurs work around the obstacles embedded in an opportunity.

> Social entrepreneurs do not let their own limited resources keep them from pursuing their visions. They are skilled at doing more with less and at attracting resources from others. They use scarce resources efficiently, and they leverage their limited resources by drawing in partners and collaborating with others. They explore all resource options, from pure philanthropy to the commercial methods of the business sector. They are not bound by sector norms or traditions. They develop resource strategies that are likely to support and reinforce their social missions. They take calculated risks and manage the downside, so as to reduce the harm that will result from failure. They understand the risk tolerances of their stakeholders and use this to spread the risk to those who are better prepared to accept it.[17]

For Dees, social value is always the ultimate goal. It is why social entrepreneurs pursue opportunities in the first place, learn and adapt as they proceed, and act boldly without regard to resources. And it is why they are called to action in the first place. Nevertheless, they could not act without the ability to recognize opportunity when it arises.

Organizations

Organizations are the fourth component of social entrepreneurship but were often an afterthought in the definitions I read. Indeed, many definitions focused on organization and management as adversaries of change.

16. Dees (1998, p. 4).
17. Dees (1998, p. 5).

James Austin, Howard Stevenson, and Jane Wei-Skillern took a neutral stance about organizations and social entrepreneurship in 2006. Writing about the opportunity, people, capital, and context involved in creating social value, the three authors noted the importance of organizational alignment in achieving results:

> Remaining attuned to how contextual changes can affect the opportunity and the human- and financial-resource environment causing the need for realignment is a critical skill for the social entrepreneur. Furthermore, practitioners should remain cognizant of a unique characteristic of the operating context, namely, that the societal demand for social-value creation is enormous. This creates a plethora of opportunities for social entrepreneurs and a concomitant ever-present temptation to address more and more of them.[18]

Although organizations impose clear operating constraints, they also provide essential capacity. As Austin, Stevenson, and Wei-Skillern continued, the challenge is to determine how much the organization can achieve with limited resources: "Seeking to address a very broad set of issues with very limited human and financial resources, may actually result in low social impact because the organization's resources are spread too thin." Simply put, organizations cannot be ignored as a component of successful social entrepreneurship and a potential source of failure.

Austin, Stevenson, and Wei-Skillern clearly understood the point— their twenty-two-page article in *Entrepreneurship Theory and Practice* used the words *organization* and *organization*s 127 times and the words *entrepreneur* and *entrepreneurs* 109 times.

Combining Components

As the reader shall see, these four components do not drift aimlessly through what Dees accurately described in 2008 as the ecosystem of social entrepreneurship. Rather, they come together on occasion in a strategy for change. Some strategies emphasize the entrepreneur's dispositions and traits, while others focus on the context created by organizations, and still others emphasize ideas and opportunities as central ingredients that are shaped and noticed by entrepreneurs and organizations.

---

18. Austin, Stevenson, and Wei-Skillern (2006, pp. 17–18).

As the reader shall also see, the key to success may be in assembling the four components together to take advantage of a specific opportunity, develop a particular idea, use an entrepreneur's special skills, or focus energy within an organization. As such, creating social entrepreneurship may be very much like solving a jigsaw puzzle. Some will start at the corners, others at the center, and still others with a color. But it is unlikely that the puzzle can be solved without some combination of all approaches, especially as the number of pieces increases.

EXPLORING DEFINITIONS

Researchers still have plenty of work to do on the components of social entrepreneurship, however. Much as we may agree that social entrepreneurship involves a search for social value, there are sharp disagreements about the characteristics of social entrepreneurs, the nature of socially entrepreneurial ideas, the number and timing of socially entrepreneurial opportunities, and the size and shape of socially entrepreneurial organizations.

Thus the challenge is no longer in specifying the goal of social entrepreneurship but in thickening the understanding about who (the entrepreneur), what (the idea), when (the opportunity), and where (the organization) shape the effort to both disturb and replace the social equilibrium. Some definitions are more inclusive, while others are more exclusive. The choice of one or the other has obvious implications for researchers, not the least of which is the estimated amount of social entrepreneurship at any given point in time. Those who use inclusive definitions invariably find more social entrepreneurship in more places than those who use exclusive definitions, thereby creating a deep inventory of examples, while those who use exclusive definitions find fewer entrepreneurs and less socially entrepreneurial activity than those who use inclusive definitions, thereby reducing the inventory of success stories to a very familiar few that almost always seem to win the national awards.

An Inclusive Definition

My definition of social entrepreneurship clearly allows more individuals, ideas, opportunities, and organizations into the tent. As I wrote in the Fall 2006 issue of *Stanford Social Innovation Review,* the question is not whether social entrepreneurs exist—that much is certain in the most cursory sampling of the Ashoka and Echoing Green fellowship winners from recent years, most notably Muhammad Yunus.[19]

Rather, the question is whether the field is too exclusive for its own good. By defining social entrepreneurship more by the characteristics of the individual entrepreneurs who forge social value through their work, I wrote that "the field may have excluded large numbers of individuals and entities that are equally deserving of the support, networking, and training now reserved for individuals who meet both the current definitional tests of a social entrepreneur and the ever-growing list of exemplars."[20]

Hence, my 2006 definition of social entrepreneurship was more inclusive. As I wrote, social entrepreneurship is *an effort by an individual, group, network, organization, or alliance of organizations that seeks sustainable, large-scale change through pattern-breaking ideas in what governments, nonprofits, and businesses do to address significant social problems*. Between 2006 and 2008, I shortened the definition to focus more precisely on *efforts to solve intractable social problems through pattern-breaking change,* thereby reserving the question about who acts as an entrepreneur and where entrepreneurial activity occurs for further research.

My old definition focused on the kind of systemic change that Martin and Osberg highlighted as essential for creating a new social equilibrium. But I also embraced a set of underlying assumptions that increased my definition's inclusiveness, most notably the notion that entrepreneurs do not always invent alone. Instead, social entrepreneurship can come from small groups or teams of individuals, from organizations, networks, or even communities that band together to create pattern-breaking change. By challenging the notion that socially entrepreneurial activity is the product of a 24/7 entrepreneur who perseveres against the odds, my old definition provided a bigger tent for social entrepreneurship.

My old definition also embraced the possibility that the quantity of socially entrepreneurial activities varies across individuals and organizations, meaning that organizations might be somewhat or moderately socially entrepreneurial, while still meeting a more traditional charitable mission. My definition also focused on the notion that some individuals and organizations might even stop their socially entrepreneurial activities

19. Light (2006, p. 48).
20. Light (2006, p. 47).

to concentrate on strengthening their operations or because of stall points, funding crises, or leadership transitions.

Not surprising, perhaps, given the field's focus on a relatively small number of social entrepreneurs, my definition provoked intense reactions within the field, especially given my assumption that social entrepreneurs might not be as rare as imagined. In questioning the "cult of personality" that surrounds charismatic entrepreneurs, I had implied that individuals were somehow unimportant to social entrepreneurship.

Drayton tried to put this debate to rest in his 2007 letter to the editor of the *Stanford Social Innovation Review.* Social entrepreneurship had to come from individuals, he wrote, in part because social entrepreneurs are unique: "Leading social entrepreneurs are remarkable. They are doing something enormously important and difficult—something that, in many ways is critical for society and, in its nature, demands much of an entrepreneur's life. These strong and often lonely human beings require and deserve our long-term understanding, loyalty, and respect."[21]

Drayton also argued that social entrepreneurs follow a predictable path into action:

Entrepreneurs capable of making profound pattern changes are rare and have a well-understood and strikingly coherent, consistent life history. After a long apprenticeship in established institutions, there comes a time when the entrepreneur is no longer able to grow or move his or her ideas ahead. In most cases, he or she must build new institutions to serve an idea that cuts across the old organizational lines, thought patterns, and disciplines.[22]

Drayton was hardly the only reader to challenge my assumptions. John Zurick, the author of the forthcoming *The Maverick's Guide to Social Entrepreneurship,* took issue with my assumption that entrepreneurship might come from pairs, teams, and networks:

If it did, we would have to cook up a new term for the individuals who are first to reach beyond their grasps, the individuals for whom the initial vision of social value is clear in finite detail, who can communicate that vision in ways that enable other people to see it just as clearly, who can inspire people to form the ranks that will

21. Drayton (2007, p. 5).
22. Drayton (2007, p. 5)

work to realize the vision, the individuals who get back up every time they are knocked down, who bring resources to bear where others see only bare bones, and who never quit and never lose sight of the greater good. These individuals are social entrepreneurs.[23]

Finally, the Manhattan Institute for Policy Research rejected my assumption that advocacy can be part of social entrepreneurship. Writing of the institute's annual award program, Howard Husock noted that "we have excluded advocacy from our criteria for social entrepreneurship, insisting, instead, that the provision of tangible services be the *sine qua non* of the field. In keeping with our emphasis on originality of approach, we exclude those who build organizations around government contracts as well."[24]

The challenges are generally resolvable through the kind of careful reading and research that I like to think underpins this book. That literature strongly suggests, for example, that Drayton was mostly right about the shared life experiences of social entrepreneurs, at least in their choice of location. As Erik Stam wrote in a 2007 article titled "Why Butterflies Don't Leave," most start-ups remain firmly embedded in the communities in which they were founded, largely because most entrepreneurs develop very similar networks that can only be found in their communities. However, they start to leave as they spot opportunities for starting their own firms, often using their new experiences to shape expansion strategies and new networks that exist far from home.

My more inclusive view of social entrepreneurship almost certainly reflects my bias as an educator. As I have argued before, the amount of social entrepreneurship can be increased by supporting more potential entrepreneurs as they cross over to actual engagement.

This is the core belief at New York University's Robert F. Wagner School of Public Service, which houses the Catherine B. Reynolds graduate and undergraduate fellows program on social entrepreneurship. The effort is based on the belief that social entrepreneurs can be identified early in their careers and given the skills and coaching to engage in socially entrepreneurial activity as soon as possible. Some will start new ventures, others will join entrepreneurial organizations, and still others will engage whole communities in the search for change.

23. Zurick (2007, p. 4)
24. Husock (2007, p. 6).

An Exclusive Definition

To the extent that my old definition was designed to provoke debate about the true amount of socially entrepreneurial activity, it accomplished its task. I received dozens of e-mails and comments about the basic definition and its underlying assumptions, many of which argued that I was diluting the true meaning of entrepreneurship.

Writing in 2007 of the need to protect social entrepreneurship from being used to describe "all manner of socially beneficial activities," Martin and Osberg made the case that inclusiveness could be a good thing: "If plenty of resources are pouring into the social sector, and if many causes that otherwise would not get sufficient funding now get support because they are regarded as social entrepreneurships, then it may be fine to have a loose definition. We are inclined to argue, however, that this is a flawed assumption and a precarious stance."

Yet Martin and Osberg suggested that the concept of social entrepreneurship must be protected. "If the promise is not fulfilled because too many 'nonentrepreneurial' efforts are included in the definition, then social entrepreneurship will fall into disrepute, and the kernel of true social entrepreneurship will be lost. Because of this danger, we believe that we need a much sharper definition of social entrepreneurship, one that enables us to determine the extent to which an activity is and is not 'in the tent.'"[25] An exclusive definition would not only allow supporters to concentrate on building and strengthening a nascent field, it would protect social entrepreneurship against the cynics who already discount social innovation as a way to change the status quo.

Martin and Osberg took an important step toward this sharper definition by focusing on the social equilibrium. According to Martin and Osberg's definition, social entrepreneurship starts with "an unfortunate but stable equilibrium that causes the exclusion, marginalization, or suffering of a segment of humanity;" engages an individual "who brings to bear on this situation his or her inspiration, direct action, creativity, courage, and fortitude;" and ends with the ultimate "establishment of a new stable equilibrium that secures permanent benefit for the targeted group and society at large."

Defined as such, social entrepreneurship involves a target (the status quo), an actor (an individual or a pair with inspiration, courage, and so forth), and an outcome (a new stable equilibrium that secures permanent

25. Martin and Osberg (2007, p. 30).

benefits). It also involves an idea for changing the status quo, an opportunity for taking action, and an organization.

Martin and Osberg drew upon Joseph Schumpeter's 1934 description of business entrepreneurship as a form of "creative destruction" that permanently disturbs the prevailing economic equilibrium. As such, it provides more depth to the search for a more precise definition of change. But Martin and Osberg's definition still leaves plenty of room for further debate about what kinds of activities actually constitute social entrepreneurship, a debate that Martin and Osberg addressed in their notion that social services and activism can coexist with social entrepreneurship in hybrid forms.

MAKING ASSUMPTIONS

My old definition of social entrepreneurship has occasionally been juxtaposed against Martin and Osberg's to illustrate the conflict between inclusive and exclusive definitions. At least that is how the editors of the *Stanford Social Innovation Review* introduced the Martin and Osberg piece in 2007. Despite the focus on differences, both definitions share common ground, not the least of which is the notion that entrepreneurship involves pattern-breaking change.

More important, both definitions also leave considerable room for debate about just where to draw boundaries about who drives social entrepreneurship, what changing the equilibrium actually means, when it is most likely to occur, and where it is housed. For one example, my 2006 definition of social entrepreneurs assumes that the entrepreneur is often plural, coming in pairs, teams, networks, alliances, or communities to create socially entrepreneurial ideas. For another example, my definition allows for the use of "old stuff in new ways" as one path to pattern-breaking change, while most definitions focus on new ideas and new organizations. Yet, even here, the definitions start with the same goal: to change the social equilibrium.

An Inventory of Assumptions

There are still issues to be resolved in the search for social entrepreneurship, however, including an effort to describe the assumptions that underpin many of the contemporary definitions that guide us. These assumptions cover the four basic components of social entrepreneurship discussed earlier in this chapter: the entrepreneurs who pursue the change, the ideas for change itself, the opportunities to disrupt the prevailing equilibrium, and the organizations that house the effort.

Readers are forewarned that my list of assumptions emerged from my forays into the literature as I began my research on social entrepreneurship in 2005 and 2006. These assumptions were drawn mostly from the literature on social entrepreneurship, which was still struggling with basic definitions at the time. They were also collected from the twenty-six highly innovative Minnesota organizations profiled in my 1998 book *Sustaining Innovation,* as well as my ongoing case studies of high-performing social benefit organizations. As such, the following discussion reflects a great deal of reading between the lines and no doubt misses many important nuances in the field.

Nevertheless, as box 1-1 suggests, I was able to discern at least forty assumptions that underpin the debate about how to define social entrepreneurship. Making these assumptions more transparent can only advance the conversation about who does what, when, and where to change the social equilibrium. In turn, each assumption provides an opportunity for deeper research on what matters most to high-impact change. Although I do not claim that these are the only assumptions about social entrepreneurship, they are the ones that most shaped my thinking about my exclusive approach to the term.

True or False?

The best way to embrace these and other questions is to make our assumptions more visible in drawing inferences about each definition. To date, we tend to make assumptions that are based on a small number of case studies, a limited research base, and intuition, all of which influenced my view of social entrepreneurship in 2006. Forced to assign a *true* or *false* to each assumption, I created a particularly inclusive definition of social entrepreneurship. Box 1-2 shows the results.

If one assumes that true assumptions lead toward exclusiveness and false assumptions toward inclusiveness, box 1-2 shows just how far from center I was when I began this study in 2005. Just six assumptions lean toward the more exclusive definition that Martin and Osberg recommended, while thirty-four lean toward the more inclusive definition that I preferred. As discussed later in this book, my assumptions changed between 2006 and 2008, moving me from a fully inclusive approach to a more balanced view of entrepreneurial activity.

FIGURE 1-1. A Continuum of Assumptions

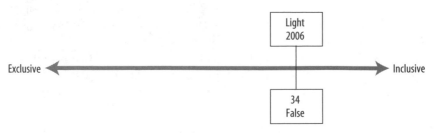

Martin and Osberg would almost certainly declare more of the 40 assumptions to be true, especially since they argue that social entrepreneurship is only achieved in final success. They also tend to see entrepreneurs as very different from other high achievers; they worry about including partial success in their definition of social entrepreneurship; they clearly believe that entrepreneurs need special skills to recognize and seize opportunities; and they would maintain that organizations must commit themselves completely to their vision if they are to change the social equilibrium.

As already noted, this divergence is healthy for the field, if only for pushing early researchers, investors, and social entrepreneurs toward testing the vulnerabilities in their definitions. Having agreed on the purpose of social entrepreneurship, which is to change the prevailing social equilibrium, researchers can work through the assumptions that are often hidden from view as they engage in aggressive empirical work. Researchers can also test the validity of their own assumptions by winnowing the list or expanding it. Figure 1-1 shows how my list of underlying assumptions forms a continuum between exclusivity and inclusivity.

Two factors reflected my decision to reject many of the assumptions that underpin an exclusive definition of social entrepreneurship. First, my prior work on innovation focused on a sample of existing organizations. If high rates of innovation were possible in my *Sustaining Innovation* cases, perhaps high rates of social entrepreneurship might be possible in other existing organizations, too.

Second, some of my decisions reflected my admittedly shallow reading of the literatures on business entrepreneurship in the two years preceding my 2006 article in the *Stanford Social Innovation Review,* which often led me to use false as the default position for assumptions that I could not prove. I knew the literature on social entrepreneurship when I began this study but was much less familiar with the literature on business entrepreneurship, nor did I have the benefit of the survey presented later in this book. Lacking evidence that entrepreneurs think differently from other high achievers, for example, I assigned a false to the assumption.

The further I explored the literature, however, the more the assumption seemed true, although it was hard to find many studies that actually compared entrepreneurs against their nonentrepreneurial peers. The most interesting study actually made the case that entrepreneurs are more like mountain climbers than not! According to Dave Valliere and Norm O'Reilly's 2007 study of a matched set of mountaineers and entrepreneurs, both groups share lofty goals (no pun intended), individualistic efforts, risky and highly uncertain environments, and severe resource constraints, which can be defined as a "mountaineering personality."

> There are many similarities in the tasks and challenges faced by entrepreneurs, particularly the corresponding similarities in the psychological traits of the individuals who pursue these paths. Entrepreneurs and mountaineers share a high level of flexibility, which helps them to deal with dynamic environments and high levels of uncertainty. They also share elevated psychosis, which helps them to persevere despite the challenges and setbacks they encounter along the way. Entrepreneurs and mountaineers share high levels of extroversion, which is manifested as assertiveness, venturesomeness, risk taking, ambition and leadership. They also share low levels of neuroticism, which help them to remain calm, stable and confident, and to demonstrate low anxiety and low reactivity to stress and criticism.[26]

At the same, Valliere and O'Reilly note that mountaineers are tougher than entrepreneurs and take greater risks but are less agreeable and have a degree of conscientiousness that mitigates their psychosis. Entrepreneurs who wonder whether they might actually be psychotic can take comfort in the relatively small samples of respondents in the study. And even if they are psychotic, at least they are not neurotic.

Many researchers had written about what makes social entrepreneurs unique, for example, but I saw little actual evidence in 2006 proving that these differences actually existed. Nor was there extensive research on

---

26. Valliere and O'Reilly (2007, p. 298).

how these differences might shape socially entrepreneurial action beyond the need for alertness and agility. I also saw plenty of persuasive theory about how social entrepreneurs differ from other high achievers, how socially entrepreneurial ideas differ from traditional social services and advocacy, why opportunities call some to action and not others, and what kinds of organizations are needed to bring ideas to fruition.

CONCLUSION

The problem with my more inclusive definition of social entrepreneurship is clear: suddenly, social entrepreneurship can be found almost everywhere. Although award and fellowship programs might yield long lists of names and organizations for possible study, such lists would not contain the "sometime entrepreneurs" or "on hold entrepreneurs" out there. Similarly, case studies might miss the once moribund organizations that have suddenly rediscovered themselves or the self-effacing entrepreneurs who prefer to remain anonymous.

Instead of searching for the proverbial needle in the haystack, my assumptions suggest that there are needles almost everywhere, thereby raising hopes that there are more social entrepreneurs that the field has yet to discover. Some of these entrepreneurs may need little more than a push to make the leap of faith into socially entrepreneurial activity. Others may need a more substantial boost in visibility and financial support to move through scale-up and sustained impact. And still others may be doing well as they are.

My assumptions suggest that any organization can produce entrepreneurial activity at least once, whether by hiring a heroic entrepreneur or by driving fear downward to the front lines. But heroes wear out and fear cannot be a motivator for long, especially in the absence of the participation, autonomy, and shared goals that we find in most innovating organizations. Thus the much greater challenge is to produce socially entrepreneurial activity twice, thrice, and more—that is, to create socially entrepreneurial activity as a natural act. As I have learned in my past research, natural innovation requires visionary leaders. But I have also learned that innovating organizations must create and sustain a socially entrepreneurial culture, which involves managerial strategies that visionary social entrepreneurs sometimes ignore.

If this culture can be created in existing organizations, the odds of socially entrepreneurial activity will surely rise from just one per ten million, as Drayton estimates, to, say, one per ten thousand, per one thousand, or even per one hundred. Just imagine what the world might look like then.

The challenge is to avoid assumptions that make social entrepreneurship just another word that gets bandied about in funding proposals and niche building. Other terms such as innovation have gone that route and may never be rescued from overuse. At the same time, social entrepreneurship should not be defined so narrowly that it becomes the province of the special few that crowd out potential support and assistance for individuals and entities that are just as special but less well known.

In the end, the research goal should be to uncover the factors that make social entrepreneurship a reality. If these factors suggest that social entrepreneurship is truly the work of a rare breed that must struggle mightily to succeed, so be it. At least the conclusion would yield insights on how to make the struggle easier. If, however, the research suggests that social entrepreneurship can be a more natural act by a much larger number of individuals and entities, all the better. Then the field can move forward to create the conditions under which social entrepreneurship can flourish and work its will on solving the great intractable problems of our times.

BOX 1-1. Basic Assumptions about Social Entrepreneurship

Entrepreneurs

1. *Social entrepreneurs work alone.* Some definitions assume that social entrepreneurs are lonely individuals who develop their ideas in isolation, while others assume that partners, teams, networks, alliances, and other groups of individuals can also innovate. A focus on the lone entrepreneur creates a more exclusive definition.

2. *Social entrepreneurs rarely rest.* Some definitions assume that entrepreneurs must be willing to sacrifice everything in a 24/7 pursuit of change, while others assume that entrepreneurs can maintain a more balanced life and still succeed. The emphasis on the heroic struggle against the odds reinforces a more exclusive, entrepreneur-centered definition that excludes less dramatic personae from consideration.

3. *Social entrepreneurs think differently from other high achievers.* Some definitions assume that social entrepreneurs bring a distinctive set of personality and behavioral characteristics to their engagement, while others maintain that entrepreneurs are simply better at recognizing or creating opportunities. The need for a special way of thinking produces a more exclusive definition.

4. *Social entrepreneurs think alike among themselves.* Some definitions assume that globalization and basic entrepreneurial qualities create a common thinking pattern among almost all entrepreneurs, while other definitions allow for variations in thinking across demographic groups and cultures. A focus on a distinct entrepreneurial quality creates a more exclusive definition.

5. *Social entrepreneurs persevere against all odds.* Some definitions assume that social entrepreneurs persevere in spite of sometimes insurmountable obstacles to their success, while others assume that entrepreneurs are no more likely to continue their pursuits than other high achievers. The focus on unrelenting faith being at the center of action is part of a more exclusive definition.

6. *Social entrepreneurs take greater risks.* Some definitions assume that social entrepreneurs are willing to take higher risks than their less entrepreneurial peers, in part because of greater personal optimism and efficacy, while others assume that social entrepreneurs are just as risk averse as any human being. The emphasis on a higher tolerance for risk creates a more exclusive definition.

7. *Social entrepreneurs share common histories.* Some definitions assume that social entrepreneurs share a similar set of work and life experiences that lead to entrepreneurship later in their career, while others

assume that there is no predictable path into social entrepreneurship. The focus on a single path to entrepreneurship generates a more exclusive definition.

8. *Social entrepreneurs are rare.* Some definitions assume that the number of actual social entrepreneurs is exceedingly low, while others assume that the number of actual entrepreneurs is much higher. The belief that entrepreneurs are rare supports a much more exclusive definition.

9. *Social entrepreneurs stay involved.* Some definitions assume that social entrepreneurs stay with their ideas until they achieve sustainable impact, while others suggest that they let go easily. The notion that entrepreneurs stay involved produces a more exclusive definition.

10. *Social entrepreneurs share "one best strategy" for success.* Some definitions assume that there is one best approach to creating change, even if it has not yet been found, while others assume that strategies vary greatly with the nature of the entrepreneur, idea, opportunity, and organization. The belief in a single strategy is part of a more exclusive definition.

Ideas

1. *Socially entrepreneurial ideas try to change the world.* Some definitions assume that social entrepreneurship only exists among ideas that aim for national, if not global change, while others assume that ideas can earn the distinction by seeking change in a city, small community, or neighborhood, whether urban or rural. The focus on sweeping change narrows to a more exclusive definition.

2. *Socially entrepreneurial ideas are radical.* Some definitions assume that ideas must be radical "new combinations" that challenge the prevailing wisdom, while other definitions assume that social entrepreneurship can exist in the expansion or more efficient application of existing models. The need for pure innovation creates a more exclusive definition.

3. *Socially entrepreneurial ideas are surprising.* Some definitions assume that entrepreneurial ideas have never been seen before, while others assume that entrepreneurial ideas are both novel and familiar. The call for surprising, completely new ideas underpins a more exclusive definition.

4. *Socially entrepreneurial ideas are complex.* Some definitions assume that socially entrepreneurial ideas must be complex to be effective, while others assume that simplicity is no barrier to change. A focus on complexity creates a more exclusive definition.

(continued)

BOX 1-1 *(continued)*

5. *Socially entrepreneurial ideas must grow to succeed.* Some definitions assume that entrepreneurial ideas start small but must grow, or scale, to their maximum reach, while others assume that entrepreneurial ideas can remain small and still disrupt the equilibrium, especially when reproduced through replication and dissemination. The requirement for maximum scale is central to a more exclusive definition.

6. *Socially entrepreneurial ideas focus on programs, not process.* Some definitions assume that entrepreneurial ideas must alter "what" the social equilibrium delivers by way of programs, while others also include ideas that focus on changes in "how" the social equilibrium delivers by way of process, including immense scale-up of existing innovations. The focus on program change alone underscores a more exclusive definition.

7. *Socially entrepreneurial ideas rarely change from inception.* Some definitions assume that the core of an idea is relatively fixed from the beginning, while others assume that ideas constantly evolve through learning and adaptation. The focus on a fixed idea from the start suggests a more exclusive definition.

8. *Socially entrepreneurial ideas are pure.* Some definitions assume that socially entrepreneurial ideas must avoid advocacy and social services, while others assume that hybrid models that include advocacy and social services can contribute both to the development and ultimate success of a new idea. The emphasis on pure innovation produces a more exclusive definition.

9. *Socially entrepreneurial ideas provoke backlash.* Some definitions assume that new ideas produce intense resistance from the social equilibrium, while others assume that ideas move forward with little notice until they succeed. The notion that the equilibrium fights back produces a more exclusive definition.

10. *Socially entrepreneurial ideas produce immediate results.* Some definitions assume that ideas must be have relatively short launch and acceleration curves to succeed in changing the social equilibrium, that the social equilibrium can be so resistant such that ideas do not show results for years, if not decades. The focus on speed underscores a more exclusive definition.

Opportunities

1. *Socially entrepreneurial opportunities are rare.* Some definitions assume that the opportunities to disrupt the social equilibrium are

rare, while others assume that the social equilibrium is riddled with constant opportunities to solve intractable problems. Fewer opportunities for action create a more exclusive definition.

2. *Socially entrepreneurial opportunities cannot be predicted.* Some definitions assume that opportunities are virtually impossible to identify through exploration, while others assume that opportunities are quite predictable in underlying trends. Fewer opportunities for action create a more exclusive definition again.

3. *Socially entrepreneurial opportunities cannot be created.* Some definitions assume that socially entrepreneurial opportunities create the incentives that start the entrepreneurial process itself, meaning that the opportunity always comes first, while others assume that opportunities can be created and opened through advocacy and other pressures, including the simple presence of a good idea. The notion that opportunities cannot be created underlies a more exclusive definition.

4. *Socially entrepreneurial opportunities occur in punctuations.* Some definitions assume that opportunities arise only at certain "tipping points" in time when the pressure for change overwhelms resistance, while others assume that opportunities exist in all periods, though they may be much more difficult in periods of economic and social quietude. The sense that change largely occurs in great punctuations forms a more exclusive definition.

5. *Socially entrepreneurial opportunities emerge in obvious places.* Some definitions assume that opportunities are the easiest to find in unregulated, less competitive corners of the equilibrium, while others assume that opportunities are evenly spread across the equilibrium. Concentration of opportunities in open space underpins a more exclusive definition.

6. *Socially entrepreneurial opportunities start the entrepreneurial process.* Some definitions assume that opportunities inaugurate the entrepreneurial process by pulling entrepreneurs, ideas, and organizations forward, while others assume that entrepreneurs can create opportunities where none exist. The notion that opportunities cannot be created where they do not already exist creates a more exclusive definition.

7. *Socially entrepreneurial opportunities appear and disappear quickly.* Some definitions assume that opportunities have relatively brief half-lives as information spreads, while others assume that opportunities can exist for long periods without diminution, even decades without a response. Limited opportunities invite less action and therefore create a more exclusive definition.

(continued)

BOX 1-1 *(continued)*

8. *Socially entrepreneurial opportunities carry degrees of difficulty.* Some definitions assume that opportunities are not created equal, while others assume that all opportunities carry roughly the same odds of success. The belief that some socially entrepreneurial opportunities are more difficult to exploit generates a more exclusive definition.
9. *Socially entrepreneurial opportunities favor competition over collaboration.* Some definitions assume that opportunities always create competition among potential innovators, while others suggest that collective action by multiple entrepreneurs with multiple ideas is essential for success. The focus on the single great idea is central to a more exclusive definition.
10. *Socially entrepreneurial opportunities appear only to the special few.* Some definitions assume that entrepreneurs must have a set of special skills such as alertness and agility to seize an opportunity, while others assume that opportunities are easy to spot. The emphasis on a set of required skills underpins a more exclusive definition.

Organizations

1. *Socially entrepreneurial organizations start from scratch.* Some definitions argue that social entrepreneurial organizations are always new and small and that they face the eventual challenge of scale-up, while others assume that old, large existing organizations are also capable of entrepreneurship, albeit under more difficult conditions. The focus on new ventures as the sole platform for social entrepreneurship is a central assumption of a more exclusive definition.
2. *Socially entrepreneurial organizations nurture a stream of new ideas.* Some definitions assume that organizations must be able to generate new ideas over time, whether held in portfolios or produced in sequence, while others assume that social entrepreneurship stands on a single idea that is fine-tuned over time. The focus on creating an "idea-generating" organization reinforces a more exclusive definition.
3. *Socially entrepreneurial organizations rarely pause.* Some definitions assume that organizations never stop pursuing change, while others assume that organizations occasionally pause to rest and rejuvenate. The need for 24/7 organizational commitment led by a 24/7 lone entrepreneur reduces the number of homes for entrepreneurship as part of a more exclusive definition.
4. *Socially entrepreneurial organizations are constructed differently.* Some definitions assume that socially entrepreneurial organizations have dis-

tinctive architectures that make them more innovative over time, while others assume they are just like other high-performing organizations in their basic operations and managerial pressures. The notion that they are constructed differently produces a more exclusive definition.

5. *Socially entrepreneurial organizations must be totally entrepreneurial.* Some definitions assume that organizations must be all entrepreneurial, all of the time, while others assume that organizations can be partially entrepreneurial. The focus on social entrepreneurship as the sole product of the organization generates a more exclusive definition.

6. *Socially entrepreneurial organizations belong in one sector.* Some definitions assume that social entrepreneurship belongs in a single sector, usually the social benefit sector, while others assume it can exist in government, social benefit organizations, businesses, and even in between. Closing off other sectors to entrepreneurship creates a more exclusive definition.

7. *Socially entrepreneurial organizations need unrestricted revenue.* Some definitions assume that socially entrepreneurial organizations need the discretionary income associated with social enterprise, while others argue that unrestricted revenue is only one of many diversified sources on which social entrepreneurship can flourish. The focus on unrestricted revenue creates a smaller set of potential platforms as part of a more exclusive definition.

8. *Socially entrepreneurial organizations need diversified revenue.* Some definitions assume that diversified revenue is essential for protecting organizations from fluctuations in the marketplace of ideas, while others assume that diversification is both difficult to achieve and a potential drag on clarity. The demand for diversification produces a more exclusive definition.

9. *Socially entrepreneurial organizations know how to fight.* Some definitions assume that organizations must be able to fight back against opposition through advocacy, coalition building, membership pressure, and so forth, while others believe that organizations should leave the fighting for others. The call for fighting strength is another requirement that leads to an exclusive definition.

10. *Socially entrepreneurial organizations insulate themselves from aging.* Some definitions assume that social entrepreneurship creates a kind of immunity from the effects of age and growth, while others assume that these organizations are subject to the same forces that encrust most organizations. The resistance to the natural consequences of aging underpins a more exclusive definition.

BOX 1-2. Making Assumptions

Assumption	Light 2006
Entrepreneurs	
1. Social entrepreneurs work alone.	False
2. Social entrepreneurs rarely rest.	False
3. Social entrepreneurs think differently from other high achievers.	False
4. Social entrepreneurs think alike among themselves.	False
5. Social entrepreneurs persevere against all odds.	False
6. Social entrepreneurs take greater risks.	True
7. Social entrepreneurs share common histories.	False
8. Social entrepreneurs are rare.	False
9. Social entrepreneurs stay involved.	False
10. Social entrepreneurs share "one best strategy" for success.	False
Ideas	
1. Socially entrepreneurial ideas try to change the world.	False
2. Socially entrepreneurial ideas always break with the past.	True
3. Socially entrepreneurial ideas are surprising.	False
4. Socially entrepreneurial ideas are complex.	False
5. Socially entrepreneurial ideas must grow to succeed.	False
6. Socially entrepreneurial ideas focus on programs, not process.	False
7. Socially entrepreneurial ideas rarely change from inception.	False
8. Socially entrepreneurial ideas are pure.	False
9. Socially entrepreneurial ideas provoke backlash.	True
10. Socially entrepreneurial ideas produce immediate results.	False
Opportunities	
1. Socially entrepreneurial opportunities are rare.	False
2. Socially entrepreneurial opportunities cannot be predicted.	False
3. Socially entrepreneurial opportunities cannot be created.	False

Assumption	Light 2006
4. Socially entrepreneurial opportunities occur in punctuations.	False
5. Socially entrepreneurial opportunities emerge in obvious places.	False
6. Socially entrepreneurial opportunities start the entrepreneurial process.	False
7. Socially entrepreneurial opportunities appear and disappear quickly.	False
8. Socially entrepreneurial opportunities carry degrees of difficulty.	True
9. Socially entrepreneurial opportunities favor competition over collaboration.	False
10. Socially entrepreneurial opportunities only appear to the special few.	False

Organizations

1. Socially entrepreneurial organizations start from scratch.	False
2. Socially entrepreneurial organizations nurture a stream of new ideas.	False
3. Socially entrepreneurial organizations rarely pause.	False
4. Socially entrepreneurial organizations are constructed differently.	False
5. Socially entrepreneurial organizations must be totally entrepreneurial.	True
6. Socially entrepreneurial organizations belong in one sector.	False
7. Socially entrepreneurial organizations need unrestricted revenue.	False
8. Socially entrepreneurial organizations need diversified revenue.	False
9. Socially entrepreneurial organizations know how to fight.	True
10. Socially entrepreneurial organizations insulate themselves from aging.	False

CHAPTER TWO

BUILDING SITES

The study of business and social entrepreneurship has long focused on newness. Study after study has defined entrepreneurship as the creation of a new venture, almost always a small business, family firm, or organization. When new ventures emerge from existing organizations, researchers have sometimes labeled it "intrapreneurship." It is an easy way to distinguish ideas developed by new ventures from those created by existing organizations.

Intrapreneurship has never quite caught on as a term, however, in part because it is generally defined as a form of entrepreneurship that just happens to occur in a different place. My recent search of the ProQuest database of academic research found just 73 articles on intrapreneurship between 1970 and 2008, compared with 5,784 on entrepreneurship.

One reason that the term *intrapreneurship* is rarely used could be that it has come to be known by a different name—*corporate entrepreneurship*. Writing in 1990, for example, Howard Stevenson and Carlos Jarillo argued that corporate entrepreneurship had become one of the fastest growing topics in the business school literature: "Yet, when reading much of the literature on entrepreneurship as such, to which corporate entrepreneurship should be somewhat related (perhaps as is a species to its genus), one finds an implicit definition of entrepreneurship as something which is radically different from corporate management. Indeed, some writers find it to be the opposite of corporate management."[1] As they concluded, corporate entrepreneurship is often viewed "as something of an oxymoron."

This is certainly the dominant view in the field of social entrepreneurship. Building in part of the business literature, which often focuses on small business, the field appears to be unalterably convinced that social entrepreneurship only springs from new ventures, in part because new ventures are easier to launch and in part because existing organizations are so difficult to change.

Consider how Moshe Sharir and Miri Lerner described Israeli social entrepreneurs in 2006: "Like business entrepreneurs, social entrepreneurs establish new organizations, develop and implement innovative programs, and organize or distribute new services. Even though they are differently motivated, the challenges and problems social entrepreneurs face during the initiation, establishment and institutionalization of their ventures resemble those faced by business entrepreneurs."[2] Defined as such, one measure of entrepreneurial success is the simple existence of a social benefit organization. (Recall that I use *social benefit organization* instead of nonprofit out of respect for Bill Drayton's request that we stop defining charitable organizations by what they are not.)

Despite the odds against success for new ventures, many scholars tend to believe that only new ventures have the agility to respond to entrepreneurial opportunities, refine and launch innovative ideas, and exploit what Drayton calls "jujitsu" leverage points needed for success. "Existing institutions are not able to make such judgments or operate on this timescale," Drayton wrote in his 2007 letter to the *Stanford Social Innovation Review.*[3]

Yet there is ample evidence that existing organizations built by social entrepreneurs continue to produce pattern-breaking change over long periods of time. Although their initial organization may have started from scratch, entrepreneurs often add to their portfolios of social innovation as these platforms develop the capacity for new ideas along different paths to have an impact.

There is also compelling evidence that existing social benefit organizations built decades, even a century or two, ago can create and maintain entrepreneurial cultures that produce social entrepreneurship,

1. Stevenson and Jarillo (1990, p. 17).
2. Sharir and Lerner (2006, p. 7).
3. Drayton (2007, p. 5).

whether as an adjunct to their primary enterprise or as part of an organization-wide transformation. These organizations create the conditions
under which new ideas develop and grow, often becoming businesses
within a business after being housed in an organizational incubator of
some kind.

Simply put, if organizations such as Environmental Defense or Share
Our Strength continue to produce innovative ideas decades after their
founding, it seems reasonable to assume that existing organizations such
as CARE might be able to produce innovations at even older ages. A pattern-breaking idea is a pattern-breaking idea, no matter where it comes
from or when it arises. Creating such ideas may be much more difficult
within an existing organization, but ample examples exist in the social
benefit and business sectors of long-established organizations that have
created the "new combinations" that Joseph Schumpeter described as
the heart of entrepreneurship in *The Theory of Development.*

THE ALLURE OF NEWNESS

Despite repeat innovation at existing firms, the field of social entrepreneurship continues to focus on new ventures as the primary, even exclusive, source of entrepreneurship. Much of this focus stems from a deeply
rooted image of entrepreneurial companies such as Hewlett-Packard,
eBay, and Apple, all of which were started in dorm rooms and garages.

The "Garage Theory" of Entrepreneurship

My 2006 assumptions about socially entrepreneurial organizations
reflected a general philosophy that social entrepreneurship can take place
for many reasons in many settings. Although I believed that entrepreneurs
are essential for changing the social equilibrium, I saw no reason to suggest
that they can begin their journey toward change only in new, small settings.

As such, my list of organizational assumptions signals an almost complete rejection of what Pino Audia and Christopher Rider called the
"garage theory" of entrepreneurship. The theory is rooted in the long list
of business entrepreneurs who started their journey to success in a garage
somewhere—Thomas Edison, Henry Ford, Walt Disney, Fred Smith, Sey-
mour Cray, Steve Jobs and Steve Wozniak, Bill Gates, Michael Dell, and
Pierre Omidyar and Jeffrey Skoll.

According to Audia and Rider's 2005 study, these stories have been
woven into "a contemporary legend that obtains its staying power not
from its accuracy but, rather, from its ability to tap common emotions in

the portion of the American public that is interested in entrepreneurship (that is, entrepreneurs, the business press, venture capitalists, and business school students and faculty."[4] In theory, what could be more powerful to the individual student, the authors imply, than the notion that fame and riches are only a garage away?

In reality, most entrepreneurs do not start imagining a new equilibrium in their garages but within organizations and industries that trained them to succeed. Moreover, they tend to locate themselves within short distances from the firms that nurtured them. As Audia and Rider argue, most are "organizational products" themselves. "The legend of the entrepreneur's garage evokes the image of the lone individual who relies primarily on his/her extraordinary efforts and talent to overcome the difficulties inherent in creating a new organization. In contrast, the process of creating new organizations is eminently social. Social relations help would-be entrepreneurs not only to garner the support needed to form the new business, but also to identify the entrepreneurial opportunities on which new businesses are built."[5]

Thomas Hellman confirmed this pattern in 2007 when he asked why employees of existing firms leave home: "Where do entrepreneurs come from? Employees of established companies turn out to be one of the most important sources for entrepreneurship. The semiconductor industry, for example, has an impressive genealogy, where, generation after generation, employees left their parent to launch the next entrant."[6] Indeed, past studies estimate that roughly 70 percent of new entrepreneurs replicated or modified an idea they encountered through their previous employment.

This research is quite consistent with Drayton's belief that social entrepreneurs share very similar life histories starting with long apprenticeships within an existing organization. In Drayton's view, organizations almost always drive entrepreneurs over the edge. But the reality may be quite different. Instead of being a source of great frustration, many organizations are what Audia and Rider call "natural incubators" for new ideas. They provide the information that helps entrepreneurs identify opportunities, the experience needed to build an effective organization, the contacts with the other employees that will form a leadership team, and the access to resources such as investors.

4. Audia and Rider (2005, p. 7).
5. Audia and Rider (2005 (p. 7).
6. Hellman (2007, p. 919).

Incubators also provide space for interaction and professional development. As Maura McAdam and Susan Marlow wrote in 2007, incubators help develop entrepreneurial talent, provide administrative services at a time when ideas must be the central concern, and provide intangible benefits such as legitimacy among stakeholders, such a buyers and new employees. Incubators become less useful over time, however, especially in a competitive environment. Developing new ideas in a more or less public space is hardly a wise method, if doing so informs competitors who can move faster. Instead of building futures, incubators can become easy targets for stealing secrets.

The Shared History of Entrepreneurs

The socially entrepreneurial process is anything but lonely, however, and need not be frustrating. To the contrary, the process itself is social, drawing the entrepreneur into teams and networks that are essential to the development of the idea and its acceleration to scale. Asking what kinds of organizations and positions entrepreneurs need for access to essential resources, Audia and Rider looked to career histories:

—Was the entrepreneur exposed to the kinds of information that signal opportunities around which a new organization might be built?

—Did the entrepreneur have opportunities to fulfill the kinds of roles crucial to the future operation of an entrepreneurial organization?

—Did the entrepreneur have close contact with colleagues with whom he or she might form a founding team?

—Did the entrepreneur have direct access to key resource providers such as suppliers, customers, or investors?

To the degree that Drayton's entrepreneurs use these resources to establish their own enterprises, they share at least part of a coherent, consistent life history. However, life history involves far more than work. It also involves what Echoing Green calls "moments of obligation," meaning life-changing events that create an unwavering commitment to change. Such moments may be common to all social entrepreneurs, but the events are often very different, suggesting that an entrepreneur's work and life histories may be anything but consistent with those of others. One size does not fit all.

Life history also expresses itself in what William Gartner, Terence Mitchell, and Karl Vesper imagined in 1989 as eight very different reasons for launching a new venture. Some entrepreneurs start their firms to escape their previous jobs for something new. These entrepreneurs may share very similar life experiences, but they tend to pick a different industry and different type of work from before. They also tend to labor during weekends and evenings as they move toward full-time commitment.

According to the three authors, other entrepreneurs start their ventures because they simply enjoy the experience of making the deal. Notwithstanding their desire for profit or social change, their primary focus is on using their considerable skills at negotiating, coordinating, acquiring, fund-raising, and motivating to build a new firm. It is almost as if they do not care what they do, just that they do it.

Still other entrepreneurs start with little or no interest in starting a new venture. Indeed, they tend to be very satisfied in their current jobs and have great opportunities for growth and upward advancement. And when they move, they solicit the help of partners and other experts who work together to supply needed expertise. "The firm is highly flexible in adapting to customer needs," Gartner and his colleagues write, "since the entrepreneur's expertise makes him or her keenly aware of changes in the environment." The result is an unrelenting focus on sales, not on research and development.[7]

The question is whether the eight types of new ventures always have to come in new firms. The answer appears to be no. Dissatisfied employees can tunnel out of their existing job into another by taking their idea to an incubator or to a particularly innovative organization such as Apple. Deals can be made in the same way: entrepreneurs with no interest in a new organization can be moved to safe spaces for developing ideas on behalf of the organization. Just as one size does not fit all new ventures, or so this argument goes, one location does not fit all new ventures either.

CORPORATE ENTREPRENEURSHIP

Creating and launching new ventures within existing organizations is hardly easy. As Jesper Sørensen wrote in 2007, bureaucracy can reduce the disposition to act by molding employee attitudes against risk. It can also hinder the development of broad entrepreneurial skills and a sense of the wider world by locking employees into narrow career paths and insulating them from the outside world. And it can make employees so secure and comfortable that they lose the will to challenge the prevailing wisdom

7. Gartner, Mitchell, and Vesper (1989, p. 180).

lest they lose their benefits. By denying both the disposition and freedom to act, bureaucracy breaks the spirit of imagination needed to innovate.

Nevertheless, the recent literature of business entrepreneurship suggests that large, old organizations must confront these patterns to survive. As Gautam Ahuja and Curba Morris Lampert wrote in 2001, established organizations are contributing to breakthroughs to a far greater extent than previously believed:

> Although the stereotype of the solitary inventor toiling in a garage adds a memorably heroic dimension to the breakthrough invention story, the fact remains that a very large proportion of R&D resources continue to be expended by established, publicly held corporations. Identifying strategies that can help such corporations to improve their record of breakthrough inventions can potentially create significant private and social value.[8]

Not only do existing firms often provide the resources for the launch of new businesses outside their boundaries, many have become obsessed with methods to increase their entrepreneurship within. "After years of downsizing and cost cutting," David Garvin and Lynne Levesque wrote in 2006, "corporations have realized they can't shrink their way to success. They've also found that they can't grow rapidly by tweaking existing offerings, taking over rivals or moving into developing companies. Because of maturing technologies and aging product portfolios, a new imperative is clear: Companies must create, develop, and sustain innovative new businesses."[9] These are not businesses outside the organization but businesses within.

Explaining an Oxymoron

Research on corporate entrepreneurship has suffered from the same identity crisis that has affected research on business and social entrepreneurship. Some scholars have defined corporate entrepreneurship as a business within a business, others as a spin-off that retains close ties to its parent, and still others as a culture that invites and accelerates new ideas from within an organization's borders.

Sally Sambrook and Clair Roberts defined corporate entrepreneurship in 2005 as "startup entrepreneurship turned inward as an antidote to the

---

8. Ahuja and Lampert (2001, p. 522).
9. Garvin and Levesque (2006, p. 102).

staleness associated with large organizations," while Robert Wolcott and Michael Lippitz defined it in late 2007 as "a process by which teams within an established company conceive, foster, launch and manage a new business that is distinct from the parent company but leverages the parent's assets, market position, capabilities or other resources."[10] But all agree that corporate entrepreneurship is fundamentally "concerned with various forms of newness," which is how Gregory Dess (not Dees) and his colleagues catalogued the term in 2003.[11] (Who would have guessed that two of the leading scholars in business and social entrepreneurship research would be J. Gregory Dees and Gregory G. Dess?)

Also like the burgeoning inventory of research on business and social entrepreneurship, the emergent field of corporate entrepreneurship is clouded by ongoing confusion about where and why it exists. Indeed, according to Sambrook and Roberts, there are at least eighteen different modes of corporate entrepreneurship that the field seems to recognize, including spin-offs, joint ventures, acquisitions, organization rejuvenation, intrapreneuring, frame-breaking change, sustained regeneration, domain redefinition, industry rule-bending, and internal corporate venturing.

Just like entrepreneurship in new organizations, corporate entrepreneurship involves many outcomes. In theory, all corporate venturing is driven by profit, which is most certainly a measure of success. But venturing may also be driven by the desire to eliminate potential competitors early, improve productivity, rejuvenate sagging reputations, or keep internal entrepreneurs from leaving. Indeed, Jeffrey Covin and Morgan Miles moved well beyond the haphazard definition of corporate entrepreneurship in 1999 to a fourfold concept that may seem very familiar to the new ventures celebrated in the field of social entrepreneurship.

Covin and Miles's first model of corporate entrepreneurship involves an effort at *sustained regeneration,* which involves the creation of new products and services or entry into new markets. This stream of ideas can be generated through increased spending on research and development. "Firms successful at the sustained regeneration form of corporate entrepreneurship tend to have cultures, structures, and systems supportive of innovation," they write. "They also tend to be learning organizations that embrace change and willingly challenge competitors in battles

10. Sambrook and Roberts (2005, p. 142); Wolcott and Lippitz (2007, p. 75).
11. Dess and others (2003, p. 352).

for market share."[12] At the same time, they are constantly abandoning failing products and services to remain fresh.

Covin and Miles's second model involves a broad commitment to *organizational rejuvenation,* which they describe as a path to greater productivity and internal performance. Such efforts do not focus on business strategy (which some scholars actually abbreviate as BS), but on the organization itself. As the authors wrote, "We believe it is important to recognize that firms need not change their strategies in order to be entrepreneurial. Rather, corporate entrepreneurship may involve efforts to sustain or increase competitiveness through improved execution of particular, pre-existing business strategies."[13]

Covin and Miles's third model is *strategic renewal* in how an organization competes. "Whereas the focal point for organizational rejuvenation is the organization *per se,*" they wrote, "the focal point for strategic renewal is the firm within its environmental context and, in particular, the strategy that mediates the organization-environment interface."[14] The basic idea for change is not a new program, but a new way of delivering existing strategies—entrepreneurship is the device for achieving gains in market share, which social entrepreneurs might label "scaling up."

Covin and Miles's fourth and final model is *domain redefinition.* Here, the organization creates a "new product-market arena that others have not recognized or actively sought to exploit." In moving to empty zones in the equilibrium, as many social entrepreneurs do, domain redefining firms seek to create the market standard against which other firms are judged. "Thus, firms that engage in domain redefinition are entrepreneurial by virtue of the fact that they exploit market opportunities in a preemptive fashion, redefining where and how the competitive game is played in the process."[15]

Some readers will be uncomfortable with these models, especially when they involve efforts to foreclose competition. After all, social benefit organizations are supposed to be collaborative, even nice, when dealing with their competitors. But to deny competition as a source of socially entrepreneurial activity is also to deny the funding realities today. Newness is not attractive by accident—it provides a path to growth.

12. Covin and Miles (1999, p. 51).
13. Covin and Miles (1999, p. 52).
14. Covin and Miles (1999, p. 52).
15. Covin and Miles (1999, p. 54).

Indeed, some researchers argue that entrepreneurship is the cause, not the product of organizational renewal, especially when the entrepreneurship requires the acquisition of new competencies. As Erwin Danneels argued in 2002, there are two kinds of innovation. The first involves the *exploitation* of opportunities using existing competencies such as research and development and customer connections, while the second involves the *exploration* of opportunities using new competencies such as information technology or the management of uncertainty. The former tends to produce incremental change, while the latter is a precursor to organizational renewal and radical change.

Based on a study of five high technology firms, Danneels concluded that "innovation activities not only draw upon existing organizations, but also serve to develop competencies, and thus contribute to firm renewal over time." Entrepreneurial engagement is not necessarily the cure for all that ails staid bureaucracies, but done well, it can spark a top-to-bottom change in business as usual. "This is particularly important in the current dynamic environment, which requires firms to renew their competencies in order to survive and prosper," Danneels continued. "Environment changes make previously acquired competencies obsolete, and call for new competencies to be built."[16] In a sense, organizations should not ask what entrepreneurship can do for the market but what it can do for their own competencies.

Shared Challenges

Whether embedded in new or existing organizations, entrepreneurship appears to thrive under certain conditions and in specific organizational cultures. As Mariann Jelinek and Joseph Litterer argued in 1995, entrepreneurial organizations are merely a species of organizations in general.

Acknowledging that the term *entrepreneurial organization* is a paradox, the question is not where entrepreneurship occurs as much as how it emerges. "Even these organizations founded by entrepreneurs often fall short," Jelinek and Litterer wrote, "becoming rigid and fixed as their founders fail to integrate other organization members around the changing goals, directions, and tasks entrepreneurship requires."[17]

All is not lost, however. Even as entrepreneurial organizations struggle to build structure and enlighten managers, as Drayton might suggest, they

16. Danneels (2002, p. 1096).
17. Jelinek and Litterer (1995, p. 137).

TABLE 2-1. Comparing Entrepreneurial and Traditional Organizations

	Response	
Situation	Entrepreneurial organization	Traditional organization
Unclear problem	Define and study the ambiguity	Ignore the ambiguity
Unclear information	Search and share information	Rely on existing data
Conflicting interpretations	Gather and compile ideas	Fight and divide with hierarchy
Different values	Negotiate differences across the organization	Create a single vision by fiat
Unclear goals	Find common ground through participation	Impose a single vision through centralization
Scarce resources	Persevere regardless of resources	Stop entrepreneuring
Vague responsibilities	Engage all participants through flat hierarchy	Specialize and formalize through tight hierarchy
Unclear measurement	Create new measures	Use old measures
Unclear cause and effect	Explore the system of cause and effect as a whole	Engage in random problem solving
Unclear communication	Create shared information systems	Control messages from the top
Fluid participation	Encourage local ownership of ideas	Control movement and interaction through rules
Risk response	Experiment	Extrapolate from past experience

must also create the conditions to create a steady stream of new ideas that permeate the inevitable rules that come with growth and transparency.

As Jelinek and Litterer argued, entrepreneurial organizations often tend to resemble traditional organizations on the surface but differ in ways not always easy to see. "Indeed, much of what makes these organizations entrepreneurial is invisible or misconstrued in traditional theory."[18] Whereas traditional theory focuses on organizational characteristics such as structure, rules, and hierarchy, the two authors focused on organizational behaviors such as shared management, "mindful alertness to anomalies," and "superior capabilities of ambiguity absorption." In short, the entrepreneurial species may look very similar to the traditional species but must behave very differently in creating pattern-breaking change. Table 2-1 shows how entrepreneurial (new or old, small or large) and traditional organizations (new or old, small or large) react to the inherent problems embedded in confronting the prevailing economic or social equilibrium.

Even when they are not the source of radical ideas, existing organizations are still involved in the process of innovation. As William Baumol

18. Jelinek and Litterer (1995, p. 138).

argued in 2004, organizations tend to specialize in incremental improvements in radical change, thereby avoiding the risks of failure, while advancing its cause by polishing breakthroughs.

According to Baumol, small, independent firms imagine and invent, while large existing firms modify and scale up. "The two types of activity are complementary, in that together they contribute more to growth than either could by itself," he wrote. "The one dreams up and inaugurates the breakthroughs, while the other contributes crucial improvements to performance. . . . The innovative process is indeed implicitly a partnership between the small entity and the large, between David and Goliath, and, in this case, both emerge victorious, and the economy gains a victory as well."[19]

Baumol is no doubt right to emphasize the incremental change that large firms often produce through alliances with new, small ventures. The literature on corporate entrepreneurship suggests that these David-and-Goliath partnerships can also emerge in large firms that create the new, small ventures inside. These large entrepreneurial organizations must be both David and Goliath simultaneously—a balancing act that can produce the breakthroughs needed to solve pressing social problems. Toyota is just such a model with its production of a hybrid car, while pharmaceuticals are using similar approaches in developing and disseminating lifesaving drugs.

Existing organizations may be quite capable of launching new ventures, but they are also quite capable of destroying them. "New ventures set up by existing companies face innumerable barriers, and research shows that most of them fail," Garvin and Levesque argued in 2006. "Emerging businesses seldom mesh smoothly with well-established systems, processes, and cultures. Yet success requires a blend of old and new organizational traits, a subtle mix of characteristics achieved through what we call balancing acts. Unless companies keep those opposing forces in equilibrium, emerging businesses will flounder."[20]

As Garvin and Levesque suggested, the very act of entrepreneurship often requires a frontal assault on existing organizations. New businesses require innovation, they wrote, innovation requires new ideas, and new ideas require mavericks: "Some degree of unconventional thinking is essential for new businesses to take hold, but many radical

19. Baumol (2004, p. 325).
20. Garvin and Levesque (2006, p. 102).

ideas are foolish or unfounded. Most mavericks, sadly, can't tell the difference between good and bad ideas. They persist in defending pet themes, demand repeated hearings, and refuse to take no for an answer."[21]

Baumol made a similar argument in 2005: "Work on breakthrough ideas clearly is beset by great uncertainty. One probably has to have a touch of madness to devote most of one's time and resources to the untried prospects that a breakthrough innovation unavoidably entails. But there is reason to suspect that the innovative entrepreneurs characteristically are self-selected risk lovers, that is, persons who are attracted by the prospect of significant prizes in disregard of the low probability of their attainment."[22]

Yet, new organizations often share similar failure rates. Writing of start-ups in 2007, John Freeman and Jerome Engel argued that entrepreneurs often demean existing management as too predictable, even as existing management often demeans entrepreneurs as too unpredictable:

> Developing a product around the new design or invention, devising the means to produce it in the predictable quantities and consistent quality required by customers, and creating the marketing and sales capabilities all require planning and coordination. These, in turn, require discipline. Organizations set up to produce that discipline have properties that are the opposite of those enhancing creativity. Conversely, organizations that are good at generating creative solutions are often not good at rapid and precise execution of plans. The problem is that innovation requires both.[23]

As the new organization grows vertically and horizontally over time, the advantages that made it so attractive to venture capitalists and philanthropists become liabilities for its own survival. The more successful it becomes, the more it must adopt the same strategies of renewal and rejuvenation needed for corporate entrepreneurship.

Shared Lessons

If entrepreneurial activity can prosper within existing organizations, lessons for entrepreneurial success can emerge from new ventures. And if entrepreneurial activity can flourish in new ventures, lessons for entrepreneurial impact can be found in existing organizations. Although new

21. Garvin and Levesque (2006, p. 104).
22. Baumol (2005, pp. 28–29).
23. Freeman and Engel (2007, p. 96).

and existing organizations may approach the entrepreneurial process from different starting points, the two can learn from each other as they move from imagining a new future to navigating the social ecosystem to protect success.

COMPARATIVE ADVANTAGES. Ideas may share the same developmental process in new and existing organizations, but clearly they create different challenges in the two settings. New ventures have greater advantages at the start of the developmental process, while existing organizations have greater strengths as ideas expand.

New organizations can clearly concentrate on the development of a powerful vision, for example, and can move quickly in developing new ideas that can achieve results, accelerating those ideas toward implementation, and creating growth. They may face greater barriers to sustained impact, particularly given scarce resources in a highly competitive funding environment, but new organizations are particularly good at spotting opportunities for impact.

In turn, existing organizations have special advantages further up the development curve, particularly in providing the resources for scale-up, ensuring sustainability, and stimulating new ideas beyond the original innovation. They may face more obstacles at the start of the entrepreneurial process, but existing organizations have greater strengths, perhaps, in moving a good idea from conceptualization to full-blown diffusion and success.

The overall development process may be similar in new ventures and existing organizations, but the challenges in the two are not always similar. The key challenges for new ventures come later in the process as they move toward scale-up: sustaining, succeeding, and imagining anew, while the key challenges for existing organizations come early in the process: imagining, start-up, and acceleration:

—Whereas new ventures are sparked by imagination, existing organizations usually start their change efforts by convincing potential entrepreneurs to act, whether through the creation of skunk works, businesses within businesses, or powerful idea generators that encourage free thinking about new products and processes. According to Julian Birkinshaw and Susan Hill, innovation used to emerge from highly centralized investments in research and development. More recently, however, they found that "ideas are as likely to crop up in Stockholm or Madrid as in Silicon Valley." Writing of the globalization of entrepreneurship in a 2005 article, Birkinshaw and Hill emphasized the role of "venture units" in sparking change, a point equally well made by Kenneth Husted and Christian Vintergaard in a 2004 discussion of "corporate venture bases."

—Whereas new ventures drive persistently toward launch, existing organizations must invest resources in protecting new ideas from internal opposition to change. New ventures often suffer from what Jodyanne Kirkwood called the "tall poppy syndrome," in which they are belittled for their innovative spirit. Writing about entrepreneurship in New Zealand in a 2007 article, she noted that entrepreneurs often keep their heads down lest they attract too much attention. The tall poppy that rises above the field is cut down first.

—And whereas new ventures have enormous energy for growth, existing organizations must invest their resources in integrating entrepreneurial ideas into their prevailing culture, oftentimes by changing the culture itself through a wrenching process of reform. These patterns suggest that existing organizations can learn a great deal from new ventures as they embark on their journey to pattern-breaking change. This journey is fraught with risk, however, and low survival rates, in part because start-ups have such difficulty in creating a reputation for impact. Writing of the "good, the bad, and the unfamiliar" in 2007, Eileen Fischer and Rebecca Reuber emphasized the need for much deeper research on this often neglected aspect of acceleration. Thus, organizations that build strong stakeholder relationships with investors such as philanthropic foundations have much greater success rates. All start-ups send signals to the rest of the world regarding their identity, image, legitimacy, and trust, but only some manage that process to their advantage.

In turn, new ventures can learn a great deal from existing organizations as they grow toward impact.

—Whereas most existing organizations already have the scaffolding of production, new ventures must build their structures from scratch as they reorganize themselves for growth. This focus on the role of managers has raised great concern within the fields of business and social entrepreneurship. Thus Drayton made the following distinction between managers and leaders in his response to my 2006 article: "It is appropriate to have a manager come in to run a franchise or manage the 13th department store in a chain, implementing a formula. A little tweak here or there will make the difference in the business's margin. But that is not what fundamental entrepreneurship is about."[24] Acknowledging the

---

24. Drayton (2007, p. 5).

potential disconnect between managers and leaders, the key is to make sure managers and their structures serve the entrepreneurship, not vice versa, which is a balancing act that corporate entrepreneurs must accept.

—Whereas most existing organizations already have the resources for sustaining momentum, even if they are unable to generate significant market share for several years or more, new ventures have very thin margins for maintaining momentum, often devoting huge amounts of time and energy to fundraising and social enterprises in an effort to provide a floor to continue their endeavor. By itself, this effort to convert reputation into cash flow can compromise the entrepreneurial idea, which is why some socially entrepreneurial organizations eschew government funding altogether. Government is simply not a reliable stakeholder, or so the theory goes, especially when the end goal of social entrepreneurship is to change government itself.

—And whereas most new organizations face great pressure to prove their success by creating measurement systems and conducting evaluations, both at significant cost, existing organizations usually have experience with tracking systems already. This pressure often produces what Freeman and Engel labeled the "paradox" of entrepreneurship in which young organizations have the advantages of newness and smallness but often lack the resources, measurement, and plain good luck to survive. However, as Michael Morris and his colleagues argued in 2007, the organizational structure of social benefit organizations has far less to do with entrepreneurship than it does with entrepreneurial orientation— that is, hierarchy is trumped by the internal culture. Transformational leadership, delegation, employee participation, and active boards produce the entrepreneurship, not the systems. Although controls are needed as a part of organizational excellence, the controls should provide enough discretion to take risks, even as the controls align autonomy with the organization's mission.

Both sets of organizations share a similar concern about resources. But whereas the new organization often raises capital from venture capitalists, existing organizations supply most of the resources from within. Nevertheless, the two can learn from each other on when and how much to invest in a new idea, and where resources can be most useful in moving an idea toward changing the social equilibrium.

LEARNING ACROSS SITES. Both sets of organizations also share the overriding need to maintain an entrepreneurial orientation over time. To the extent they copy existing organizations in the world writ large, even the

most entrepreneurial venture can develop organizational sclerosis, especially if it spends too much time admiring the large, old organizations
that dominate the Fortune 500. This isomorphism, as sociologists call it,
is a form of mimicry that can strip a new venture of its entrepreneurial
orientation, while lowering the risk of being different.

There is no question that entrepreneurs pay attention to the behavior
and structures of their competition—and little doubt that socially entrepreneurial organizations pay attention to the award winners in their
field. After all, imitation is the sincerest form of flattery. As Heather
Haveman argued in 1993, the question is not *whether* organizations imitate their peers, but *whom* they imitate. "There is some evidence that the
actions of organizations with high visibility and prestige influence other
organizations," she wrote. "The difficulty is determining which organizations are most visible, most prestigious, and most successful."[25]

Once the most visible, prestigious, and successful organizations are
found, the question is no longer *which* organizations to imitate, but
what to imitate. At least for business and social entrepreneurship, the
answer is entrepreneurial organization. As Tom Lumpkin and Gregory
Dess defined it in 1996, the term *entrepreneurial orientation* refers to
the organizational characteristics that lead to new entry, which in turn
is the essential act of entrepreneurship. Described as "purposeful enact-
ment," Lumpkin and Dess argued that the term "involves the intentions
and actions of key players functioning in a dynamic generative process
aimed at new-venture creation." According to Dess and Lumpkin's
2005 definition, entrepreneurial orientation involves five organizational
behaviors:

　　—*Autonomy*: "Independent action by an individual or team aimed at
bringing forth a business concept or vision and carrying it through to
completion."

　　—*Innovativeness*: "A willingness to introduce newness and novelty
through experimentation and creative processes aimed at developing
new products and services, as well as new processes."

　　—*Proactiveness*: "A forward-looking perspective characteristic of a
marketplace leader that has the foresight to seize opportunities in anticipation of future demand."

　　—*Competitive aggressiveness*: "An intense effort to outperform
industry rivals . . . characterized by a combative posture or an aggressive

25. Haveman (1993, p. 598).

response aimed at improving position or overcoming a threat in a competitive marketplace."

—*Risk-taking*: "Making decisions and taking action without certain knowledge of probable outcomes; some undertakings may also involve making substantial resource commitments in the process of venturing forward."[26]

The five behaviors are remarkably similar to Dees's 1998 definition of social entrepreneurship, in part as a commitment to a process of continuous innovation, adaptation, and learning—perhaps Dees and Dess share more than a similar name after all. Socially entrepreneurial activity is clearly the product of socially entrepreneurial orientation, even in the form of competition for funding.

By focusing on entrepreneurial orientation, the fields of business and social entrepreneurship can move away from the debate about new as opposed to existing organizations and toward a much more productive debate about maintaining the entrepreneurial orientation into the future. Assuming that socially entrepreneurial organizations must maintain a stream of new ideas and insulate themselves from aging, the question is not *what* they should imitate but *how* to maintain the entrepreneurial orientation over time and through growth.

THE ENTREPRENEURIAL ORGANIZATION

Viewed as a whole, these findings suggest that social entrepreneurship flourishes in robust organizations, whatever their age or location. Applied to social entrepreneurship, robustness describes an organization's ability to bend, stretch, and adapt over time.

It also involves an organizational state of being that is essential for sustaining change. According to *Webster's New Collegiate Dictionary,* being robust means "having or exhibiting strength or vigorous health"; "having or showing vigor, strength, or firmness"; "strongly formed or constructed, sturdy"; "capable of performing without failure under a wide range of conditions"; "rough, rude"; "requiring strength or vigor"; and "full-bodied, hearty."

In other words, robustness is essential for sparking and sustaining an effort to change the prevailing social equilibrium. It describes a setting in which high performance and innovation reinforce each other to create

26. Dess and Lumpkin (2005, p. 148).

tight *alignment* around a vision of the future, *adaptability* in moving pattern-breaking ideas through the developmental process, *alertness* to opportunities for attacking the prevailing social equilibrium, and *agility* in their organizational responses to these opportunities. Each of these characteristics increases the likelihood that organizations will support the entrepreneurship that their entrepreneurs create.

—*Alignment.* Entrepreneurs, ideas, and opportunities rarely cohere unless they are tightly aligned around a specific vision for change. Once housed within an entrepreneurial organization, they can easily interact to create a clear strategy for generating impact. Although opportunities may be the first component of social entrepreneurship, it is always possible that entrepreneurs, ideas, and organizations are already scanning the outside environment for opportunities to combine their strengths to identify an opportunity or create one where none currently exists.

—*Adaptability.* Sustaining entrepreneurial fervor long enough to create pattern-breaking change requires a great deal of organizational adaptability. Unless the idea is already so tightly developed that it is ready to work its will immediately, the business and social entrepreneurship literatures suggest that learning and adaptation are essential for actually disturbing the equilibrium. This ability to adapt the idea, whether led by the entrepreneur or the organization, is essential for exploiting the opportunity for change whenever it arises. Adaptation is also essential in the battle to change the social equilibrium as it fights back against change.

—*Alertness.* Alertness is a critical resource as entrepreneurs identify weaknesses in the social equilibrium. As such, existing organizations sometimes identify an opportunity first and empower an entrepreneur, a unit, or a business within a business next, while new ventures may reflect an entrepreneur's quick reaction to a new opportunity for change. And ideas may circulate through "entrepreneurial space" looking for an attachment to an entrepreneur, opportunity, or organization. Within the agenda-setting literatures, plenty of studies suggest that entrepreneurship emerges from a kind of primordial soup of entrepreneurs, ideas, opportunities, and organizations, all seeking a new combination à la Schumpeter's 1934 conceptualization.

—*Agility.* Given that opportunities open and close quickly, entrepreneurs and organizations must be able to use speed to their advantage. They cannot wait long to apply their creativity in exploiting a particular opening for change. Rather, they must prepare themselves to move quickly. But agility does not just apply to the emergence of a specific opportunity. It also resides in the ability to move quickly in response to replication and dissemination openings, learning and adaptation pressure, funding and capacity-building needs, and information technology and training requests. Agility also encompasses a general organizational confrontation with the natural consequences of aging. To the extent that agility remains a core value of entrepreneurs and their organizations, it acts as a device for staying lean and fast in the midst of extraordinary pressure to bulk up with needless bureaucracy.

Together these four attributes of entrepreneurial organizations create a culture in which social entrepreneurship can thrive as entrepreneurs quickly identify opportunities, ideas find entrepreneurs, and opportunities open and close. This fluid model of social entrepreneurship creates enormous potential to increase the amount of activity by studying, nurturing, and sustaining synapses among the four components of equilibrium-disturbing action. As Dess, Lumpkin, and Jeffrey McGree described this model in 1999, entrepreneurial organizations are barrier free:

> The internal structures of barrier-free organizations are often characterized by fluid, ambiguous, and deliberately ill-designed tasks and roles. Barrier-free organizations also typically feature fewer layers of management, smaller-scale business units, and advocate the creation of process teams and interdisciplinary work groups, empowerment of first-line personnel, open communications vertically and laterally, and accountability for results rather than an emphasis on activity.[27]

In a word, such organizations create a culture of entrepreneurship and sustain it through rejuvenation.

Because the entrepreneurs, ideas, and opportunities move in and out of barrier-free organizations over time, spending precious resources looking for each other, the focus should be on the least expensive way to create connections. This might mean greater investment in helping entrepreneurs explore potential ideas through such programs as Harvard University's Social Entrepreneurship Collaboratory and other planning entities that provide training and education. Or it might require a stronger infrastructure designed to identify opportunities and ideas for action through environmental scanning and devices for assessing weaknesses in

27. Dess, Lumpkin, and McGee (1999, p. 93).

the equilibrium. It might even involve the development of organization designs that appear to work well in scaling up new ventures that entail further analysis of the process for scaling up and sustaining growth, managing success, or reigniting the search for entrepreneurial ideas.

But whatever the device, we should accept the notion that social entrepreneurs are not always the starting point of change. They may be, as Drayton argues, essential for keeping an idea alive, but they occupy only part of the socially entrepreneurial space. This is why Ashoka provides a range of technical assistance as ideas develop, whether on its own or through partners in the advertising and management consulting industries.

CONCLUSION

Some readers will still argue that existing organizations cannot produce sustainable social entrepreneurship, and they are no doubt right that entrepreneurial behavior is extremely difficult to produce within the stifling bureaucracies that emerge over time in many industries. But if new ventures such as Teach For America can remain entrepreneurial as they grow into large organizations, there is no reason that existing organizations cannot do so as well. As such, Bostijan Antoncic and Robert Hisrich wrote in 2003 that entrepreneurship in organizations is a matter of degree: "Pure forms, in absolute terms, such as totally entrepreneurial or totally non-entrepreneurial organizations are abstractions that help us understand reality, but do not actually exist in the real world."[28]

Defining intrapreneurship as "entrepreneurship within an existing organization," Antoncic and Hisrich endorsed the distinction between risk-averse and reactive organizations on the one hand and risk-taking and proactive organizations on the other. They also argued that such entrepreneurship occurs beyond the organizational core. As they wrote, "the major concern is with existing routines, their repetition, and with the efficiency of existing production and support operations," while intrapreneurship "can be viewed as a curious, constantly searching activity at the frontier." Although such entrepreneurship may be much more difficult in existing organizations, especially if they have to transform themselves to produce new ideas, it is nonetheless a source of potential equilibrium-changing entrepreneurship.

28. Antoncic and Hisrich (2003, p. 9).

The choice of organizational platform, be it a new venture or an existing organization, is just a choice, not an absolute determinant of eventual success. Indeed, there may be situations when an existing organization is the preferred location for social entrepreneurship, whether because of its resource base, overall reach, and readiness to support new ventures within its boundaries. As Audia and Rider argued, organizations do not have to watch helplessly as employees exit with intellectual capital in the form of new ideas and market knowledge. Rather, they can create conditions that allow entrepreneurship to flourish in existing settings, such as incentive systems, career development, or start-up resources for internal action. They can also create the space for imagination by setting up incubators or other protected units. Existing organizations may face great barriers to entrepreneurship, but they can and do produce it. Witness Intel's effort to leapfrog itself or Apple's deep investment in a culture of surprise.

Given this view and the supporting literature, it seems reasonable to reject the assumption that socially entrepreneurial organizations always start from scratch. There is ample evidence that entrepreneurship can emerge from within existing organizations, especially if these organizations maintain an ongoing stream of ideas. This requires occasional pauses along the way for renewal and rejuvenation, not to mention basic capacity building toward improved organizational performance.

Entrepreneurship also appears to require a commitment to management excellence, especially in creating the conditions for ideas and their champions to survive long enough to produce sustainable change. And given the evidence supporting the use of incubators and businesses within businesses, it seems reasonable to argue that entrepreneurship need not be the sole purpose of an organization. These conclusions confirm many, though not all, of my assumptions about socially entrepreneurial organizations.

CHAPTER THREE

CREATING STRATEGIES

Looking at the United States over the past fifty years, it is impossible to ignore the dramatic changes produced by social entrepreneurship. Led in part by social benefit organizations, the United States launched massive new programs to reduce disease, increase health care access for children and the elderly, guarantee civil rights, explore space, build an interstate highway system, help the working poor, and improve air and water quality. Some of these endeavors involved single great programs such as Medicare, the Civil Rights Act, and the Clean Air and Water Acts; others involved a string of smaller programs such as increased funding for medical research, incremental increases in the minimum wage, and protection of specific wilderness areas. If greatness is measured in part by a commitment to solving important, difficult problems, the United States measures up very well indeed. Every effort produced social entrepreneurship.

Yet, just as one can look back with awe at what society accomplished over the past half century, so, too, can one look forward with considerable doubt about whether the United States will ever be so bold again. Are the nation's leaders so worried about losing their jobs that they will not take the chances embedded in the kinds of inherently risky projects that produced new rights and liberties? Are Americans so impatient for success that no endeavor, however well designed and justified, can outlast the early difficulties that face so many entrepreneurial efforts? And are both so addicted to stories of failure that no endeavor, however noble and well designed, can survive long enough to achieve results?

These questions would not be so troublesome but for the fact that many of the most important problems are still out there to be solved. The nation has far to go in increasing access to health care, reducing the dangers of nuclear war, improving air and water quality, reducing hunger, and so on down the list. To the extent that the nation converts the marathon of achievement into little more than a series of exhausting wind sprints, the list of breakthroughs over the next half century will be meager indeed.

Moreover, many of the world's greatest achievements are now imperiled by a host of threats such as global climate change, the growing divide between rich and poor, population growth, renewed marginalization, the return of once-conquered diseases such as polio, and lack of access to the instruments of production. Social entrepreneurship has a role here, too. Changing the social equilibrium is only part of the process—the changes must be protected. Even as we explore the four components of social entrepreneurship, it is always important to remember the ultimate goal—it is not entrepreneurship for entrepreneurship's sake, but lasting change to the betterment of humankind.

The rest of this chapter examines the logic of social entrepreneurship and strategies for tying entrepreneurs, ideas, opportunities, and organizations together at various stages of the entrepreneurial process. Readers should note that I have searched for lessons from business and social entrepreneurship, often combining insights from the two fields as if they are interchangeable. Some readers will be uncomfortable with the back-and-forth, but it is necessary to draw as much out of the available research as possible, especially given the many choices for investigating social entrepreneurship.

THE LOGIC OF SOCIAL ENTREPRENEURSHIP

The logic of social entrepreneurship is both simple and complex. On the one hand, most logic chains contain a relatively small number of variables and proceed directly from what Roger Martin and Sally Osberg called "a stable but inherently unjust equilibrium" to a "stable ecosystem around the new equilibrium ensuring a better future for the targeted group and even society at large."[1] This simple chain is illustrated in figure 3-1.

---

1. Martin and Osberg (2007, p. 34).

FIGURE 3-1. A First Logic Chain of Social Entrepreneurship

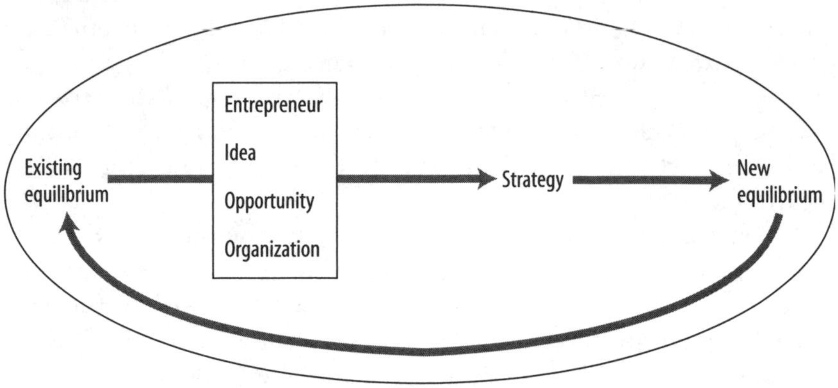

On the other hand, there are dozens of untested assumptions in the chain as well as substantial chaos both within and between each link. Because the entrepreneurial process is burdened by uncertainty, achieving sustainable change involves a host of choices that influence eventual success, almost all of them related to the way in which the four components are linked together by strategy.

The Order of Things

It is important to note that the four components are not numbered in any particular order. It could be that entrepreneurs always come first, bringing that zeal, ambition, and unwavering perseverance to the search for pattern-breaking ideas and opportunities for impact. It could also be that opportunities come first, thereby creating the incentives that spark the entrepreneurial process. Or ideas could come first and merely wait to be discovered by entrepreneurs, encouraged by opportunities, and implemented by organizations. Finally, it could be that organizations come first, marshalling enough resources to move quickly against an entrenched problem when the entrepreneur appears, the idea emerges, and an opportunity arises.

The order in which the four components interact is not a trivial issue, especially if it determines ultimate success. If the order varies in measurable ways across change efforts, it may be a key determinant of ultimate impact. If so, order might be a key variable in efforts to increase the amount of social entrepreneurship. If entrepreneurs come first, one might be wise to put much more funding into finding potential entrepreneurs and providing enough resources to convert their passion into action; if ideas come first, one might argue for a deeper investment in research and development regarding potential interventions for challenging the existing equilibrium; if opportunities are the key driver of change, for example, one might invest more in environmental scanning to help nascent entrepreneurs see below the horizon; and if organizations come first, one might invest more in idea generators, such as incubators or other structures that encourage risk-taking and experimentation.

Unfortunately, the entrepreneurial process is usually so chaotic that it is difficult to determine which of the four components comes first, second, and so forth. Since every innovation is different, learning is the only way to get from one side of the chasm to the other. Those who believe that entrepreneurship can be programmed need only read Douglas Polley and Andrew Van de Ven's 1996 description of the "rugged landscape" of action:

> We want to cross the dark valley to reach the peak on the other side. A broad goal galvanizes us to action. To reach the other side we must explore the valley at the same time we are constructing a path to the other side. We utilize our collective and individual skills by dividing up and sending scouts to pick specific paths from among the visible details of the valley (game paths, open versus thickly wooded areas, caves and canyons, etc.). Some are detoured in the maze of a cave, some get chased up a tree by wild beasts, others become preoccupied with cataloguing the vegetation along the trails, while others discover that the peak on the other side consists of a mountain range with many peaks. As we move forward and exert efforts in clearing our paths we discover more about the terrain as well as ourselves. We become good at trail blazing, at learning what we like and dislike, but not necessarily at knowing where we will end up.[2]

Van de Ven clearly viewed the process as anything but linear. The process does have a starting point of a sort but progresses in often unpredictable ways. As such, there can be no one best strategy for success. "In an ideal world, managers could formulate a long-term strategy, methodically implement it and then sustain the resulting competitive advantage,"

2. Polley and Van de Ven (1996, p. 880).

Donald Sull wrote in 2007. "Reality, however, is rarely so neat and tidy. Technologies evolve, regulations shift, customers make surprising choices, macroeconomic variables fluctuate and competitors thwart the best-laid plans."[3]

Using a single, linear strategy is not only impossible in such a world, it is dangerous. First, it splits the formulation of strategy from its implementation—formulation occurs at the start of the journey before the stumbling begins. Second, it produces escalation of commitment to failed strategies—the longer an organization stays on a given path, the less it is willing to change. Third, it ignores timing and feedback—there are times to move fast, times to go slow, and times to take a rest.

It is little wonder that so much of the innovation literature has coalesced around a much looser approach, which Sull calls "inherently iterative." Entrepreneurship occurs in stages, but with ample feedback and correction. Unlike the old stage models, in which innovation moved forward through gates from one stage to the next, newer models assume that innovation starts with chaos and ends with a semblance of order once a product or process has achieved some level of validation and profitability.

Traveling Alone

The question is whether entrepreneurs must endure the chaos alone. As Van De Ven wrote in 1993, Joseph Schumpeter's view of the individual entrepreneur as the sole source of creative labor and vision, antagonist, opportunity seeker, and persuader is just the ideal type, not the reality: "A common bias in Western culture is to attribute innovations to a particular individual entrepreneur, who at a particular date and place came up with the innovation through a stroke of genius or fortune. Although examples exist to support this bias, historical studies clearly show that most innovations are collective achievements of the efforts of many actors working over an extended period, often in parallel and independent locations."[4]

The reason for collaboration was clear to Van de Ven:

Conventional wisdom is that entrepreneurs act independently and compete to be the first into the market with their new product or service. There are many technologies and industries in which this

3. Sull (2007, p. 30).
4. Van de Ven (1993, p. 212).

may lead to successful monopoly profits. However, this practice may lead to unsuccessful results when the innovation involves a new technology for a new industry. Running in packs means that entrepreneurs coordinate, i.e., simultaneously cooperate and compete, with others as they develop and commercialize their innovation. Running in packs is analogous to bicycle racers who cue their pace to one another.[5]

Social entrepreneurship may involve a great demand for collaboration, especially if resistance to large-scale change is greater in the social sector. According to John Thompson, Geoff Alvy, and Ann Lees, social entrepreneurship requires a combination of different kinds of individuals who complement each other. Writing of natural and latent entrepreneurs in 2000, the authors argued that "social entrepreneurship requires a combination of people with visionary ideas, people with leadership skills and a commitment to make things happen, and people committed to helping others."[6]

As Thompson, Alvy, and Lees suggested, this mix of behaviors and skills can exist in what these authors called the "true entrepreneur" but can also emerge when "enterprising or intrapreneurial people are linked up with the visionary idea and opportunity. Arguably, if the idea or need is strong enough, appropriate champion will be attracted."[7]

The notion that ideas might emerge before champions is a staple of the agenda-setting literatures in political science. As John Kingdon argued in 2002, the policymaking environment consists of a number of "streams" that move through institutions such as Congress and the presidency simultaneously. Some contain solutions, others contain participants, and still others contain problems, resources, and organizations. The agenda gets set as these streams come together. Focusing on "ideas whose time has come," Kingdon refers to a primordial soup that produces opportunities for action in which ideas, participants, and problems finally join.

This view is hardly unique to the study of business entrepreneurship. Indeed, Chihmao Hsieh, Jack Nickerson, and Todd Zenger easily could have cited Kingdon in their 2007 study of how entrepreneurs discover opportunities: "Entrepreneurs deliberately select or otherwise stumble

---

5. Van de Ven (1993, pp. 223–24).
6. Thompson, Alvy, and Lees (2000, p. 332).
7. Thompson, Alvy, and Lees (2000, p. 332).

on problems to solve. Thereafter, they seek high-valued solutions—sets of valuable and complementary design and commercialization choices—which are discovered either by sheer luck or through a deliberately organized search."[8] The question is whether there are strategies that might make the stumbling more successful and luck more likely.

STRATEGY STEP BY STEP

Social entrepreneurship involves a relatively simple but dynamic process that demands complicated strategies for success:
   —Imagining a new equilibrium
   —Discovering an opportunity
   —Inventing the idea for change
   —Launching the idea into action
   —Scaling up for high impact
   —Diffusing the idea
   —Sustaining momentum
   —Navigating the changing social ecosystem
Each step carries its own risks and rewards, distinctive tasks, and chaos. One cannot create too many feedback loops both within and across the eight steps. Each step may also require very different kinds of entrepreneurs, ideas, opportunities, and organizations. The wildly optimistic entrepreneur who imagined the new equilibrium may need a more conservative style for scaling up and diffusing, for example, while the radical new idea that emerged from invention may need a touch of the familiar to gain momentum. Figure 3-2 shows the process.

Imagining

Some of the most interesting work in the study of business entrepreneurship focuses on the role of entrepreneurial imagination in sparking initial action. Entrepreneurs must believe that change is both essential and possible. They must also be inspired to act and create, two of Martin and Osberg's prime characteristics of social entrepreneurs. They must also withstand chaos. As James Quinn wrote in 1985, new ideas advance through a

> series of random—often highly intuitive—insights frequently triggered by gratuitous interactions between the discoverer and the

8. Hsieh, Nickerson, and Zenger (2007, p. 1286).

FIGURE 3-2. The Socially Entrepreneurial Process

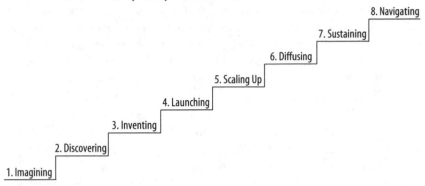

outside world. Only highly committed entrepreneurs can tolerate (and even enjoy) this chaos. They adopt solutions whenever they can be found, unencumbered by form plans or PERT charts that would limit the range of their imaginations. When the odds of success are low, the participation and interaction of many motivated players increase the chance that one will succeed.[9]

The question is what might be done to improve the odds that entrepreneurs will actually imagine a world worth fighting for. The answer is still out of reach, largely because imagination is such a difficult psychological construct. The creative process is nothing if not emotional. As Teresa Amabile and colleagues wrote in 2005, "Creative activity appears to be an affectively charged event, one in which complex cognitive processes are shaped by, co-occur with, and shape emotional experience. The biographies, letters, and journals of well-known creative individuals abound with emotional drama."[10]

The research on imagination is so broad that it is nearly impossible to describe. There is no doubt that it exists at the very front end of the entrepreneurial process, but considerable debate remains about what prompts some individuals to imagine.

Thus Amabile and her colleagues wrote of the link between affect and imagination. "If, as suggested by the experimental literature, positive mood enhances creativity at work, we would expect a given day's

9. Quinn (1985, p. 76).
10. Amabile and others (2005, p. 367).

creativity to follow reliably from the previous day's mood, above and beyond any carry-over of the previous day's mood." After interviewing 222 individuals who were serving as members of twenty-six project teams in seven different companies, they concluded that positive affect is, indeed, an antecedent of creativity: "That is, when positive affect increases, the scope of attention broadens and cognitive flexibility increases, increasing the probability that diverse cognitive effects will be associated."[11]

Affect also influences the incubation of new ideas. "Theoretically, the incubation process could be quite brief, with effects on creative thought manifested the same day. Or it could be a more lengthy process, playing out overnight, over the course of several days, or even over weeks and months."[12]

Translated, feeling good about the future increases the odds that an individual, pair, team, network, and so forth will believe in both the essential and the possible. It also produces joy, a rarely used term in either business or social entrepreneurship. "People reported feeling passionately involved with their work, deeply interested in it, positively challenged by it, and enjoying it as it was unfolding," Amabile and her colleagues wrote. "The feelings of enjoyment that arise in the course of doing an activity creatively may set up a virtuous cycle of enhanced creativity and enhanced intrinsic enjoyment."[13]

Joy, or positive affect, is hardly the only source of creativity that has been identified over the years. Pamela Tierney and Steven Farmer wrote about creative self-efficacy in 2002, for example, arguing that employees are more creative when they have job tenure, organizational support, and enough job complexity to believe that they can actually change the future.

In turn, Todd Thrash and Andrew Elliot wrote about the link between inspiration and creativity in 2003, suggesting that psychology has mostly ignored motivation (activation and energy), evocation (feeling overtaken, openness, calling), and transcendence (positive affect and clarity) as sources of inspiration and the creativity that follows. "Inspiration implies *motivation*, which is to say that it involves the energization and direction of behavior; inspiration is *evoked* rather than initiated directly

11. Amabile and others (2005, p. 376).
12. Amabile and others (2005, p. 392).
13. Amabile and others (2005, pp. 393–94).

through an act of will or arising without apparent cause; and inspiration involves *transcendence* of the ordinary preoccupation or limitations of human agency."[14] These factors are triggered by a set of events or possibilities that evoke creativity.

In addition, a number of researchers have struggled to find the source of the creative climate that allows imagination to flourish. According to Samuel Hunter, Katrina Bedell, and Michael Mumford, writing in 2007, creativity has been linked to a host of sources, including expertise, information processing strategies, abilities, personality characteristics, collaboration, group interactions, leadership, and organizational structure. But after culling through eighty-eight of the most rigorous articles on these sources, the authors concluded that strong interpersonal relationships, intellectual challenge, and challenge are the strongest predictors of a strong climate for creativity. And they wrote that creativity and inspiration are strongly related to challenging work and an intellectually stimulating environment.

Before readers say "duh" about some of these findings, it is important to note that they provide insights for creating a climate of creativity. As Hunter, Bedell, and Mumford concluded, managers can easily do something about the resources and autonomy needed to imagine. They can allocate more time and resources for imagination, encourage participation, avoid micromanagement, build diversity into the creative process, and set goals that challenge their employees. They can also create a sense of urgency surrounding innovation, though such urgency may actually undermine the positive affect associated with dreaming.

Discovering

Imagination leads directly, albeit chaotically, into the discovery of an opportunity for change. Even opportunities that exist before imagination must be discovered, in part because entrepreneurs are motivated to create the new equilibrium they imagine. Opportunities may be like dollar bills blowing in the wind just waiting to be caught, but they will never be caught unless entrepreneurs look up.

Many entrepreneurship scholars tend to view discovery as a process within a process. Entrepreneurs scan the environment and existing knowledge, match a problem to a solution, and decide whether they should proceed to invention. Although the number of stages varies from study

14. Thrash and Elliot (2003, p. 871).

to study, discovery is generally viewed as the product of a deliberate, proactive search. Entrepreneurs do not want just any dollar blowing in the wind; they want ones that match their problem. As Vesa Puhakka argued in 2007, finding the right opportunity involves three related strategies:

—First, entrepreneurs must constantly scan the competitive environment. "Entrepreneurs should know who their competitors are, what their products are and how they acknowledge future technologies and trends."

—Second, entrepreneurs should be proactive. "Entrepreneurs should vision the future (based on competitive scanning and existing knowledge) and in terms of the most probable future trends in the business. Further, entrepreneurs should grab the near future trends that others are not yet capable of seeing."

—Third, entrepreneurs should engage in collective search with trusted advisers. "Out of this active social dialogue, entrepreneurs can then locate those people whom they can really trust." Much as entrepreneurs are often described as mavericks that only trust themselves, Puhakka argues that team entrepreneurship may be the best way to develop a trusted cadre of fellow searchers.[15]

Knowledge is the critical link across these stages. As Mark Casson and Marina Della Giusta also argued in 2007, "opportunity seeking" is about gathering information. "In opportunity seeking, much of the information gathered will be 'spillover' information acquired from people who cannot use the information themselves," the two authors wrote. "The entrepreneur is not looking for commercial secrets acquired by eavesdropping on business rivals, but rather information obtained from non-competing sources that is surplus to their requirements."[16]

This kind of knowledge is often found in broad social networks. Even as they protect their ideas from poachers, entrepreneurs can learn a great deal about potential opportunities from interacting with each other, as well as mentors, investors, suppliers, and customers. These networks are particularly important in the search for social value. Although social entrepreneurs most certainly compete with each other in the search for funding, they also benefit from interactions that improve the odds of successful invention. Assuming that there is no shortage of opportunities, interaction is a collective good that helps the field as a whole advance.

15. Puhakka (2007, pp. 46–47).
16. Casson and Della Giusta (2007, p. 230).

Inventing

Despite its critical impact on entrepreneurship, imagination is necessary but insufficient for successful entrepreneurship. Imagination must be converted into invention. Although there are plenty of legends about mad scientists and "eureka moments," most inventions occur through a more mundane process of trial and error that leads to a specific product or process.

This is certainly what Julian Birkinshaw and Michael Mol found after studying 11 management innovations such as total quality management and the balanced scorecard. According to their case studies, new ideas rarely involve eureka moments. Instead, they involve traditional methods of problem solving. "The management innovator brings together the various elements of a problem (that is, dissatisfaction with the status quo) with the various elements of a solution (which typically involves some inspiration from outside, plus a clear understanding of the internal situation and context). . . . While not able to identify a 'eureka moment' per se, most management innovators could point to a clear precipitating event that provided them with a focal point around which to coordinate their efforts."[17]

Again, this highly iterative process often defies linear description. It varies with the nature of the problem and the availability of solutions, investments in research and access to knowledge. It also involves variations in the same factors that create an entrepreneurial orientation. Indeed, according to Robert Wolcott and Michael Lippitz, there are at least four strategies for creating a new idea:

—*The Opportunist Model:* According to Wolcott and Lippitz, all companies start as opportunists: "Without any designated organizational ownership or resources, corporate entrepreneurship proceeds (if it does at all) based on the efforts and serendipity of intrepid 'product champions'—people who toil against the odds, creating new businesses often in spite of the corporation."[18] This has been the emphasis in new venturing outside the organization and is the dominant model within the field of business entrepreneurship.

—*The Enabler Model:* Whatever their initial success, organizations eventually hit stall points that weaken their entrepreneurial spirit. In the enabler model, organizations assume that employees will develop new

17. Birkinshaw and Mol (2006, p. 85).
18. Wolcott and Lippitz (2007, p. 76).

ideas if given adequate support: "Dedicating resources and processes (but without any formal organizational ownership) enables teams to pursue opportunities on their own insofar as they fit the organization's strategic frame."[19] This has been the central hope in creating incubators.

—*The Advocate Model:* Instead of letting a thousand flowers bloom by merely fertilizing the soil, organizations can put their faith in a highly protected internal operation: "In the advocate model, a company assigns organizational ownership for the creation of new businesses while intentionally providing only modest budgets to the core group. Advocate organizations act as evangelists and innovation experts, facilitating corporate entrepreneurship in conjunction with business units."[20] This has been the core construct in spin-offs.

—*The Producer Model:* Instead of creating a separate business within a business, organizations can create internal incubators for new ideas. "As with the enabler and advocate model, an objective is to encourage latent entrepreneurs. But the producer model also aims to protect emerging projects from turf battles, encourage cross-unit collaboration, build potentially disruptive businesses and create pathways for executives to pursue careers outside their business units."[21] This has been the key emphasis of organization-wide rejuvenation.

Launching

Scholars of business and social entrepreneurship tend to view the launch process as a brief moment in entrepreneurial time. Although organizations devote substantial resources to creating attention for new products such as the iPhone, research on launch strategies is left largely to marketing departments, as is corporate social responsibility. Entrepreneurship is about new ideas, or so it seems, while launching is about marketing. However, there are hints of potential strategies in the growing inventory of descriptive work on why some new products succeed while others fail.

The bulk of this work focuses on product characteristics. The most aggressive study of how organizations can exploit opportunities was conducted as part of the Panel Study on Entrepreneurial Dynamics research program, a ten-year effort that began in 1995 led by William

19. Wolcott and Lippitz (2007, p. 77).
20. Wolcott and Lippitz (2007, p. 78).
21. Wolcott and Lippitz (2007, p. 79).

Gartner and his colleagues. Among the hundreds of measures used to describe the creation of new businesses, the study team included a handful that described potential lever points for building launch strategies:

—*Market research:* responding quickly to changes in markets, serving niches missed by others, and more effective marketing and advertising

—*Products and process:* developing new and advanced product and process technologies, utilizing new product and process technology

—*Product diversity:* creating more attractive products, distinctive goods and services, and more product choices for the customer

—*Facilities and convenience:* finding superior locations and providing more customer convenience and more attractive facilities

—*Price:* setting lower prices compared with similar products

—*Cost containment:* lowering the cost of production, creating more effective channels of communication, minimizing administrative and sales costs, and enhancing employee participation in management

Most of these measures tap into a relatively small business literature on the characteristics of a successful product launch. According to Anthony Di Benedetto's 1999 study of 200 product launches, for example, success involves both strategy and tactics. On the strategic side, Di Benedetto found that successful launches generally involve "superior skills" in marketing research, sales, distribution, promotion, R&D, engineering, as well as "the use of cross-functional teams making key marketing and manufacturing decisions, and getting logistics involved early in planning." On the tactical side, he also found that success was also related to the quality of the selling effort, advertising, technical support, good launch management, support programs, and excellent launch timing relative to customers and competitors, as well as "information-gathering activities of all kinds (market testing, customer feedback, advertising testing, etc.)."[22] Timing turns out to be of particular note in explaining success—organizations can do everything right in bringing a product to the launch, but the timing must be right.

Di Benedetto is not the only researcher to look for the path to survival:

—Analyzing sixty studies of successful product launches in a 2001 study, David Henard and David Szymanski found significant relationships between success and product (price, innovativeness, and so on), strategy (order of entry, marketing synergy, among others), process (including customer input, the use of cross-functional teams), and market

22. Di Benedetto (1999, p. 540).

(opportunity, competition, and so forth). The two authors also noted that surprisingly there are few studies of the relationship between product quality and success and concluded that "few attempts have been made to model how firms generate ideas for new products and how successful idea and success at each of the other phases of the new product initiative eventually translate into new product success. This void in research attention persists even though the generation of new product ideas is arguably the first step in a cumulative new product development process."[23]

—Reviewing the commercialization of 1,700 new products, Gerald Udell and Mike Hignite found that product failures were highly related to perceptions of potential success by large buying organizations such as Wal-Mart. As the authors reported in 2007, new products are often introduced to these pass-through agents with little thought about what might make the product appealing to a buyer: "The best laid plans of entrepreneurial product champions often go awry, not because of product flaws, or even resource shortcomings, but because of the entrepreneur's failure to reconcile the needs of the new product with their experiences and those of their firm."[24]

—Exploring a sample of 11,250 new technology ventures launched between 1991 and 2000, Michael Song and colleagues found that only 22 percent were still alive five years later. According to their 2008 analysis, the authors found eight significant factors that predict survival: supply chain integration, market scope, the organization's age, the size of the founding team, financial resources, the founder's marketing experience, the founder's industry experience, and level of patent protection. Here, older organizations actually enhance the odds of survival, in part by providing needed capital as the new venture bounces along during its early years.

—Reporting on 33 Israeli social ventures in 2006, Moshe Sharir and Miri Lerner found eight significant contributors of success: the social network, total dedication of the entrepreneur, the capital base at the establishment stage, the acceptance of the idea of the venture in the public discourse, the venturing team, long-term cooperation, the ability of the service to stand the market test, and previous managerial experience. Of the eight predictors, Sharir and Lerner concluded that just two were

23. Henard and Szymanski (2001, p. 363).
24. Udell and Hignite (2007, p. 75).

necessary for success: total dedication to the venture's success and the venture's social network.

These findings echo much earlier work on the creation of new ideas by Peter Drucker. According to Drucker, entrepreneurial success depends on three very different factors. First, successful ideas often, but not always, offer the "fustest with the mostest." As he wrote in 1985, this strategy may carry great reward, but also comes with high risk, making it the "greatest gamble." "And it is unforgiving, making no allowances for mistakes and allowing no second chance."[25] The first to attack and exploit opportunity may do little more than provide an inventory of what not to do.

Second, successful ideas involve "creative imitation." Acknowledging that creative imitation might seem like a contradiction in terms, Drucker wrote that the entrepreneur copies a new idea but applies it in a way that is better, faster, more economical, and more inviting than the original.

Third, successful ideas involve what Drucker called "entrepreneurial judo," a form of organizational maneuvering that fits well with Bill Drayton's notion of the importance of managing the "jujitsu points" of change. According to Drucker, entrepreneurial judo "first aims at securing a beachhead, one which the established leaders either do not defend at all or defend only half-heartedly. . . . Once that beachhead has been secured, that is, once the newcomers have an adequate market and adequate revenue, they move in on the rest of the territory."[26] In other words, they look for opportunities in open space.

Scaling Up

Scaling up is a multistep process of its own that focuses on expanding the impact of a new idea. Defined as mix of internal capacity building and as external diffusion, the concept taps into a large inventory of research, some of which is referenced elsewhere in this book.

Some of the best work on the relationship between capacity and scaling up has come from within the social entrepreneurship community, most notably from Steven LaFrance, Michael Lee, Rick Green, Jaclyn Kvaternik, Andrew Robinson, and India Alarcon. With support from the Skoll Foundation, LaFrance and his associates searched for lessons on scaling up among twenty-eight organizations, including Ashoka, City

25. Drucker (1985, p. 13).
26. Drucker (1985, p. 23).

Year, College Summit, Doctors Without Borders, Environmental Defense, Heifer International, and TransFair USA.

Scanning the field in 2006, LaFrance and his associates defined scaling as an effort to increase social impact to more closely match demand. After noting that creating new branches was the most common form of scaling up among the twenty-eight organizations, LaFrance and his team turned to the seven organizational assets that affect scaling:

—*Defining and adhering to core mission*: "Clearly defining and adhering to the mission provides focus for decision-making and resource deployment during the scaling process."

—*Balancing control and flexibility*: "Scaling, particularly when it entails organizational expansion, places great challenges on organizational and management structures. The challenge is to balance control with flexibility for innovation and impact."

—*Codifying what works*: "Impact can be scaled more effectively by clearly articulating essential components of the model so that it can be more easily and faithfully replicated."

—*Cultivating and perpetuating the culture*: "For scaling to succeed, organizations must cultivate and perpetuate during the scaling process those aspects of the culture—shared values, behaviors and norms—that are critical for mission achievement."

—*Collecting and using data*: "The ability to gather and use data can be critical for informing important scaling-related decisions such as establishing needs in new issue or geographic areas, demonstrating the effectiveness of a model, setting priorities, and choosing strategies."

—*Connecting fundraising to the mission*: "Successfully-scaled social entrepreneurs are able to expand their resource base by viewing fundraising as a way to achieve mission and by finding ways to connect supporters to programmatic work."

—*Making the right decisions for scaling*: "Strong leadership and governance means making sure the right decisions are made to foster greater mission achievement during what is often a period of rapid organizational change." [27]

Each of the seven characteristics of scaling stands as a best practice, but each also interacts with the other six to improve the odds of success. "In planning for capacity-building work," LaFrance and his associates wrote, "organizations will need to prioritize the scaling capacities that

---

27. LaFrance and others (2006, p. 3).

will provide the most leverage at the present moment. . . . The scaling capacities do not dictate what is needed at a particular moment per se. Rather, they provide general principles that inform an organization's capacity-building strategy and should be reflected on periodically to define what capacity building is needed now."[28]

This sentiment is echoed throughout the business literature. One of the very best summaries of building entrepreneurial organizations involves Google, which was the subject of a 2008 article by Bala Iyer and Thomas Davenport. Looking back on how Google became a $250 billion company, Iyer and Davenport focus in part on the company's "built to build" infrastructure. By investing in the organization itself, Google has created the capacity not just to adapt and learn but to put that adapting and learning to immediate effect in generating new ideas and scaling them to immediate profitability. It has the organizational architecture, employee commitment, and technical resources to create a constant stream of ideas. "While few organizations can match the magnitude of Google's infrastructure investments," Iyer and Davenport wrote, "many can achieve the kind of purposeful design that allows the company to roll out innovations very rapidly."[29]

At the same time, Google does not expect every innovation to produce immediate results. To the contrary, Iyer and Davenport argued that Google practices "strategic patience." This patience produces an ongoing commitment to scalability, an accelerated product development life cycle and support for third-party development and "mashups." The company then builds to build by making innovation part of everyone's job description, eliminating friction at every turn, letting the market choose, and cultivating a taste for failure and chaos.

Diffusing

Diffusion has long been considered a key measure of successful innovation. The greater the diffusion, the greater the replication; the greater the replication, the greater the impact. "Replication is not the only sign that an idea has spread," Ashoka's Noga Leviner, Leslie Crutchfield, and Diana Wells explained in 2006. "But it is one indication that an idea has taken root. Social entrepreneurs who succeed on this front have moved beyond their direct impact to influence the way other groups in society

---

28. LaFrance and others (2006, p. 4).
29. Iyer and Davenport (2008, p. 62).

approach a social problem."[30] In short, imitation is not only the sincerest form of flattery; it is one of the fastest methods for reshaping the social equilibrium.

Diffusion begins with a choice between what Trisha Greenhalgh and her colleagues described in 2004 as three very different approaches: "let-it-be" diffusion, which is unpredictable, uncertain, emergent, adaptive, and self-organized; "help-it-happen" diffusion, which is encouraged, supported, influenced, and negotiated; and "make-it-happen" diffusion, which is scientific, orderly, regulated, and programmed.

Unfortunately, the choice of one form of diffusion over another is difficult given the factors that influence successful spread. The innovation has a significant impact on potential adoption—after all, some ideas are easy to understand, while others are complex; some are easily appended to existing practice, while others require new infrastructure. Adopters also have a significant impact on diffusion—some are highly motivated to change, while others resist; some have the tolerance to handle ambiguity, while others value routines. The organization plays a significant role, too—some organizations have a commitment to learning, while others are filled with confusion; some have the time and energy to experiment, while others are too tight to fail.

Having read more than 500 articles and books on diffusion, Greenhalgh and her colleagues offered a number of conclusions on why these individual factors matter, but few on how the factors might be used to improve the odds of success. Indeed, the authors complained that the lack of research on implementation was the single most striking finding of their detailed literature review. Nevertheless, they did find at least some explanations for managing the "nonlinear process" of spreading an idea in the research on system readiness for adoption, including funding, communication, networks, and feedback. After examining a long list of possible leverage points for increasing the odds of diffusion, the authors also focused on a set of organizational factors that can be manipulated by entrepreneurs and their advocates:

—*Organizational structure:* "An adaptive and flexible organizational structure, and structures and processes that support devolved decision making in the organization (e.g., strategic decision making devolved to departments, operational decision making devolved to teams on the

---

30. Leviner, Crutchfield, and Wells (2006, p. 97).

ground) enhance the success of implementation and the chances of routinization."

—*Leadership and management:* "Top management support, advocacy of the implementation process, and continued commitment to enhance the success of implementation and routinization. . . . If the innovation aligns with the earlier goals of both top management and middle management and if the leaders are actively involved and frequently consulted, the innovation is more likely to be routinized."

—*Human resources:* "Successful routinization of an innovation in an organization depends on the motivation, capacity, and competence of individual practitioners. The early and widespread involvement of staff at all levels, perhaps through formal facilitation initiatives, enhances the success of routinization."[31]

Sustaining

Sustaining momentum is a central concern for social entrepreneurship, if only because the prevailing equilibrium can be highly resistant to change. But much of the knowledge about sustaining change is yet to be distilled from the case studies that now circulate throughout the field— the stories of Ashoka innovators, Echoing Green fellows, Skoll Foundation grantees, *Fast Company* and Monitor Group award winners, among others. But there is a growing body of work that is starting to pull together strategies from what might be called "biographies of change."

Writing in 2007 of twelve high-impact nonprofits they selected by reputation, for example, Heather McLeod Grant and Leslie Crutchfield emphasized six factors that create "forces for good" from imagination to success:

—*Blending social services and advocacy:* "High impact organizations may start out providing great programs, but they eventually realize that they cannot achieve large-scale social change through service delivery alone."

—*Using the market to affect change and generate revenues:* "High-impact nonprofits have learned that tapping into the power of self-interest and the laws of economics is far more effective than appealing to pure altruism."

---

31. Greenhalgh and others (2004, p. 611).

—Creating evangelists who support the new idea with volunteer time and energy: "High-impact nonprofits build strong communities of supporters who help them achieve their larger goals."

—Building networks of other nonprofits to create alliances for change: "Although most nonprofits pay lip service to collaboration, many of them really see other groups as competition for scarce resources. But high-impact organizations help their peers succeed, building networks of nonprofit allies and devoting remarkable time and energy to advancing their fields."

—Adapting to uncertainty: "High-impact nonprofits are exceptionally adaptive, modifying their tactics to increase their success. They have responded to changing circumstances with one innovation after another."

—Sharing leadership throughout the organization through participatory management: "The leaders of these 12 organizations all exhibit charisma, but they don't have oversized egos. They know that they must share power in order to be stronger forces for good."[32]

Although the authors never describe these characteristics as an ordered set, the first two characteristics appear to focus on imagination, the second two on launch and acceleration, and the last two on maintaining success.

Navigating

As already suggested, business and social entrepreneurship do not occur in a vacuum. They may occur at the intersection of policy streams or within David-and-Goliath partnerships, among evangelists or across networks, and in lonely garages or noisy incubators.

But as Paul Bloom and J. Gregory Dees argued in early 2008, entrepreneurship involves an ecosystem in which players (individuals and organizations) and the environment (norms, markets, laws) interact to move ideas forward. Writing first about players, for example, Bloom and Dees focused on resource providers, competitors, complementary organizations, beneficiaries and customers, opponents and problem makers, and affected or influential bystanders. Writing next about the environment, Bloom and Dees emphasized politics and administrative structures, economics and markets, geography and infrastructure, culture and social fabric.

---

32. Grant and Crutchfield (2007, pp. 35–39).

Imagining this ecosystem as a governing environment, Bloom and Dees argued that there are four practices that drive "systemic ecosystem change":

—Coalitions: "Systemic ecosystem change is usually created by coalitions of social entrepreneurs and organizations, not by the unilateral actions of a single entrepreneur or organization. Creating successful coalitions, however, is challenging because it is often difficult to attract the right partners, agree on a joint strategy, select the best leaders (or leading organizations), hold the coalition together, and make strategic adjustments as the situation unfolds."

—Communications: "Many potentially powerful innovations never take hold or create lasting systemic ecosystem change because they were not effectively communicated. The key to effective communication is for social entrepreneurs to frame the issues so that they help build support for their cause."

—Credibility: "It is often hard for social entrepreneurs to convince others that a systemic change is needed . . . to make the case that the change they propose will work. That is why it is important for social entrepreneurs to find ways to establish their credibility."

—Contingencies: "Biological and social ecosystems are complex . . . which makes it difficult to predict all of the consequences of any significant intervention. Because of this, creating systemic change is often an experimental and learning process. It is important for social entrepreneurs to forecast how their ecosystem and the players in it might react to any change—and be prepared with potential countermoves to ameliorate or capitalize on the situation."[33]

What makes Bloom and Dees's model so compelling is that it is responsive to changing conditions. Their four practices vary greatly with changing conditions. One cannot know which approach to networking, communicating, convincing, or anticipating will work—each strategy is dependent on the nature of the ecosystem, which is always in flux. This work leads to a second logic chain that puts the ecosystem first, not the problem. This amended chain is illustrated in figure 3.3.

This ecosystem approach is well supported by the traditional literature on business entrepreneurship. Indeed, Van de Ven wrote of a similar "infrastructure for entrepreneurship" in 1993. According to his study, this infrastructure is composed of resources such as knowledge,

33. Bloom and Dees (2008, pp. 52–53).

FIGURE 3-3. An Amended Logic Chain of Social Entrepreneurship

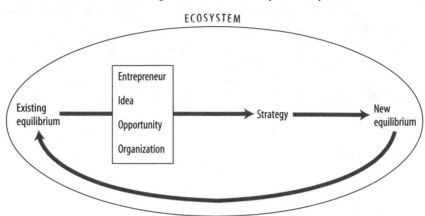

financing, and human capital; institutional arrangements that regulate public and private collaboration and technology standards; and processes such as research and development, networking, commercialization, and marketing.

Images of infrastructure may be much more architectural than are images of an ecosystem. Yet, different though the two metaphors are, they focus on the same result, again largely through a shared effort to change the prevailing equilibrium. "By engaging in cooperative and competitive relationships in the development of alternative technological possibilities," Van de Ven argued, "groups of entrepreneurs in both the public and private sectors increasingly isolate themselves from traditional industries by virtue of the interdependencies, growing commitments to, and unique know-how of a new technology. Isolation frees the actions from institutional constraints of existing technologies and industries. . . . As the number of entrepreneurs gains a critical mass, a complex network of cooperative and competitive relationships begin to accumulate."[34]

This focus on partnerships is in sync with emerging views of social entrepreneurship as a cooperative, not competitive, process. Whereas business entrepreneurship eventually produces a single winner, social entrepreneurship appears to require "swarming" to succeed, which will be discussed at the end of chapter five.

34. Van de Ven (1993, p. 220).

As Sally Osberg told the Skoll World Forum in March 2008, the next chapter of social entrepreneurship involves collaboration and common purpose:

> More and more social entrepreneurship is not only about the power of the brilliant individual, increasingly it's about the power of partnerships, the coalitions that take the solutions you envision and bring the impact of those solutions to scale, not necessarily one organization to scale, the impact of the solution to scale. This is the direction we are headed, toward a dynamic open-source model of social change.[35]

STILL SEARCHING FOR STRATEGY

Most of these efforts to unlock the secrets of success may be inspiring to those about to begin an entrepreneurial journey, but they do not necessarily sum to a strategy for tying entrepreneurs, ideas, opportunities, and organizations together into an effective campaign for changing the social equilibrium. Except for the emerging effort by Bloom and Dees to highlight the highly interactive role of the social ecosystem and systemic change, most research offers long checklists of possible factors that *might* underpin successful change but little guidance on what matters most at which stage of the process.

As Grant and Crutchfield would surely acknowledge, for example, successful organizations have many choices in how they attack the social equilibrium, but the choices may be very different depending upon the entrepreneur's ability, the idea itself, the nature of the opportunity, and the organization's capacity. Such lists also create the expectation that organizations must be perfect in every way, a myth that Grant and Crutchfield rightly debunk.

More important, it is one thing to argue that organizations should share leadership or pump resources into innovation and quite another to link those choices with a specific target, such as ending hunger. Even Grant and Crutchfield acknowledged the problems in deciding which of their six practices are essential to high impact: "The 12 high-impact nonprofits that we studied use a majority of these six practices. But they

---

35. Remarks at the Skoll World Forum, Oxford University, United Kingdom, March 28, 2008.

didn't always, and they don't all employ them in the same ways. . . . Yet they all converge on using more of these practices, not fewer."[36]

Unfortunately, it is not clear which of these practices matter most in creating "forces for good," or how combinations fit particular types of entrepreneurs, ideas, opportunities, and organizations. Even as these lists describe a range of paths to high impact, we need to push forward with conversations about which strategies fit with what kinds of systemic change. Such conversations obviously enrich theory whenever they involve comparison groups of like organizations. After all, thousands upon thousands of organizations have evangelists, but many fewer change the social equilibrium.

Notwithstanding the need for further research on their six practices, Grant and Crutchfield's study produced persuasive evidence directly relevant to confirming at least some of the forty assumptions about social entrepreneurship. According to their research, high-impact organizations such as Environmental Defense do not discount advocacy. "Ultimately, all high-impact organizations bridge the divide between service and advocacy," they wrote. "They become good at both. And the more they serve and advocate, the more they achieve impact."

Grant and Crutchfield's study also showed the importance of partnerships to success—high-impact organizations rarely act alone:

> Regardless of whether they have formal or informal affiliates, all of these nonprofits help build their respective fields through collaboration rather than competition. They share financial resources and help other nonprofits succeed at fundraising. They give away their model and proprietary information in an open-source approach. They cultivate leadership and talent for their larger network, rather than hoarding the best people. And they work in coalitions to influence legislation or conduct grassroots advocacy campaigns, without worrying too much about which organization gets the credit. These nonprofits realize that they are more powerful together than alone and that large-scale social change often requires collaborative, collective action.[37]

Grant and Crutchfield also confirm the need for adaptation and the steady stream of ideas and development that goes with it: "All of the

36. Grant and Crutchfield (2007, pp. 39–40).
37. Grant and Crutchfield (2007, p. 38).

nonprofits in our sample have mastered what we call the *cycle of adaptation*," they wrote. "First, they listen to feedback from their external environments and seek opportunities for improvement or change. Next, they innovate and experiment, developing new ideas or improving upon older programs. Then they evaluate and learn what works with the innovation, sharing information and best practices across their networks."[38]

Finally, despite debunking the myth of perfection in management, the analysis confirmed the need for "reliable internal infrastructure" as a foundation for sustaining impact. According to Grant and Crutchfield, all of their organizations were willing to invest in organizational capacity, including all aspects of management. At the same time, however, Grant and Crutchfield argued that management comes second. At least for their small group of organizations, "greatness has more to do with how non-profits work *outside* the boundaries of their organizations than with how they manage their own *internal* operations. The high-impact nonprofits we studied are satisfied with building a 'good enough' organization and then focusing their energy externally to catalyze large-scale change."[39]

My question about Grant and Crutchfield's description of management is whether "good enough" is actually good enough. Would the Nature Conservancy or the American Red Cross have made the list of high-impact nonprofits if they had been more than good enough when they were confronted by both figurative and literal hurricanes?

At least in recent years, good enough in the social benefit sector has not been good enough for most Americans. Confidence in charitable organizations remains low, and ratings of charitable performance in spending money wisely, helping people, running their programs and services, and being fair have hit bottom, while the percentage of Americans who think charities waste a great deal or fair amount of money is soaring.

Perhaps this is why LaFrance and his colleagues put such a great emphasis on capacity building as an essential ingredient of the entrepreneurial success: "Developing organizational capacity is essential for social entrepreneurships to reach the full promise of their ideas. By turning inward, one lays the necessary foundation for sustaining and growing the organization's impact, which ultimately means more prosperity, equity, and sustainability for this world we share."[40]

38. Grant and Crutchfield (2007, p. 39).
39. Grant and Crutchfield (2007, p. 35).
40. LaFrance and others (2006, p. 20).

FIGURE 3-4. A Final Logic Chain of Social Entrepreneurship

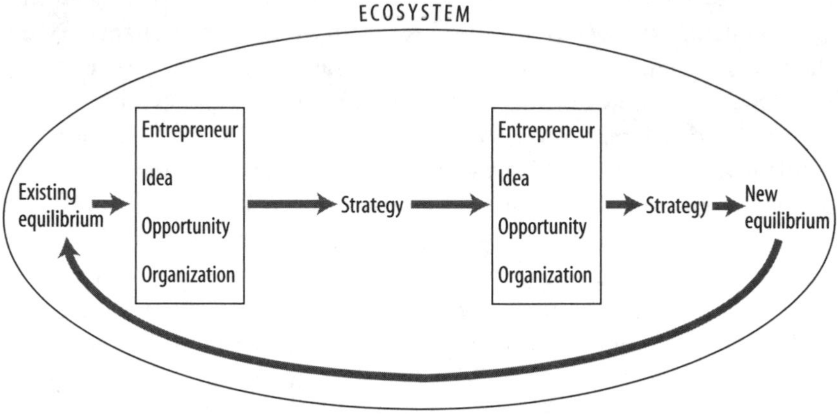

THE LOGIC OF SOCIAL ENTREPRENEURSHIP REVISITED

As this quick review of entrepreneurial strategies suggests, the four components are both cause and consequence of impact, independent predictors of social entrepreneurship and dependent outcomes of that action.

Described as such, proof of concept becomes a key mediating factor in socially entrepreneurial activity. It is certainly one of the most important factors to "mezzanine" investors as they make their decisions about fellowships, loans, and grants.

A Final Logic Chain

As the socially entrepreneurial activity adapts over time, so does the entrepreneur, idea, opportunity, and organization. In a sense, success reflects a "virtuous cycle" in which learning and adaptation create greater impacts, which in turn create more learning and adaptation, which in turn again create even greater impacts. Along the way, this cycle may produce a new entrepreneur, a stream of very different ideas, sensitivities to emerging opportunities, and increased organizational capacity. Figure 3-4 shows this final logic chain.

Readers should note that social entrepreneurship can have immediate impacts through proof of concept. It is quite possible, for example, that early impact affects the organization more than the entrepreneur, idea, or opportunity do or that it affects the entrepreneur more than it does the organization. At least in business entrepreneurship, for example, the entrepreneur is often jettisoned in favor of a more traditional executive as the idea moves toward scale. As such, this second logic chain is highly dependent on the stage of entrepreneurial impact, from start-up to scale-up to maturity.

Readers should note that this final logic chain is difficult to validate given the current state of research on social entrepreneurship. Not only is further research essential for identifying meaningful interactions between the four components, it is also essential for asking whether and how differences and changes in any or all of the four components affect actual impact. At what point, for example, does the new idea become the prevailing wisdom? And what can or should be done to protect that new equilibrium from the creative destruction that it once created?

This final logic chain raises three questions about the assumptions that underpin strategies of entrepreneurship. First, how fast does the logic chain progress from beginning to end? Second, how does stress affect movement through the chain? And third, does experience matter to mastery of the process?

Time and Logic

My final logic chain does not include a time line from start to finish, nor are there any definitive studies of just how long it takes to move from imagination to launch or, more important, from launch to success.

There is a reason for the lack of such research, of course. Time is almost impossible to measure across the entrepreneurial process. Although most researchers assume that entrepreneurial activity must pass through one phase (such as imagining) to the next (recognizing), most also allow for considerable motion within each phase of the process. As Ajay Vohora, Mike Wright, and Andy Lockett described the "critical junctures" that face university spin-outs as they move from conducting basic research to framing opportunities, planning launches, and producing sustainable returns, "each phase involves an iterative, non-linear process of development in which there may be a need to revisit some of the earlier decisions and activities."[41]

This is not to argue that time is irrelevant to success. As Vohora and his coauthors explained in their 2004 analysis, the longer a venture dawdles at each critical juncture between the phases, the more vulnerable it becomes: "Unless each critical juncture is overcome, the venture cannot

---

41. Vohora, Wright, and Lockett (2004, p. 147).

move to the next phase of development and hence will stagnate."[42] According to their study of nine high technology ventures, successful movement through the entrepreneurial process involves access to physical, financial, human, or technological ventures; the ability to generate those resources through persuasion and reputation; and the organizational capacity to convert resources into performance. Other linear models make the same case, including the "spin-out funnel" presented by Bart Clarysse and four of his colleagues in 2005.

The time between phases also varies greatly according to the amount of learning and adaptation that occurs along the chain. According to Céline Druilhe and Elizabeth Garnsey's 2004 research, successful university spin-outs can change direction many times en route to formal launch, often driven by the entrepreneur's relevant knowledge and experience and the resource requirements of the idea. The higher the demand for knowledge and resources, the longer is the time between imagination and success. Petra Andries and Koenraad Debackere found the same effect in their 2006 study of technology ventures, except in this instance, time between phases varied according to uncertainty and ambiguity. The higher the need for adaptation and learning, the longer the time between imagination and success.

Studies of time and success lead inevitably to strategies for being the "fustest with the mostest." All things being equal, Ans Heirman and Bart Clarysse argued that software development depends almost entirely on speed for success. Unfortunately, speed is often beyond reach because of "sticky information" that is expensive to transfer from customers to developers. Looking at almost 100 research-based start-up firms in their 2007 study, the authors concluded that speed depends on "rapid and flexible iterations with customers," "employing people who previously worked together," and, sadly, avoiding collaboration with universities. In other words, not all ideas move through the logic chain at the same speed, meaning that some entrepreneurial ideas have immediate impacts, while others can take years to reach launch velocity.

Stress and Logic

Just as my final logic chain does not include a time line, it does not include a stress line. Nevertheless, there is no question that stress varies as the entrepreneurial process advances. Indeed, according to Minet

---

42. Vohora, Wright, and Lockett (2004, p. 148).

Schindehutte, Michael Morris, and Jeffrey Allen, entrepreneurship is an "extreme experience" that tests the limits of entrepreneurial commitment: "The entrepreneurial context can be characterized in terms of peaks and valleys, or periods of relatively high pressure, stress, uncertainty, and ambiguity and periods of relative stability and predictability," the authors wrote in their 2006 study.[43]

Past research suggests that three psychological characteristics shape the response to stress. One is peak performance, which involves a period of objective high performance that exceeds expectations. A second is peak experience, which involves a period of perceived high performance that exceeds what Schindehutte and her colleagues described as the "usual level of intensity, meaningfulness, and richness." A third is flow, which involves a state of focused energy that is sometimes described as an almost mystical experience that produces exceptional feats of action.

Peak performance, peak experience, and flow are all related, and all rise and fall over time. This research provokes a number of questions, according to Schindehutte and her colleagues: Can entrepreneurs prepare themselves to experience peak moments more effectively? Can they create flow? Can they make peak performance a common response? Can they "smooth" the entrepreneurial experience to avoid the inevitable lows and perhaps temper the highs? As least for Schindehutte and her colleagues the joys of "being in the zone" may outweigh caution about the ultimate stress involved.

This research does not imply that entrepreneurs are superhuman, even though it does suggest that entrepreneurs can summon great strength when needed. Yet, it supports the considerable evidence that entrepreneurs experience great stress. In fact, they may experience much of the same physical and psychological stress that athletes, professional coaches, and even polar explorers experience. Indeed, one of my favorite articles on stress and leadership involves a study of Artic and Antarctic expeditions. Obviously, participants in such expeditions experience great physical and emotional stress—exertion, fatigue, isolation, and confinement. As Lawrence Palinkas and Peter Suedfeld wrote in their 2008 *Lancet* article, even short escapes from these pressures involve great risk. Consider the following excerpt from *North to the Pole*, an account of the 1986 Steger International Polar Expedition:

---

43. Schindehutte, Morris, and Allen (2006, p. 349).

Sitting there cold and hungry as the wind snapped the tent walls like a whip, we grumbled among ourselves, certain that the other group was hoarding more than its share of the additional supply we had gotten from Deep Camp. With a storm raging outside, another one was about to erupt in our tents. As our suspicions evolved into anger, we shouted over to the other tent group, demanding our full share of the soup. As the accusations shot back and forth like darts, it slowly became apparent to all of us that, in our state of perpetual stress, hunger, and exhaustion, it was impossible for us to look at the issue objectively. When the smoke cleared, it proved to be an innocent matter with a simple explanation.[44]

Such extreme experiences may be intensified by different perceptions of time. Entrepreneurs tend to view the past and future through a compressed lens. According to Allen Bluedorn and Gwen Martin, entrepreneurs in general consider thirty days as a short-term future, and three years as their long-term future. Entrepreneurs also think of their immediate past as fourteen days, their middling past as six months, and a long-term past of five years. The further entrepreneurs saw into the past, the further they saw into the future, but all tended to calculate time in short increments. And the younger the entrepreneur, the shorter are the past and future horizons.

All entrepreneurs do not see the past, present, and future in similar terms. According to Bluedorn and Martin's 2008 study of 181 new ventures, the further entrepreneurs looked into the past, the less they preferred to work fast. However, the more entrepreneurs engaged in what psychologists label polychronicity, or multitasking, the less they focused on being punctual and on schedule, but the more they preferred to work fast. Although preferring to work fast was not a source of stress for these entrepreneurs, time compression was. The further these entrepreneurs looked into the future, the less they reported high levels of stress, perhaps because long futures permit greater planning.

Mastery and Logic

There is good reason to believe that mastery of the entrepreneurial process increases with experience—after all, entrepreneurs learn and adapt over time, or so the theory goes, which should increase the odds of future success. This is certainly the theory that underpins investment

44. Palinkas and Suedfeld (2008, p. 156).

in serial and portfolio entrepreneurs, both of which are habitual entrepreneurs. As suggested by the terms, a *serial entrepreneur* founds entrepreneurial organizations in order, disposing of one before the next, while
a *portfolio entrepreneur* founds multiple entrepreneurial organizations
at once and maintains a steady supply over time.

As Paul Westhead and Mike Wright reported in 1998, past evidence
produces a variety of hypotheses about the differences between novice
and habitual entrepreneurs:

—Novice founders are less likely to be as educated as habitual entrepreneurs and more likely to be women and older.

—Novice founders are less likely to have experience with more than
one organization before launch.

—Novice founders are more likely to found an organization in familiar territory, meaning the industry where they last worked.

—Novice founders are more likely to emphasize a need for independence when starting their first organization.

—Serial founders may be more cautious in their entrepreneurship,
while portfolio founders may be more likely to spread their risk across
their organizations.

—Habitual founders are more growth oriented than are novice
founders.

—Habitual founders have greater success than novice founders do.

According to their 1998 study of 389 novice, 157 serial, and 75 portfolio founders, Westhead and Wright confirmed almost all of their
hypotheses and concluded that serial and portfolio founders are not only
different from novice founders but from each other. However, the
authors could not find any difference in success, in part because habitual
founders bring certain biases to their work that may favor the conventional wisdom that existed when they first began their careers.

The fact that novice founders succeed as often as habitual founders
has obvious implications for social entrepreneurship, especially for
investors. At a minimum, investors should discount past experience as a
criterion for placing bets. "Habitual entrepreneurs may be sufficiently
competent covering less routine areas of entrepreneurship," Westhead
and Wright concluded. "However, beyond the start-up phase they may
be less competent at growing their business above a modest size and scale
of development."[45]

45. Westhead and Wright (1998, p. 200).

This does not mean that novice founders are the best bet, however. They have their own liabilities. Writing in 2005, Westhead, Deniz Ucbasaran, and Wright concluded that novices may have problems in adapting to changing environments, in part because of their relative inexperience, while portfolio founders may have the greatest strengths in spotting opportunities in other industries.

Of the three types of entrepreneurs, serial founders emerge as the poorest bet. "Serial entrepreneurs exhibit more cautious behavior with regard to their subsequent ventures, possibly because they do not want to tarnish their reputation," the coauthors wrote. "This may be a barrier to more innovative behavior in subsequent ventures. Some serial entrepreneurs are likely to try to repeat past successes, rather than to key into changing market opportunities the next time around."[46] At least for serial entrepreneurs, the first investment may be the best. A good case can be made that the first investment should also be the last.

LINKING STAGES AND COMPONENTS

None of the logic chains in this chapter contains an explicit link between the seven stages described above and the four components of social entrepreneurship, if only because there is almost no research suggesting how to sort through the 7-by-4 table that would emerge.

Nevertheless, there are three reasons to pursue the links. First, if the four components have different impacts at each stage, the field may need to target its scarce resources more effectively. Entrepreneurs might matter most at the front end of the process but are less important than organizations as the idea gains momentum. In turn, ideas might matter most at the invention and launch stage but may be far less important in scale-up or navigation. In turn again, organizations may be least important for imagination but essential for sustaining. Second, if the four components carry different weights across the seven stages as a whole, the field may need to spread some of its resources over a longer time line. Instead of making the traditional two-year grant at the start of the entrepreneurial process, the field might make additional one-year grants at key stage gates over the next ten years. Entrepreneurs may need a different set of skills for the launch and diffusion of ideas from those skills they used for imagination and discovery; organizations may need new

46. Westhead, Ucbasaran, and Wright (2005, p. 413).

TABLE 3-1. Linking Stages and Components

Stage	Stage impact			
	Entrepreneurs	Ideas	Opportunities	Organizations
Imagining	++++	+	+	+
Discovering	++++	+	+++	+
Inventing	+++	++++	++	+
Launching	+++	+++	++	+++
Scaling up	++	+++	++	+++
Diffusing	+++	+++	++	++
Navigating	++++	+	+++	++
Total process impact	23 +	16 +	15 +	13 +

+ = impact.

networks and better planning tools to sustain momentum compared with what they needed at the launch and scale-up phase; ideas may need to adapt as they move from scale-up to diffusion. Third, if learning and adaptation are essential as all four components vary through the process, then the field must ask whether and how capacity building can improve the odds of eventual breakthroughs. Total dedication to the venture must include total dedication to strengthening the entrepreneur, fine-tuning the production process, exploring opportunities, and insulating the organization from aging. Social entrepreneurs cannot spend time, energy, and funding wisely unless they have the time, energy, and funding to do so. To the extent that the field worries about being a target for cynics, as Martin and Osberg caution, it must be ready to invest in raw capacity.

The question of links between stages and components remains, however. At least for now, the best one can do is to speculate on the potential role of each component as the entrepreneurial process moves forward through an uncertain future. Table 3-1 shows a simple way to begin.

The table shows just how important entrepreneurs are to the process as a whole and suggests at least some stage effects. Entrepreneurs matter most at the beginning and at the end of the entrepreneurial process when their traits and characteristics have the greatest effects, but they matter less at the invention, launch, and scale-up phases when they may need the kind of capacity building that Ashoka and Echoing Green give their fellows.

Ideas have a greater impact in the middle of the entrepreneurial process. Once entrepreneurs imagine a new equilibrium, they must create an idea for getting there. Ideas are the key product of invention and must be launched, scaled up, and diffused effectively. Although Drayton is no doubt right to suggest that ideas will collapse without the entrepreneur, the idea must be able to stand on its own, which implies the value of research and development support.

Opportunities have their greatest effects at just two of the seven stages: discovery and diffusion. It is important to note, however, that Schumpeter and many contemporary scholars believe that opportunities may have their greatest impact on imagination—that is, opportunities create the incentive to imagine, not vice versa. If true, the weight of opportunity would be much greater than suggested in table 3-1.

Finally, organizations tend to matter much more as the process moves forward. However, organizations can be critical factors if the entrepreneurial process occurs within an existing organization. Whereas imagination and discovery can occur without any organizational engagement at all, they are more difficult in existing organizations, which either drives the entrepreneur out or suppresses entrepreneurship completely.

CONCLUSION

The effort to find convergence on the logic of social entrepreneurship is more than just an academic enterprise. It is essential to the basic development of the field and influences everything from making grants and selecting fellows to sorting case studies and outlining future research. Although divergence is healthy as a field matures, it must involve transparency. Basic terms, assumptions, and biases must be clear.

In turn, definitions must be precise. It is nearly impossible to draw inferences from research without clarity about what is under investigation. It is also impossible to draw the growing inventory of research together into a body of knowledge without further clarity about samples and cases, which in turn must involve more detailed analysis about who, what, when, and where concerning social entrepreneurship and whether and how it actually occurs.

Once again, readers should note that socially entrepreneurial activity can occur in new organizations as well as in existing organizations. Although scholars of business entrepreneurship often separate the two, I believe that socially entrepreneurial activity can take place in many places, including government, businesses, social benefit organizations, and hybrid organizations in between, as well as in new and existing organizations.

This is what makes the search for the "one best" strategy so difficult. Although the field of social entrepreneurship is certainly making progress in defining the basic components of strategy, it still needs to work on both the theory and actual practice of creating change under different conditions. Because the ecosystem is so complex, it is unlikely that this work will produce major breakthroughs. Rather, it is more likely that it will produce a series of conditional statements about success and failure, which means that we must study both.

Social entrepreneurship may be more difficult in existing organizations, especially ones that have become evermore bureaucratic over time, but it still takes place within these organizations nonetheless. It also takes place in organizations such as the Grameen Bank, Teach For America, Share Our Strength, and ACCION, which were originally created for social entrepreneurship and which have learned and adapted as their organizations have aged gracefully.

CHAPTER FOUR

EXPLORING THE EVIDENCE

The questions are interesting, the territory immense, and the chance to influence social change significant. In a field hungry for rigorous research on what works, scholars have an extraordinary opportunity to make an immediate impact.

Researchers can do so through every method imaginable—quantitative or qualitative studies, small samples or large, simple statistics or computer modeling, literature reviews or studies of studies, and longitudinal analyses or single-case studies. But researchers can only be a force for good if they let the evidence take them where it will. They must confront the field with hard questions about its assumptions, tough analysis of the facts, and a readiness to speak truth to power. No matter how much they might believe in one assumption or another, and no matter how much they want to be invited to celebrate the great potential of social entrepreneurship, researchers must maintain enough distance to make sure they focus on what they know, not on what they hope.

Researchers must also resist the temptation to tell the field what it wants to hear. By their nature, researchers are contrarians. They are at their very best when they confront the prevailing wisdom to prove it right or wrong. In a very real sense, they must be part of the continuous upset that moves a field forward—not so much through the creative destruction that renders entire industries obsolete, but through a readiness to challenge the dominant theories that are too often used to explain success and failure after the fact. They must use their own entrepreneurial qualities to help the field advance on solid evidence. Bluntly put, they must persevere when the prevailing ideologies of social entrepreneurship push back.

Researchers cannot play this role without hard evidence, however, much of which may exist well beyond the boundaries of their nascent field. They must also be just as concerned about the reliability and validity of their measures as social entrepreneurs must be about their business assumptions, as rigorous about their analysis as social entrepreneurs must be about their growth, and just as transparent about their findings as social entrepreneurs must be about their results. Researchers must also be just as ready to enter the marketplace of ideas and peer review as social entrepreneurs must be courageous about exposing their ideas to competition.

COMPARING BUSINESS AND SOCIAL ENTREPRENEURSHIP

Readers are forewarned that the following pages draw heavily on the field of business entrepreneurship. This is not to suggest that business and social entrepreneurship share the same environments, pressures, and goals, however. As Eleanor Shaw and Sara Carter warned us in 2007, business and social entrepreneurship differ in at least five important ways:

—Business entrepreneurship focuses on profits, while social entrepreneurship addresses unmet social needs.

—Business entrepreneurship engages market forces, while social entrepreneurship draws upon and builds community support.

—Business entrepreneurship involves financial risk, while social entrepreneurship depends on organizational and personal credibility.

—Business entrepreneurship produces individual financial gain, while social entrepreneurship generates collective public goods.

—Business and social entrepreneurship both involve creativity, but business entrepreneurship uses creativity to enter new markets, while social entrepreneurship uses creativity to solve intractable problems.

There are other differences buried in this list. Hard as I searched, I failed to find any credible research on the ethics of business entrepreneurship, for example. Business entrepreneurs surely have at least some "ethical fiber," as Bill Drayton would describe it, but they rarely use it to ask their customers to make the leaps of faith required for systemic social change—they expect their products to move the market, not their calls for change.

I also found little research comparing business and social sector financing. Writing of "the looking-glass world of nonprofit money" in 2004, Clara Miller argued that the social benefit sector does not follow business rules: "The rules, when they apply at all, are reversed, and the science turns topsy-turvy. Not only are the nonprofit rules governing money—and therefore business dynamics—different from those in the for-profit sector, they are largely unknown, even among nonprofits. Or at the very least, they remain unacknowledged and unspoken."[1]

In this looking-glass world, consumers do not buy the product, cash is rarely liquid, price is not determined by supply and demand, price rarely covers costs, profits do not drop to the bottom line for reinvestment, infrastructure is deemed a luxury, and administrative costs are treated as wasted money, not reasonable costs.

In this world, it is easy to see why social benefit organizations might struggle to survive. It is also easy to understand why scaling up is so hard to do—everyone wants to pay for the mission, but few are ready to invest in the organizational infrastructure—and why social entrepreneurship might be doubly difficult. According to Miller, something has to give:

> All the good will, brain power, capacity-building, finger-waggling, stand-setting evaluation and impact measures will not change the fact that the underlying financial system we have put in place and support is the worst enemy not only of the improvements everyone is trying to make, but of the socially critical programs and services this system is meant to support. All efforts to improve the sector will be merely palliative without essential, systemic reform of the way the rules of finance work.[2]

Despite these differences, there are good reasons to blend the business and social entrepreneurship literatures in the search for lessons learned. First, the business literature is much deeper—the field may be in its adolescence, but it is producing rigorous research at a rapidly accelerating rate, much of which is directly relevant to the underlying assumptions of social entrepreneurship.

1. Miller (2004, p. 1).
2. Miller (2004, pp. 7–8).

Second, business and social entrepreneurship share a long list of concerns. Both are driven by profit, for example, albeit financial profit for the former and social for the latter. Writing of a world populated entirely by altruists in 2005, Israel Kirzner challenged his readers to think of two entrepreneurs who decide to help the world by making cheese and bicycles. Contrary to the prevailing wisdom that altruists are not motivated by profit, Kirzner argued that both entrepreneurs would seek to maximize profit by paying market wages:

> More important, both the cheese manufacturer and the bicycle manufacturer—precisely because they are the altruists that they are—will be on the lookout for pure profit opportunities. . . . They will be continually alert to opportunities to buy inputs (including labor) at lower than most prevailing prices. They will be continually alert to opportunities to sell their cheese or their bicycles at higher prices in newly discovered markets. And they will be alert to possibilities of switching from the production of cheese or of bicycles to that of sweaters or of golf lessons—all, of course, with the overpowering objective of in some way channeling pecuniary profits to the altruistic improvement of the human condition.[3]

For Kirzner, the profit may be social, but it is profit nonetheless.

Third, as James Austin, Howard Stevenson, and Jane Wei-Skillern argued in 2006, most of the differences between the sectors are best viewed on a continuum ranging from purely business to purely social. Business entrepreneurship may be more concerned with meeting new needs; sensitive to market pressure, not constituents; effective at managing financial and human resources; and connected to the customer, but the three Harvard Business School professors argued that social entrepreneurship must reflect business realities, while business entrepreneurship must still generate social value.

Readers are free to discount the business literature as they wish, but there are important insights to be found in the field. To the extent that social entrepreneurship hopes to make up for lost time in building its knowledge base, it must borrow insights from other fields. The next four sections of this chapter are structured to do just that by exploring the evidence on many of the assumptions underpinning the four components of social entrepreneurship.

3. Kirzner (2005, p. 468).

ENTREPRENEURS

It is safe to argue that researchers have invested their greatest energy in the study of individual entrepreneurs. Yet, despite the mounds of evidence summarized below, we are still some distance from defining that entrepreneurial quality that seems to distinguish social entrepreneurs from other high achievers.

This research has produced at least one agreement and one caveat. The agreement focuses on the nature of the entrepreneur as an unconventional thinker. Focusing on scientific breakthroughs in her 1995 study, Carol Steiner identified practicality, authenticity and creativity, and teamwork as the three markers of unconventional thinking among scientists and engineers. For Steiner, science is a necessary component of the innovative idea. "Yet innovation needs visionaries able to take in the big picture. It needs individuals confident enough to shake off the straitjacket of specialist paradigms. Most of all, it needs free agents to creatively and individually interpret a complex world through a complicated interpersonal process."[4]

The only problem is that there is little hard evidence to make this case. Virtually every recent article on the difference between entrepreneurs and other high achievers ends with a call for more research. "What lies beneath?" Norris Krueger asked in the title of his 2007 article. "The experiential essence of entrepreneurial thinking," he answered.

But that essence of entrepreneurial thinking has yet to be defined. "Like Newton," Krueger concluded, "I hope I have offered the reader a few shiny pebbles; and while I hold some of those pebbles quite dear, it is very clear to me that cognitive science offers an ocean of great ideas, theories, and methods that entrepreneurship scholars and educators can explore for many years. There are smoother pebbles and prettier shells yet to be found."[5]

Introducing the Entrepreneur

The search for the prototypical entrepreneur is a path well worn by scholars of business entrepreneurship, but one that has yielded very little hard evidence of deep personality differences that might mark the social entrepreneur. Indeed, the lack of durable findings on the distinctive

4. Steiner (1995, p. 439).
5. Krueger (2007, p. 134).

characteristics of business entrepreneurs prompted William Gartner to write a seminal article in 1988 urging researchers to stop asking who is an entrepreneur.

Gartner's work did not condemn all of the research on individual entrepreneurs, however. Rather, it focused on the lack of progress in identifying the personality traits of entrepreneurs. According to Gartner, the trait approach assumes that entrepreneurs are "a describable species" that one might find in a field guide of some kind.

Describing his search for "this entity known as the entrepreneur," Gartner collected the available research on everything from the willingness to take risks to age, marital status, fear, intelligence, "delinquent associations," the need for achievement and autonomy, conformity, benevolence, optimism, and reactions to tension. With the evidence, or mostly the lack thereof, in hand, Gartner concluded that personality characteristics were "ancillary" to the entrepreneurial task of creating new combinations and organizations. "How do we know the dancer from the dance?" he quoted Yeats.[6]

Gartner clearly understood why the search for core characteristics is so appealing. "Entrepreneurs often *do* seem like special people who achieve things that most of us do not achieve. These achievements, we think, must be based on some special inner quality. It is difficult *not* to think this way."[7]

His colleagues Howard Aldrich and Martha Argelia Martinez pushed the same argument forward more than a decade later: "As intellectually stimulating as it may be to find out what motivates entrepreneurs and how they differ from ordinary mortals, the more critical question is how these individuals manage to create and sustain successful organizations, despite severe obstacles."[8] Later in the same article, they posed the central question for their field: "Can we really get to know the key features of those individuals who enter the heaven of successful entrepreneurship if we do not see the actions and circumstances of those who 'were not chosen'?"[9]

Nevertheless, the search for the entrepreneurial "type" continues unabated and drives much of the contemporary study of social entrepreneurship.

6. Gartner (1988, p. 11).
7. Gartner (1988, p. 22).
8. Aldrich and Martinez (2001, p. 41).
9. Aldrich and Martinez (2001, p. 52).

Loner at Work

This book has already suggested that social entrepreneurship can occur in existing organizations, largely by arguing against the "garage theory" of business entrepreneurship and for the concept of corporate entrepreneurship and team-based invention.

The question here is not whether entrepreneurs work alone, however, but whether entrepreneurs *should* work alone. Although there is very little evidence about the answer, there is potential consensus that lone entrepreneurs actually have higher failure rates than partners, teams, or networks have, for example.

We all know that new ventures often fail, but at least one recent study suggests they fail more frequently when lone entrepreneurs are in charge. According to Lee Fleming in 2007, loners such as Alexander Graham Bell (program innovator), Henry Ford (process innovator), and Thomas Edison (program and process innovator) have long been celebrated as the source of breakthroughs. However, after studying a sample of U.S. inventors who received patents between 1975 and 2005, Fleming found that lone inventors were also a source of many failures.

> My fieldwork consistently indicates that innovators working by themselves can be the source of more failures as well as more breakthroughs. Their output at both extremes of the distribution suggests that the impact of lone inventors' work is highly variable. . . . The models indicate that lone inventors generate few novel combinations and the combinations they create are less likely to be used, on average, by inventors. Those results call into question whether lone inventors are truly the creative geniuses that they are reputed to be.[10]

However, it could be that inventors who have failed have the right idea but the wrong locations, marketing skills, production technology, or peers. Their ideas might have been successful but for the lack of the kind of support that Ashoka and Echoing Green fellows receive. Nevertheless, the findings suggest that the fields of business and social entrepreneurship may spend too much time focusing on the heroic innovator—the key is to look at the heroism, not the hero.

Lone inventors should not be ostracized, however. According to Fleming, lone innovators were responsible for more than 20 percent of

10. Fleming (2007, p. 70).

corporate patents. "As such, they are an important resource in the corporate lab despite their reputation (sometimes deserved) of difficult work habits and lack of social skills. It therefore behooves companies to figure out ways to motivate and compensate the prickly but prolific lone inventor and to integrate the creative breakthroughs of such individuals."

Lone inventors may take fewer shots on goal, using Fleming's hockey metaphor, but the research shows they are also more likely than collaborators to create the biggest breakthroughs. The question for investors is how to identify the breakthrough early enough to make a difference in pushing it forward.

It is interesting that Fleming's work suggests that managers may be much more important to entrepreneurship compared with what Drayton and others have suggested. As Fleming, Santiago Mingo, and David Chen argued in 2007, managers are particularly important in determining the structure of a collaborative effort. "Our results have particular implications for the care and feeding of boundary spanners, also known as gatekeepers," Fleming and his coauthors wrote. "Based on our results, brokered conceptions are fundamentally more likely to fail; managers need to ensure that the expertise behind the creativity is widely distributed, encourage perceptions of group ownership, and see that the idea gets effectively transferred for development."[11] Managers are not mere ciphers who blindly follow leaders: they design and operate cohesive collaborations, while protecting lone innovators from their adversaries.

Thinking Differently

Even though Gartner is no doubt right about the need to focus on what entrepreneurs do to change the prevailing equilibrium, the thought process in doing so cannot be written out of the equation. As Scott Shane, Edwin Locke, and Christopher Collins argued in 2003, the entrepreneurial process involves human agency, which means that entrepreneurship involves the basic decision to act:

It is often said that a person cannot win a game that they do not play. In the context of entrepreneurship, this statement suggests that success depends on people's willingness to become entrepreneurs. Moreover, because the pursuit of entrepreneurial opportunity is an evolutionary process in which people select out at many

11. Fleming, Mingo, and Chen (2007, pp. 469–70).

steps along the way, decisions made after the discovery of opportunities—to positively evaluate opportunities, to pursue resources, and to design the mechanisms of exploitation—also depend on the willingness of people to "play" the game.[12]

Taking the entrepreneur out of entrepreneurship is like removing the Prince of Denmark from Hamlet.

Instead of being buried in early childhood, these characteristics can be activated by opportunity and enhanced by experience, a point emphasized in Robert Sternberg's 2004 analysis of "successful intelligence." According to Sternberg, entrepreneurs draw on much more than analytic intelligence (IQ) in their drive for breakthroughs. They also draw upon practical and social intelligence, which sum to successful intelligence. "One needs the creative intelligence to come up with new ideas," he wrote, "the analytical intelligence to evaluate whether the ideas are good ones, and the practical intelligence to figure out a way to sell these ideas to people who may not want to hear about them."[13]

This focus on a blend of experience fits well with the career histories of business entrepreneurs. As one study after another has shown, entrepreneurs almost always come from the industries they intend to change. They also tend to share similar training, networks, and organizational experience. Some of that experience is no doubt negative, driving entrepreneurs to start their own ventures, while some is positive, especially in organizations that have created an entrepreneurial culture.

Entrepreneurs even share geographic histories. As Pino Audia and Christopher Rider found, entrepreneurs tend to rely on local social ties, partnerships, and friends. As a result, they are often dependent on the very industries they seek to change for insights on how to crack a given product equilibrium.

At the same time, there is little research to suggest that this experience must be acquired in the same way. It is not the path that is similar but the accumulated skills, alertness, and other characteristics that are. Many entrepreneurs acquire these assets through the long apprenticeships in moribund organizations that Drayton describes but may develop their intention to exit or impatience for impact earlier. Simply put, the shared history must be converted into action.

12. Shane, Locke, and Collins (2003, pp. 257–59).
13. Sternberg (2004, p. 196).

The *experience-centered* approach pairs well with a focus on opportunities. "Why do some people and not others discover particular entrepreneurial opportunities?" Scott Shane and Sankaran Venkataraman asked in 2000. The answer cannot be blind luck, if only because luck favors the prepared mind. Rather, it involves a mix of access to information, personal ability, and the decision to exploit an opportunity, which J. Gregory Dees translates as the recognition and relentless pursuit of opportunity, continuous innovation, adaptation, and learning, as well as bold action without concern for limited resources.

Despite this general movement toward experience-centered and opportunity-centered characteristics, the literatures on business and social entrepreneurship continue to generate more questions than answers about what makes entrepreneurs unique. Are core characteristics malleable, or are they forged early in life as basic motivations? Are core characteristics shrouded by the subconscious or just within reach of a viable opportunity? And do core characteristics vary with stages of the entrepreneurial life cycle—that is, is one set of characteristics essential for launch, another for scale-up, and still another for ongoing operations?

The Entrepreneurial Personality

The literatures may generate more questions than answers, but the studies do pile up. Perhaps this is just an artifact of academic incentives—social psychologists study entrepreneurial behavior because they are social psychologists; psychologists study personality because they are psychologists; economists study social incentives because they are economists.

But whatever the motivation, researchers have made at least grudging progress in winnowing the vast number of personal characteristics that might influence entrepreneurship. According to Hao Zhao and Scott Seibert's 2006 study, entrepreneurs differ from managers on four of the "big five" personal dimensions—neuroticism, extroversion, openness to experience, agreeableness, and conscientiousness. Entrepreneurs will be happy to know that their brethren were more open and conscientious than managers were and less neurotic but perhaps a bit troubled that their brethren were also less agreeable. Summed as such, entrepreneurs are an amalgam of obstinence and perseverance. At least in this meta-analysis of forty-seven different studies, social entrepreneurs are "unreasonable people," which is how John Elkington and Pamela Hartigan described them in their book of the same title in 2008.

It is important to note that the biggest difference between entrepreneurs and managers was not in the degree to which one or the other was disagreeable. Rather, the difference was in conscientiousness, which Zhao and Seibert described as "an individual's degree of organization, persistence, hard work, and motivation in the pursuit of goal accomplishment."[14]

The importance of personality was confirmed by Andreas Rauch and Michael Frese in 2007 in their article titled "Let's Put the Person Back into Entrepreneurship Research." Searching through 116 different samples of entrepreneurs, the authors found at least fifty-two personal characteristics that might matter to success, including benevolence, conformity, humility, impulsiveness, optimism, rigidity, risk-taking, shyness, sobriety, skepticism, and tolerance for ambiguity.

Although some experts argue that research on personal dispositions has produced few insights, Rauch and Frese found otherwise. The characteristics with the strongest relationship with entrepreneurial behavior, defined as business creation and business success, were need for achievement (perhaps developed in childhood), self-efficacy (perhaps in adolescence), innovativeness (perhaps at birth in the form of creativity), stress tolerance (perhaps in basic DNA), need for autonomy (perhaps in early learning), and proactive personality (perhaps in childhood).

The findings have practical implications for investors. "For example, people interested in starting a business might evaluate their traits and use this information to support their career choice and to match themselves to the task of running a business or to decide on partners who compensate for their weaknesses," Rauch and Frese suggested. "Similarly, government agencies may use task-specific traits to select political entrepreneurs more successfully."[15] Certainly, these kinds of findings can help socially entrepreneurial investors discipline themselves as they look for characteristics that might help them choose between competing proposals.

Sorting Characteristics

Entrepreneurs may be central to entrepreneurial activity, but it is still not clear which characteristics matter most under what circumstances and when. The point is well made in 2008 by the study of polar expeditions in *Lancet*. Having described the nature of the task, Lawrence

14. Zhao and Seibert (2006, p. 265).
15. Rauch and Frese (2007, p. 372).

Palinkas and Peter Suedfeld compared the ideal personality type for short and long expeditions:

—The ideal person for a short expedition is easily described as someone who has high achievement motivation, a high sense of adventure, and a low susceptibility to anxiety.

—The ideal person for a long expedition is more complex, in large measure because personality has more time to affect success. Thus, the ideal type is someone who has few symptoms of depression; has low neuroticism; is introverted but socially adept; is satisfied with social support; is not greatly extroverted or assertive; has no great need for social interaction; has low demands for social support; is sensitive to the needs of others; has a desire for optimistic friends; has a high tolerance of boredom, a high tolerance for a lack of achievement, and a low need for order.

As these comparisons show, characteristics may be more or less important over time. Shifting from polar expeditions to entrepreneurial explorations, one can easily argue that entrepreneurs might need one set of personal characteristics to imagine a new idea (creativity, for example), sense an opportunity (alertness), develop an idea (intellect), launch a new venture (risk-taking), accelerate it toward the tipping point (optimism), and so forth.

Characteristics may also become more or less visible over time. A sense of adventure is likely to be more noticeable to an investor or potential partner than is neuroticism; a low tolerance for boredom is likely to be more visible than is depression. Indeed, one of the easiest ways to sort, and therefore test, the impact of an entrepreneur's core characteristics is simply to ask which are closest to the entrepreneurial decision and work downward from there.

According to figure 4-1, doing so involves at least some effort to link deeply held and often shrouded characteristics such as personality, intelligence, and motivation to more visible, even teachable characteristics such as skills, entrepreneurial assets, access to networks, commitment to an idea, alertness to opportunity, and even core values. As entrepreneurs move up the pyramid, they convert skills, beliefs, and personal capacity into the behaviors that produce action.

As readers will note, deep personality traits are found at the bottom of the pyramid—although these traits *may*, and I emphasize *may*, affect action-oriented characteristics such as alertness, they are so deeply held that they are mostly invisible to investors. The top of the pyramid

FIGURE 4-1. Sorting Core Characteristics

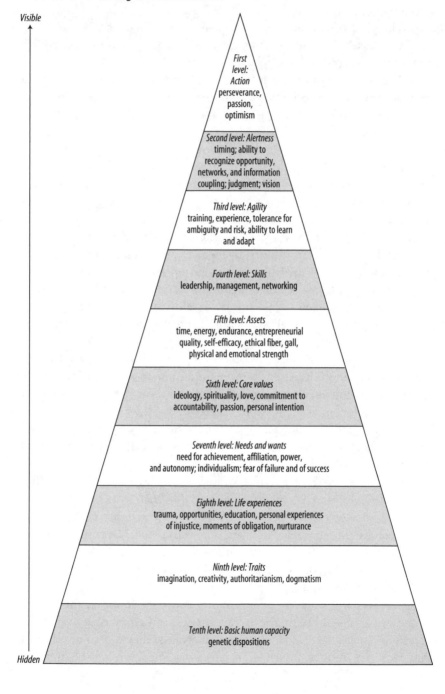

Visible

First level: Action
perseverance, passion, optimism

Second level: Alertness
timing; ability to recognize opportunity, networks, and information coupling; judgment; vision

Third level: Agility
training, experience, tolerance for ambiguity and risk, ability to learn and adapt

Fourth level: Skills
leadership, management, networking

Fifth level: Assets
time, energy, endurance, entrepreneurial quality, self-efficacy, ethical fiber, gall, physical and emotional strength

Sixth level: Core values
ideology, spirituality, love, commitment to accountability, passion, personal intention

Seventh level: Needs and wants
need for achievement, affiliation, power, and autonomy; individualism; fear of failure and of success

Eighth level: Life experiences
trauma, opportunities, education, personal experiences of injustice, moments of obligation, nurturance

Ninth level: Traits
imagination, creativity, authoritarianism, dogmatism

Tenth level: Basic human capacity
genetic dispositions

Hidden

focuses more closely on cognitive characteristics, which is just a term that captures behaviors and beliefs that are quite directly related to action. "Entrepreneurs *imagine* a different future," Jerome Katz and Dean Shepherd wrote in 2003. "They *envision* or *discover* new products or services. They *perceive* or *recognize* opportunities. They *assess* risk, and *figure out* how to profit from it. They *identify* possible new combinations of resources. Common to all of these is the individual's use of their perception and reasoning skills."[16] To a great extent, the discussion of personality traits is driven by nouns, while the list of behavioral characteristics is based on verbs.

Readers may disagree about where to rank one characteristic or another, but such an array forces much closer examination of the purported relationship between any given characteristic and the decision to act. If a given characteristic cannot be traced ever upward to action, then it cannot be at the core of social entrepreneurship.

Readers may also disagree on the direct or indirect relationship between lower-level characteristics such as imagination or creativity. After all, these and other deep characteristics seem to play a direct role in the actual entrepreneurial decision. As Roger Martin and Sally Osberg argued, it is creativity that produces the idea for creating a new social equilibrium and fortitude that fuels action. At least until further research shows otherwise, one can assume that deep characteristics provide the foundation for each level above them.

Thus some of these characteristics have been validated by empirical research on business and social entrepreneurship, while others are based on hunches about the relationship between a given characteristic and the decision to act. In general, the higher a characteristic rises on the pyramid, the better is the evidence of a connection to entrepreneurial behavior. The research on basic human capacity, personality traits, life experiences, and motivation is particularly problematic—each characteristic is well argued, but the lack of evidence is what prompted Gartner's original complaint and the movement toward more measurable experience-centered and opportunity-centered characteristics such as alertness, agility, assets, and skills.

It is important to note that demographic characteristics and culture are not listed in the pyramid. This is not because they are irrelevant to entrepreneurship, however. Rather, they appear to be relevant to all levels

16. Katz and Sheperd (2003, p. 1), authors' emphasis.

of the pyramid—they affect early motivation and access to networks, skills and values as well as the basic readiness to act. As Susan Davis argued in 2002 after her own literature review, "Entrepreneurship is not bound by rigid concepts of age nor plagued by homogeneity. . . . Entrepreneurs (like youth) are diverse, found in every culture, class, race, ethnicity, gender, sexual orientation, physical agility, and age."[17] Indeed, demographic characteristics and culture are so important to entrepreneurship that they deserve separate consideration below.

Perseverance

Perseverance is generally viewed as one of the most significant characteristics of successful entrepreneurs. As Gideon Markman, Robert Baron, and David Balkin explained in 2005, the link between perseverance and entrepreneurship is not new. Whether viewed as a personality trait or an entrepreneurial behavior, perseverance not only increases the odds of success, but it reduces the hazards of failure. Just knowing that one has done everything possible to succeed reduces the frustrations of early failure, while increasing subsequent tenacity and perseverance. Thus does perseverance produce perseverance.

Defining perseverance as the tendency to "persist and endure in the face of adversity," Markman, Baron, and Balkin argued that the effort to control events "provides innumerable personal, financial, and social benefits: Perseverance influences individuals' courses of action, the level of effort they put forth while pursuing their endeavors, the length of their endurance and their resilience in the face of setbacks and repeated failures. Perseverance also influences how much stress individuals can endure while they cope with setbacks, and the level of accomplishments they eventually realize."[18]

OPTIMISM. If perseverance is so important to entrepreneurial success, the question is where perseverance comes from. Does it reside in deep personality traits such as physical strength or the need for achievement? Is it embedded in the "moments of obligation" that Echoing Green believes spark action? Is it a consequence of believing that anything is possible? Or is it even a product of what Shane, Locke, and Collins call love?

The answers are unclear. According to Robert Baum and Edwin Locke's 2004 analysis, for example, perseverance, or tenacity, is best

17. Davis (2002, p. 3).
18. Markman, Baron, and Balkin (2005, p. 3).

viewed as the product of passion: "We measured passion for work in terms of the emotions of love, attachments, and longing; however, passion can be witnessed over time in the long hours worked during venture start-up and growth phases and in the tendency for entrepreneurs to experience their venture's successes and difficulties as personal events."[19] In turn, passion is driven by a vision of what might be, a belief in one's own ability to succeed (self-efficacy), and personal goals forged in social values.

Once again, therefore, the question is where perseverance comes from. At least by my reading, the central predictor of perseverance is optimism. It may flow from deeper traits, but it appears to be the most visible resource for sustaining action. This notion is well supported in recent research by Thomas Asterbro, Scott Jeffrey, and Gordon Adomdza. In 2007 their study of more than 1,100 Canadian inventors showed that roughly a third of independent inventors continued to spend time on their projects after being told they would fail, and almost two-thirds continued to spend money. The difference was optimism.

These findings echo earlier work by other scholars. In 1995, for example, Leslie Palich and Ray Bagby reported that business entrepreneurs did not differ significantly from their less entrepreneurial peers in their willingness to take risks. Where entrepreneurs did differ significantly was in their basic optimism about success. Entrepreneurs may not necessarily prefer to engage in more risky behavior, Palich and Bagby wrote. Rather, they simply may frame a situation more positively than negatively, adopting a rose garden scenario when more caution might be warranted.

There is even evidence that optimism may be a core characteristic of entrepreneurial success. Summarizing twenty-five years of research, Frederick Crane and Erinn Crane argued in 2007 that successful entrepreneurs are optimistic, goal oriented, and persistent. In particular, successful entrepreneurs tend to be both "little" and "big" optimists. "Little optimism involves specific expectations about positive outcomes such as finding a convenient parking spot in a crowded shopping center. Big optimism deals with larger and less specific expectations such as believing our economy is on the verge of tremendous growth."[20]

Although Crane and Crane suggested that little optimists can be big pessimists, and vice versa, it is the combination of little and big optimism that produces the perseverance, or fortitude, that may ensure success.

---

19. Baum and Locke (2004, p. 2).
20. Crane and Crane (2007, pp. 15–16).

Successful entrepreneurs do not suffer from unrealistic or destructive optimism, they wrote. "In fact, the literature demonstrates that successful entrepreneurs are not high-rolling gamblers, and do not delude themselves or distort reality."[21]

Finally, optimism may be the central factor in surviving failures and setbacks, even to the point where it might be used for the "grief counseling" that Smita Singh, Patricia Corner, and Kathryn Pavlovich recommended in 2007. Although there is little research on how often socially entrepreneurial ventures fail, there is no doubt that there are great setbacks and failures en route to impact. Optimism may allow entrepreneurs to learn from their setbacks and failures—the key is not how they grieve per se but how they learn.

OVERCONFIDENCE. Just as optimism can drive success, it can trump warnings of failure—indeed, it may be the most important reason why many inventors keep going after receiving credible evidence that they should quit. As Asterbro, Jeffrey, and Adomdza argued, perseverance appears to be related to the concept of sunk costs. Having invested so much of their time and money before their moment of choice, inventors may keep going just because they cannot accept an alternative future.

Although overconfidence has its benefits, it clearly has costs. "Without over-optimistic judgments," Phillip Koellinger, Maria Minniti, and Christian Schade wrote in 2007, "we would probably see fewer business start-ups but higher average success rates and returns among those who become entrepreneurs. . . . In addition, new entry, albeit unsuccessful, might help spur competition and push incumbent businesses toward efficiency."[22] However, failed entry has social costs, not the least of which is the personal impact on nascent entrepreneurs who might have succeeded with better advice.

Thus some of the characteristics that might lead to failure are ones that are no doubt essential for success. Perseverance in the face of resource constraints might not be particularly wise for the individual entrepreneur, particularly if the resources never arrive, but it may be essential for pattern-breaking change. Optimism about the future may increase the tolerance for risk, but it may also blind the entrepreneur to potential threats along the path to a new social equilibrium. Entrepreneurs may not be high-rolling gamblers, but their investors often are.

21. Crane and Crane (2007, p. 22).
22. Koellinger, Minniti, and Schade (2007, p. 521).

Thus Mathew Hayward, Dean Shepherd, and Dale Griffin argued in 2006 for a "hubris theory of entrepreneurship." According to their hypothesis, this theory might explain why overconfident entrepreneurs are more likely to initiate new ventures and also more likely to fail. "Greater overconfidence provides founders with the bravado to undertake and persist with more challenging tasks and the conviction that they will have the necessary resources for the ventures to succeed. The number of ventures present in an economy, therefore, depends on the supply of overconfident actors who are willing to start ventures."[23]

It is interesting that some psychologists believe that a more realistic optimism can be taught, especially during childhood. Despite this evidence, there has been almost no research on optimism as a teachable skill, even though Frederick Crane and Erinn Crane report at least some evidence that optimism can actually be taught: "Optimism training, it seems, may just be what the doctor ordered to improve the success rates of entrepreneurial ventures and to ensure the future of entrepreneurship."[24] Perhaps it is time to field test the curriculum among the nascent entrepreneurs identified in national fellowship programs such as Ashoka and Echoing Green. Call it a boot camp for believing in the impossible.

A Rare Breed?

Drayton was no doubt right when he argued in 2002 that entrepreneurial quality is the most important criterion in the selection of an Ashoka fellow and the toughest to define. "There are many creative, altruistic, ethically good people with innovative ideas," he wrote in 2002. "However, only one in many thousands of such good people also has the entrepreneurial quality necessary to engineer large-scale systemic social change. Entrepreneurial quality does not mean the ability to lead, to administer, or to get things done; there are millions of people can do these things. Instead, it refers to someone who has a very special trait— someone who, in the core of her or his personality, absolutely must change an important pattern *across her or his whole society*. . . . It is only the entrepreneur who literally cannot stop until he or she has changed the whole society."[25]

Drayton has long taken the most exclusive stance on the core characteristics of social entrepreneurs, estimating the number of social entrepreneurs

23. Hayward, Shepherd, and Griffin (2006, p. 160).
24. Crane and Crane (2007, p. 23).
25. Drayton (2002, p. 124).

at just 1 per 10 million in 2007. But the pyramid of characteristics suggests a somewhat different course that might occasionally involve a pair, team, network, or community composed of individuals with different characteristics that add up to the entrepreneurial quality that Ashoka seeks in its fellows. "The entrepreneur in entrepreneurship is more likely to be plural, rather than singular," Gartner and his colleagues wrote of business entrepreneurship in 1994. "The locus of entrepreneurial activity often resides not in one person, but in many."[26]

The same holds for social entrepreneurs. Writing in 2002 on the need for entrepreneurs to *envision, engage, enable, and enact* change, John Thompson argued that entrepreneur is plural: "True social entrepreneurs contribute to all four of these," he wrote of his list. "However, there is nothing to prevent the roles being split and shared. The opportunity spotter and the project champion may be different people, who combine to make an entrepreneurial team."[27] Indeed, the more one peruses the list of potential characteristics, the more one cannot escape the potential value of a team, if only for the physical endurance and high performance one finds in an Olympic relay team.

The critical question is not how many entrepreneurs make an entrepreneur, but what kinds of characteristics are most important to eventual success. Should researchers concentrate more on skills such as the bridging and adaptive leadership that Susan Alvord, David Brown, and Christine Letts wrote about in 2004? Should they search the wreckage of early trauma and other "deeply transformative" experiences that Lynn Barendsen and Howard Gardner described in 2004 as factors in the "righteous anger" and sense of injustice that may provoke socially entrepreneurial action later in life? Should they concentrate on the moments of obligation that Echoing Green addressed in its 2006 book, *Be Bold,* or the "spiritual entrepreneurs" that Alfredo Sfeir-Younis wrote about in 2002?

The answer is all of the above and more, but only to the extent that such characteristics actually matter in converting potential entrepreneurs into actual successes. Given the range of intractable problems yet to be solved, the field should worry less about how many entrepreneurs there are per 10 million and much more about making sure that every potential entrepreneur has the chance to succeed.

26. Gartner and others (1994, p. 17).
27. Thompson (2002, p. 416).

The Demography of Entrepreneurship

Alertness, agility, and other characteristics are not the only factors that matter to social entrepreneurship. In fact, they may be the product of demography and culture. Although researchers sometimes describe entrepreneurs as a relatively homogeneous group that comes from the "right" schools with the "right" networks, many researchers are now turning to the relationship between demographic characteristics, such as age, gender, race, class, and marital status, and entrepreneurial action.

Gender is now seen as so important to entrepreneurship, for example, that the U.S. National Science Foundation set aside additional funds to ensure an oversample of women in the Panel Study of Entrepreneurial Dynamics (PSED), which involved a sample of 64,000 adults. Analysis of the voluminous database showed that gender is related to a number of assets needed for successful entrepreneurship including economic, social, and political resources.

Moreover, gender helps explain differing entrepreneurial intentions, behaviors, biases, and skills. As Nancy Carter and Candida Brush explained in 2004, there are a number of reasons why women might be less likely to become entrepreneurs, which is defined in PSED as anyone who starts a new business. However, women's self-efficacy, work values, financial capital, access to opportunity, and entrepreneurial intensions may present the greatest barriers to engagement. "Gender differences occur not in the composition of opportunity structures," Carter and Brush wrote, "but in access to those structures. . . . In addition to education and experience disparities, women are more likely to have careers frequently interrupted or work only part-time. These labor force interruptions can disadvantage an individual and they miss opportunities to gain new job skills or incur erosion in previously attained skills."[28]

It is no surprise, therefore, that the intention to launch and manage a start-up varies by gender: "Research shows that men stress the desire to be their own boss in starting a new business, women stress the desire to be personally challenged or to create employment in which they can balance work and family. Women tend to deal with career or manage a business and family simultaneously, often with mixed success."[29]

Somewhat different patterns hold for race and ethnicity. On the one hand, earlier research on entrepreneurial intent showed that Blacks and

28. Carter and Brush (2004, p. 16).
29. Carter and Brush (2004, p. 17).

Latinos were starting new businesses at rates that far exceeded Whites. On the other hand, Whites were much more likely to keep their businesses alive. Although it is too early to know what causes so many Blacks and Latinos to fail, the initial research suggests that these nascent entrepreneurs face many of the same barriers as women face. According to Patricia Greene and Margaret Owen's report in 2004, strong social networks and fewer existing job opportunities within minority communities may encourage higher levels of entrepreneurial intent, while lower levels of education, less access to start-up capital, and limited markets for small businesses may act as significant barriers.

The Panel Study on Entrepreneurial Dynamics has found a number of other demographic patterns that are important to entrepreneurial intent such as age, net worth, work experience, and family encouragement. Younger adults (aged twenty-five to forty-four) are more likely to start new businesses, for example, as are people who spend less time on leisure activities, have larger families with more children, and work more hours.

Culture and Entrepreneurship

Culture is also becoming a more visible topic in the fields of business and social entrepreneurship as researchers challenge the notion that entrepreneurs are drawn from a single culture. As Alexander Kessler asked in 2007, can theories developed by North American researchers in a North American context be generalized to the rest of the world?

One might assume it likely, for example, that Austrian and Czech entrepreneurs would share common entrepreneurial experiences, if only because they share a border. But according to Kessler, successful entrepreneurship is driven by very different forces in each country. In Austria, success depends on access to capital, which winnows the number of potential entrepreneurs. In the Czech Republic, however, success depends on personality characteristics such as the need for achievement and the landscape of entrepreneurial resources. Whereas Austrian entrepreneurs go to the right schools and have the right networks to be judged worthy of support early in their entrepreneurial careers, Czech entrepreneurs must fight every step of the way.

Clearly then, if differences across a shared border can have a significant impact on entrepreneurial success, differences across regions, even continents, must have a significant impact too. Moreover, they must address the possibility that entrepreneurs act very differently as they move forward. Some may arrive in finery, while others come with boxing gloves.

Researchers are already engaging in more comparative analysis, although much of the work is in Asia or in Europe. Nevertheless, comparative analysis is becoming much more frequent in both business and social entrepreneurship. In 2007 alone, there were fifty-seven studies of entrepreneurship and culture cited in the ProQuest database, including the following titles:

—"A Tale of Two Politico-Economic Systems: Implications for Central and Eastern Europe"

—"Environmental Perceptions and Scanning in the United States and India: Convergence in Information Seeking?"

—"Tall Poppy Syndrome: Implications for Entrepreneurship in New Zealand"

—"Selling the Race: Culture, Community, and Black Chicago, 1940–1955"

—"The Merchants of Zigong: Industrial Entrepreneurship in Early Modern China"

—"Doing Business in the Torres Straights: A Study of the Relationship Between Culture and the Nature of Indigenous Entrepreneurs"

—"Entrepreneurship in Egypt and the U.S. Compared: Directions for Further Research Explored"

—"Makin' It, by Keeping It Real: Street Talk, Rap Music, and the Forgotten Entrepreneurship from 'the 'Hood'"

—"A Comparison of Indigenous and Non-Indigenous Enterprise in the Canadian Sub-Arctic"

—"The Needed Globalization for African Countries: A Case for Entrepreneurship"

Many of these articles call for more research even as they demonstrate a remarkable sensitivity to ethnic and cultural differences. Noting that past research on start-ups makes only passing reference to culture, Marina Zhang and Mark Dodgson in their case study in 2007 of a failed company called Avaro confirm the potential contributions of further research to search for patterns among new studies and reassess conclusions from the past. According to Zhang and Dodgson, "aspects of the business system in Korea and its specific culture led to the loss of potential international value-added for the firm, allowing, in the Chinese idiom, 'a roasted duck to fly away.'"[30] More significant perhaps, a 2002 study by Ronald Mitchell and five colleagues showed that there might

30. Zang and Dodgson (2007, p. 349).

well be a "universal culture of entrepreneurship," but there are still meaningful differences among entrepreneurs from different countries.

IDEAS

The core characteristics of entrepreneurs may have received the greatest attention in recent years, but the idea is still considered the "knockout test" in making investments in pattern-breaking change. As Drayton described the nature of entrepreneurial action in 2002, "there can be no entrepreneur without a *powerful, new, system change idea*. The entrepreneur exists to make his or her vision society's new pattern. He or she is married to that vision, in sickness or in health, until it has swept the field."[31]

As their websites attest, the Schwab and Skoll foundations use a similar test in making grants to social entrepreneurs. The Schwab Foundation for Social Entrepreneurship describes social entrepreneurs as individuals who have "a practical but innovative stance to a social problem, often using market principles and forces, coupled with dogged determination, that allows them to break away from constraints imposed by ideology or field of discipline, and pushes them to take risks that others wouldn't dare," while the Skoll Foundation defines them as individuals who "pioneer innovative, effective, sustainable approaches to meet the needs of the marginalized, the disadvantaged and the disenfranchised," and, in doing so, create "solutions to seemingly intractable social problems, fundamentally improving the lives of countless individuals, as well as forever changing the way social systems operate."

Introducing the Idea

Despite the importance of the idea, or product, to entrepreneurial success, few studies have looked at how ideas vary. Some scholars distinguish between large and small ideas, others between programmatic innovation and process, and still others between truly radical and incremental ideas. Although differences in the consumer appeal of ideas have proved only modestly useful at best in predicting the success of new ideas, the fields of business and social entrepreneurship generally assume that a good idea must be new, large, and radical to produce the creative destruction that sweeps away the status quo.

There is a somewhat larger literature on the difference between innovations in what a product delivers (technical innovation) and how a

---

31. Drayton (2002, p. 123).

product is delivered (administrative innovation). The classic statement on the difference is now forty years old, but it is still quite relevant to the discussion of social entrepreneurship. In 1978 Richard Daft argued in his seminal article that the difference is driven by "dual cores," one composed of engineers and other program specialists and the other of managers. "Each group tends to produce innovation within its primary task. Innovative ideas may be moving through the hierarchy in different directions, and the direction taken may affect changes for adoption," Daft wrote. "A new idea thus will be brought into the organization by organization experts who are interested in and aware of that particular kind of development. Experts in the technical aspect of an organization will tend to be those people working on or near the core technology."[32]

Not surprising, technical ideas from technical experts have a greater chance of adoption and success compared with technical ideas from managers, and vice versa. To the extent investors believe that new programs are the key to changing the economic or social equilibrium, they should bet on program experts; to the extent they believe new processes are the key, they should bet on administrators. The choice is a simple function of who has the appropriate expertise, not whether one likes program people more than they do managers.

Researchers have used Daft's insights to study the sequence of the two kinds of innovation. Some researchers argue, for example, that technical innovations almost always trigger administrative innovations, which in turn create the organizational capacity that provokes further technical innovations, which in turn prompt even more administrative innovation. However, it is not clear just which innovation should come first. Should an entrepreneur or organization focus first on nurturing a technical innovation such as welfare reform in the hope that the organization will have to change its administrative procedures as a result? Or is it best to start with an administrative innovation such as a laptop-based case management program and wait for the program innovation to follow? No one knows, even though such findings would clearly help both fields develop strategies for success.

To Change the World

Social entrepreneurship does not exist in just any size or scope. Although some researchers believe a socially entrepreneurial idea can involve a relatively small target such as a neighborhood or rural town,

32. Daft (1978, p. 195).

the field tends to believe that entrepreneurship only occurs when Joseph Schumpeter's gales of creative destruction are released. After all, Schumpeter did not write of breezes but gales, not incremental reform but creative destruction. Most of the literature on social entrepreneurship follows Schumpeter's lead: the threshold of change should be high enough to exclude incremental adjustment:

—Sandra Waddock and James Post defined social entrepreneurship in 1991 as "catalytic change." "The activities of social entrepreneurs can thus be distinguished from those of other types of public entrepreneurs by (1) the fact that social entrepreneurs are private citizens, not public servants, (2) their focus on raising public awareness of an issue of general public concern, and (3) their hope that increased public attention will result in new solutions eventually emerging, frequently from those same organizations already charged with dealing with the issue. It is this latter aspect that gives rise to the term 'catalytic.'"[33]

—Franklin Buttel defined biological breakthroughs in 1989 as "locomotive technologies" that originate in innovative bursts: "A new technical form can be said to be revolutionary in the neo-Schumpeterian sense if it meets several criteria. First, of course, the technology must have relatively wide applicability, which biotechnology sure does. Second, a technology will tend to be revolutionary if it is applicable in both the sphere of production (to reduce production costs) and consumption or circulation (to create large new categories of consumer and producer goods, thereby providing a dynamic for capital accumulation). Third, a revolutionary technology should be applicable to the leading or ascendant economic sector(s), or to sectors likely to be leading ones in the future."[34]

—David Francis, John Bessant, and Michael Hobday defined innovation in 2003 as a spark for the "transformational imperative." "Winning formulae are, almost always, time-bound and often rendered obsolete by technical change. This pattern is ancient. For example, for thousands of years, in stone-aged societies, arrowheads were made by 'knappers' (early stone masons). Flint knapping was replaced when it became possible to make arrowheads using the then new technology for casting bronze. Later the bronze arrow-head makers were swept away by the new technology of iron making. A similar story has been repeated in almost all industries, from construction to cosmetics. From

33. Waddock and Post (1991, p. 394).
34. Buttel (1989, p. 251).

the perspective of incumbent players, when such disruptive changes occur, 'business as usual does not work any more.'"[35]

The broadest assumption about the size and scope of an entrepreneurial idea is also the most recent. Writing in 2007, Mariano Corso and Luisa Pellegrini argued that organizations face a balancing act between exploitation of old certainties through incremental change and exploration of new possibilities through radical ideas. Incremental exploitation involves continuous improvement in existing technologies and can be distinguished from radical exploration by its type of change (cumulative, not discontinuous), its frequency (high as opposed to occasional), type of knowledge involved (spread evenly and not concentrated among inventors), and workforce participation (also high rather than concentrated). In contrast, radical exploration involves the creation of capabilities that lead to innovation in "new and uncharted territories." According to Corso and Pellegrini, organizations do not have to choose between the two forms of change. Indeed, they should aim for a balance between incremental and radical innovation by creating a "fully dexterous organization," meaning an organization that has the capacity to produce both radical and incremental innovation.

Radical Combinations

Social entrepreneurship may aim for large-scale change, but the change can come in many forms. Even though social entrepreneurs focus on intractable problems such as poverty, hunger, and disease, they have many choices in shaping a specific solution. Indeed, Schumpeter's "new combinations" come in at least six forms: changes in an existing product, changes in an existing production process, innovative combinations of existing products and production methods, invention of entirely new products or processes, better use of by-products and improved waste disposal, and improved customer service. Any one of the innovations can produce significant changes in the prevailing equilibrium.

Many, if not all of these combinations can produce social change. No doubt there are differences between product and process, as well as changes in application (old stuff used in new ways) and in technical services such as the wraparound services used in the Grameen Bank's microfinance approach. But the goal is clearly not the lowest possible price. It is sustainable change in the prevailing social equilibrium.

35. Francis, Bessant, and Hobday (2003, p. 18).

According to Robert Baron, for example, ideas have three features that affect their attractiveness to potential adopters: value, newness, and desirability. Writing in 2006 of how entrepreneurs shape ideas, Baron noted that ideas are matched to opportunities on the basis of pattern-recognition—that is, entrepreneurs operate in a fluid environment in which changing conditions create opportunities to match prototypes and specific knowledge to a specific pattern. Entrepreneurs often have their own concept of "newness" stored in memory, for example, and bring that image to the surface as they select among potential innovations.

U.S. presidents face a similar set of choices in shaping the domestic legislative agenda. As I wrote in 1981, they must decide whether to send a specific legislative package to Congress or build innovative policies through vetoes, executive orders, rule-making, and signing statements. Second, they must choose between large initiatives such as Medicare or smaller programs such as the Polio Vaccine Assistance Act that might open a wedge in the social equilibrium. Third, they must decide whether to present an entirely new idea such as the Voting Rights Act that creates an entirely new equilibrium on its own or a significant modification to an existing act such as the increasingly stringent amendments to the original Clean Air Act.

Interest in social entrepreneurship has risen in part because Congress and the president, as well as other world governments, have become less interested in innovation. As I wrote in 2008 of the nearly 400 major proposals that presidents submitted to Congress during the past five decades, the absolute number of proposals hit a modern high under President Johnson from 1965 to 1968 and dropped steadily under the next seven presidents.

The content of the president's domestic agenda has also changed over time, as presidents have turned away from large-scale expansions in the federal mission. They have moved toward modifications of existing programs (old ideas) over changes in existing missions (new ideas) and modest adjustments (small-scale ideas) over significant proposals (large-scale ideas).

It is particularly important to note that radical change often involves the combination of incremental ideas with large packets of reform. This is certainly the case in government. As Mary Bryna Sanger and Martin A. Levin wrote in 1992, most government innovation is anything but surprising:

We found that public sector innovations generally did not spring anew as if from blueprints, but evolved through an adaptive process. Their novelty more often was in their assemblage—often of familiar parts. Like natural selection, the evolutionary tinkering that ultimately produces innovation is messy. Organisms change and adapt; their ultimate fate is tested in the field. Evolutionary tinkering—using bits and pieces of what is around in new ways to meet changing circumstances—is iterative, incremental, and disorderly. Failure—error—becomes the basis for evolutionary learning. Analysis occurs at the implementation stage, after a process that is begun to "do the doable."[36]

Having examined twenty-eight winners of the Ford Foundation's prestigious Innovation in Government Award, Sanger and Levin also concluded that the innovation is often built on "old stuff" used in new ways. The innovation comes from the new combination of familiar elements.

Managers innovate through a process of wandering around, informally listening and looking. They pick up old stuff through an adaptive, trial-and-error process of Aim-Fire-Ready. New plans change and adapt in response to assessments of actual field performance. We argue that this is both how successful practitioners in fact behave to develop innovative initiatives *and* how they ought to behave. They ought to because it is more effective and more realistic.[37]

Robert Behn famously described this process in 1988 as "management by groping along."[38]

Surprise and Familiarity

This view of groping along toward impact fits well with the notion that entrepreneurial ideas involve a mix of novelty and familiarity. As Thomas Ward argued in 2004, ideas only "stick" when they strike a balance between novelty and familiarity: "new and different enough to capture consumers' attention, but familiar enough to not be misunderstood or rejected out of hand as too radically different."[39]

36. Sanger and Levin (1992, p. 104).
37. Sanger and Levin (1992, p. 89).
38. Behn (1988, p. 648).
39. Ward (2004, 173).

Even though these perceptions adhere to the idea, they are shaped by the core characteristics of entrepreneurs, including their creativity and persistence. This combination is essential in shaping an idea for maximum impact, a point well made in studies of specific innovations, such as the electric light. Andrew Hargadon and Yellowlees Douglas wrote in 2001 that "Edison's design strategy enabled his organization to gain acceptance for an innovation that would ultimately displace the existing institutions of the gas industry."[40]

Edison's commitment to novelty wrapped in familiarity affected a long list of implementation decisions. Although his lights produced steadier, clearer illumination, they mimicked gas lights in their strength; although Edison could have run his electric wires above ground, he chose to bury them; and although he could have used new lighting features, he insisted on light sockets that could be placed in the now-useless gas fixtures. "For entrepreneurs attempting to introduce novelty within or outside organizations," Hargadon and Douglas wrote, "this history suggests they should choose their designs carefully to present some details as new, others as old, and hide still others from view altogether. The challenge ultimately lies in finding familiar cues that locate and describe new ideas without binding users too closely to the old ways of doing things."[41] Thus does the packaging of the idea bear great influence on its ultimate diffusion to a wider audience of adopters.

Specifically, innovators must also address a number of practical questions about their idea. Although the answers may be affected by the entrepreneur's own biases—tolerance for risk and ambiguity, access to information, willingness to accept negative answers—the idea carries its own questions. Is there a market for the product or service? Can a market be created if it does not exist? How difficult is the product or service to implement? Can it be marketed successfully? How much money, time, and energy will the idea require, meaning how large an investment will it require? How quickly must it achieve results to produce a reasonable rate of return? And can it be marketed to potential investors?

Backlash

Without exception, all twenty-six of the Minnesota organizations profiled in my 1998 book *Sustaining Innovation* faced external opposition

---

40. Hargadon and Douglas (2001, p. 476).
41. Hargadon and Douglas (2001, p. 499).

of one kind or another. When a teacher in Cyrus, Minnesota, mentioned the benefits of transcendental mediation in an innovative introduction to world religions, several parents organized a phone tree to protest this assault on Christianity. When the Walker Art Center introduced performance art to the community audience, the community fought back against the HIV/AIDS program that it sponsored. And when the Domestic Abuse Project (DAP) announced that it would expand its program to cover gay and lesbian abusers, religious conservatives went on the offensive against this further legitimization of an unholy lifestyle.

The fact is that true innovation makes the outside world uncomfortable. Investors may reward it, governors may applaud it, vice presidents of the United States may even call for much more of it, but innovation creates discomfort. Breaking down the status quo is its purpose. It criticizes the prevailing wisdom even as it defines a new possibility. Entrenched interests rarely embrace an idea that might unseat them. The more an idea challenges the status quo, therefore, the more the status quo will fight back.

None of the *Sustaining Innovation* organizations had more conflict with the status quo than the A Chance to Grow–New Visions School. Established in 1983 by the parents of a brain-injured child, A Chance to Grow was designed to help children exercise their brains much as they might exercise their bodies. Alongside more traditional classes, students would also spend time in the "brain gym" improving their body-eye coordination. In theory, learning skills would improve with practice.

The founders, Bob and Kathy DeBoer, made no pretense of their basic impatience with the learning establishment. "They said 'get used to it' when we asked about our daughter," said Kathy DeBoer. "We just felt we could do better. There are a lot of ideas out there on what might work—biofeedback, the healing touch, colored glasses—but not much solid research. We decided to act and experiment at the same time. Time is the enemy of these kids."

The more the DeBoers learned, the more they wanted to help other brain-injured students. And the more they wanted to help, the more the educational establishment pushed back. It was one thing to try the brain gym on their daughter but quite another to seek funding from Minneapolis Public Schools. Skepticism changed to outright hostility; curiosity changed to investigation. Still, A Chance to Grow persevered in its effort to win a public school charter. "You have to learn how to count votes," said Bob DeBoer of his strategy for winning school board approval. "You also have to learn to analyze data. You'd better be able to defend what you're doing." For A Chance to Grow, that meant data, data, and more data, much of them based on experiments that compared the old with the new.

No matter how hard my *Sustaining Innovation* entrepreneurs tried to smooth the rough edges, all of their efforts produced hardball. Some of the hardball started with simple jealousy, while some was disguised as caring worry. Nevertheless, hardball is hardball, however played. Socially entrepreneurial organizations must be aware that innovation is risky. Courage is essential, and a good public relations strategy is always a help. Being prepared for the inevitable is most certainly one way to fight it.

Immediate Results?

Ultimately, these questions go to the heart of the idea itself and the most basic question raised by Schumpeter about the basic natures of invention (the idea) and innovation (the effort to change the prevailing equilibrium). Writing in 1939 about his own theoretical, historical, and statistical analysis of business cycles, Schumpeter argued that innovation was not synonymous with invention:

> The making of the invention and the carrying out of the corre-sponding innovation are, economically and sociologically, two entirely different things. They may, and often have been, performed by the same person; but this is merely a chance coincidence which does not affect the validity of the distinction. Personal aptitudes—primarily intellectual in the case of the inventor, primary volitional in the case of the businessman who turns the invention into an innovation—and the methods by which the one and the other work, belong to different spheres.[42]

Viewed as different terms, invention would involve the nature of the idea itself—its value, newness, desirability, and so forth—while innova-tion would involve the building of a new venture driven by entrepreneurs working either inside or outside an existing organization. Thus the indi-viduals who create the idea in the first place might decide not to innovate at all, leaving that task to the entrepreneurs who take the idea forward.

The key question thereby becomes how successful ideas differ from failed ideas. Do new products have the same success as new applications? Do unique ideas have more success than adjustments to existing ideas

---

42. Schumpeter (1939, p. 85).

do? Which ones work under what kinds of innovation processes? And do the core characteristics of the entrepreneur change with the type of pattern-breaking idea? One might argue, for example, that tolerance for risk and ambiguity would be more important to a new product than to a new application. But only further research comparing entrepreneurs and types of ideas will help answer the question. Unfortunately, the business and social entrepreneurship literatures have produced more questions than answers about what matters most to success in actually altering the economic or social equilibrium. In fact, I count at least fifty open hypotheses on the characteristics of successful products alone, of which twenty-four were contained in David Henard and David Szymanski's 2001 article, which was titled simply "Why Some New Products Are More Successful than Others."

Matching Ideas with Problems

The results leave readers longing for more research, especially given the tendency of most studies to assume that product quality is uniform across the spectrum of new ideas. More important, readers remain perplexed about the lack of attention to the way individuals and firms generate ideas for new products and to how idea generation and resulting implementation might affect success no matter who the entrepreneur might be. If ideas are the knockout test of social entrepreneurship, it seems reasonable to ask for more research on whether some carry a greater punch than do others.

At least for social entrepreneurship, Sarah Alvord, David Brown, and Christine Letts provided an excellent starting point in their case studies of seven socially entrepreneurial organizations. Despite the small sample size, the authors were able to describe at least three different kinds of ideas. One involves building social capacity by "working with poor and marginalized populations to identify capacities needed for self-help and helping to building those capacities." A second focuses on disseminating a package of innovations by reconfiguring information and technical resources "into user-friendly forms that will make them available for marginalized groups." A third is concerned with building a movement that mobilizes "grassroots alliances to take on abusive elite or institutions."[43]

Despite these differences, all of these approaches to mobilization "treat the assets and capacities of the marginalized groups themselves as

---

43. Alvord, Brown, and Letts (2004, pp. 267–70).

vital to the development initiative, thereby creating the necessity for sharing control and mobilization resources with the local partners— without whose willing cooperation the initiative will fail—while increasing the likelihood of sustainable change because of its grounding in local commitment and capacities."[44] At least for development, opportunities for change appear to favor collective action.

OPPORTUNITIES

Opportunity may be the most confusing term in the study of social entrepreneurship, in part because opportunities are difficult to see and even more difficult to exploit. Opportunities are often a mere figment of an entrepreneur's imagination and may not be visible to anyone else. Moreover, researchers have generally taken opportunity for granted. Yosem Companys and Jeffrey McMullen summarized the problem in their 2007 analysis, "There have been surprisingly few recent studies that explore the nature of opportunities. . . . Indeed, scholars have yet to develop an integrated theoretical framework that explains the emergence and development of entrepreneurial opportunities. Without such a framework, little can be said about the relationship between opportunity, innovation, and performance and the strategies that are needed to discover and exploit new opportunities."[45]

This framework may be elusive, but opportunity can still be defined. As Jonathan Eckhardt and Scott Shane wrote in 2003, "We define entrepreneurial opportunities as situations in which new goods, services, raw materials, markets and organizing methods can be introduced through the formation of new means, ends, or means-ends relationships."[46] Similarly, Robert Singh wrote in 2001 that "an entrepreneurial opportunity should be defined as a feasible, profit-seeking, potential venture that provides an innovative new product or service in a less-than-saturated market."

Defined as such, business opportunities share a number of features, including their durability, attractiveness, timeliness, and openness. They must also be real, not simply the product of conjecture by the hopeful entrepreneur. Instead of asking "who is an entrepreneur?" Singh argued that researchers should ask "what is an entrepreneurial opportunity?"[47]

44. Alvord, Brown, and Letts (2004, p. 270).
45. Companys and McMullen (2007, p. 302).
46. Eckhardt and Shane (2003, p. 336).
47. Singh (2001, p. 10).

One answer is clear: an opportunity is a moment in time and place that allows entrepreneurs to challenge the prevailing equilibrium. Even if an opportunity cannot be precisely identified, at least researchers know that it exists in the ecosystem that surrounds the entrepreneurial activity.

It is essential to recognize that entrepreneurs need resources to exploit this ecosystem. Aldrich and Martinez explained the challenge as follows:

> The creation of a new firm requires a certain amount of knowledge that can be obtained by formal education, previous experience, or informal training. Entrepreneurs also require financial capital in order to obtain the inputs (labor, raw materials, information, etc.) necessary for the production of their goods or services and to sustain them during the unavoidable period in which their efforts do not produce profits. Finally, entrepreneurs must also develop social networks to gain access to the information, knowledge, financial capital, and other resources that they do not possess.[48]

Introducing the Opportunity

Opportunities come in many shapes, sizes, and locations. It is a point well made by J. Gregory Dees in his work on social enterprise, which is distinguished from social entrepreneurship by its focus on business-like operations and revenue generation. As Dees argued in 1998, leaders of social benefit organizations must understand the full range of available options for generating new funding opportunities: "As they evaluate their organizations' potential to operate at the commercial end of the spectrum, nonprofit leaders should begin by identifying all potential commercial sources of revenue. Potential paying customers include the organization's intended beneficiaries, third parties with a vested interest in the mission, and others for whom the organization can create value."[49]

Dees and Beth Battle Anderson made a similar argument in 2006 in asking a series of questions about the alignment of markets with social outcomes in "socially-enterprising innovation":

> How and under what conditions can commercial markets be aligned with social purposes? When commercial market forces are not aligned with social impact, how can philanthropic methods help soften pressure to compromise social mission? In what ways

48. Aldrich and Martinez (2001, p. 51).
49. Dees (1998).

can philanthropic market forces undermine intended social impact? How is it possible to "internalize" social costs and benefits? In what ways could commercial market-based approaches undermine the creation of social value?[50]

These questions go to the heart of matching a profit-making opportunity with an organization's underlying social mission, and they strongly suggest that entrepreneurs have a choice regarding the opportunities they exploit. What might work for one goal might not work for another; what might work for one organization might not be right for another. William Foster and Jeffrey Bradach made a similar argument in 2005 in asking whether social benefit organizations should seek profits. The answer generally depends on the nature of the opportunity and the pressure to reduce dependence on any given source of revenue. Some socially entrepreneurial organizations can generate substantial revenues, while others should never try. But the effort to generate revenues, however attractive doing so might be, is neither necessary nor sufficient for social entrepreneurship.

Rare Events

We have only begun to examine similar patterns in social entrepreneurship, though Waddock and Post raised the issue of opportunities more than fifteen years ago in 1991. According to Waddock and Post, "A problem is probably ripe for attack by catalytic social entrepreneurship only when a series of efforts by individual organizations or public agencies have failed and the multifaceted dimensions of the problem and their reach into society have become obvious, at least to the social entrepreneur. It is that individual who reframes the problem in a new way and develops a temporary structure for increasing public awareness of the issue through his or her vision."[51]

Defined as such, an opportunity is based on market failures, which generate clear social needs such as protecting endangered species, caring for the homeless, attacking hunger, preventing child labor, strengthening human rights, treating intractable diseases (through new or existing medicines, vaccines, and practices), and more. As Christian Seelos and Johanna Mair argued in 2004, such needs do exist on a continuum from

50. Dees and Anderson (2006, p. 55).
51. Waddock and Post (1991, p. 395).

more to less social. Or as Martin and Osberg would argue, opportunities come from the prevailing social equilibrium.

This vision of social entrepreneurship fits well with the literature on how business entrepreneurs find opportunities. According to Lawrence Plummer, Michael Haynie, and Joy Godesiabois, the search process flows in three simple steps. The opportunity is discovered, it is evaluated, and it is exploited. The authors argued in 2007 that discovery and exploitation do not necessarily "exhaust" an opportunity, meaning that a single opportunity itself can be exploited by other entrepreneurs either because the original opportunity is big enough to accommodate multiple ideas or because it was underexploited by the first actor. Instead of being a rare event, entrepreneurship can beget further entrepreneurship. The challenge is to exploit the opportunity when it first opens, not when it is about to close.

Predictably Ephemeral

If one visualizes the social equilibrium as a kind of aurora borealis that contains the prevailing wisdom about the world, the question is how social entrepreneurs might locate and exploit a given opening in the span. Visualized as such, social entrepreneurs would need special skills to break through the barriers that lay ahead. Jeffrey Robinson made this case in his 2006 work on how social entrepreneurs navigate the barriers to entry. Robinson made three important points in using his navigation metaphor to define the entrepreneurial process:

> First, social entrepreneurship opportunities are different from other types of opportunities because they are highly influenced by the social and institutional structures in a market/community. . . . Second, social entrepreneurship is not only a process by which social problems are solved using entrepreneurial strategies but it is also a process of navigating social and institutional barriers to the market/community they want to impact. . . . Third, social entrepreneurs find opportunities in areas and under circumstances they understand.[52]

As Robinson's definition of social entrepreneurship suggests, opportunities exist *before* the entrepreneur acts—the challenge is to find the opportunity, not create it. However, his list of social and institutional barriers

52. Robinson (2006, p. 187).

fit strategies designed either to create a new opportunity or to exploit it. According to Robinson, entrepreneurs are often hampered by social barriers such as a lack of access to local networks of business owners and other social ventures, business organizations and resources, community-based and social organizations, as well as the political infrastructure and pool of labor and talent. In turn, entrepreneurs are also limited by local norms, values, the culture, government and quasi-government.

Creating Chances

Opportunities constitute a critical area for future study, particularly to the extent that they vary in size, visibility, and so forth. Researchers must not examine only the relationship between opportunities and the core characteristics of entrepreneurs, however. They must also ask whether entrepreneurs can actually create opportunities when none already exist. To date, the business and social entrepreneurship literatures have invariably assumed that alertness is the key to recognizing opportunities. But alertness may involve the use of advocacy and other tools to create a wedge in the social equilibrium.

Such wedges are particularly important for social entrepreneurship given the balkanization of the status quo against providing opportunities for action in the first place. Thus entrepreneurs may have to create the opportunity before they exploit it, whether by placing a given issue on the agenda through lobbying, raising consciousness through media coverage, attacking government corruption, or otherwise lifting the veil on marginalization. Thus opportunities do not always precede imagination, especially if imagination involves the creation of opportunities for accidental innovations such as the not-too-sticky adhesive that led to Post-it Notes. Researchers must also ask when and how frequently the opportunity to create opportunities occurs. Schumpeter believed that periods of stability were punctuated by periods of upheaval, most of which were created by the introduction of new information.

Although there seems to be some agreement in the business literature that opportunities have half-lives, meaning that opportunities surface intermittently and open and close quickly, there is less agreement on just how long the half-lives are. And although there also seems to be agreement that opportunities arise in long cycles of relative economic stability followed by intense periods of action, there is less agreement on how long the periods of disequilibrium last. "The very notion of equilibrium suggests an economy that will continue on its path undisturbed until it is shocked out

of equilibrium," Randall Holcombe argued in 2003.[53] In a stagnant economy, there are few opportunities to be exploited and high risks of failure.
Hence, entrepreneurial activity will be at a minimum. But when the economy is being battered by shocks such as financial volatility, there are many
more opportunities and much greater incentives to be entrepreneurial.

Perhaps the most important theoretical work on this subject was done
recently by Eckhardt and Shane in 2003. According to their reading of
the research, opportunities are likely to be transient because of external
and internal factors. First, they wrote, the shocks that initially generate
the opportunity are often replaced by other shocks that open up new
opportunities and close up the existing ones. And second, even when
new shocks do not immediately follow, the opportunities are often taken
by competitors.

However, as the authors also wrote, the half-lives of opportunities can
be shorter depending on mechanisms that limit imitation, such as patents
or concentrations of limited resources on a market leader, for example,
Teach For America. At the same time, the half-life can be longer depending on the amount of information available to create new ideas. Limited
information creates limited opportunity, while a surplus of information
about slightly different variations on a similar theme creates longer
opportunity. Given the lack of deep resources for social entrepreneurship, one can easily argue that the half-life of socially entrepreneurial
opportunities is relatively short. But whatever the length of the half-life,
opportunities do open and close, driven by intermittent disturbances that
create openings in the equilibrium.

Punctuations!

There are many articles in the business entrepreneurship literature that
focus on Schumpeter's waves of creative destruction. These disruptions
pulse through the economy in what researchers call long waves, rising and
falling away as a new equilibrium forms and stabilizes. They also course
through the public policy process, which is more relevant perhaps to the
discussion of social entrepreneurship. "The common core of policy
agenda research," Frank Baumgartner, Christopher Green-Pedersen, and
Bryan Jones wrote in 2006, "is attention to the dynamics of how new
ideas, new policy proposals, and new understandings of problems may or
may not be accepted in the political system. . . . New issues or ideas may

53. Holcombe (2003, p. 30).

well meet resistance from the prevailing political arrangements, but they sometimes break through to create dramatic policy changes."[54]

According to Baumgartner, Green-Pedersen, and Jones, such break-throughs reflect a "disjointed and episodic trace" of policy activities that build up over time. "As new participants with fresh ideas break into the inner circle of policy-making, the system is jolted; there is nothing smooth about the process of adjustment in democratic societies."[55] In short, the opportunity for systemic change involves punctuations in time that tend to close relatively quickly as the policy system either realigns around the new ideas or musters the support to reject them. This cycle of destruction and potential rejection was unmistakable from 1987 to 1989 when Congress first provided breakthrough catastrophic health benefits for Medicare recipients then abolished it two years later under pressure from the AARP.

These punctuations launch the waves of change that Drayton described in 2002:

> A big pattern-change innovation triggers years of follow-on change as the innovation is adapted to more and more social and economic sub-sectors and spreads geographically. This dynamic is one of the reasons leading social entrepreneurs are so critical. They are at the cutting edge of the social sector's transformation—both because each of their innovations agitates everyone in the sector with new ideas and opportunities and because each wave also makes standing still ever more perilous.[56]

Degrees of Difficulty

This focus on needs almost invariably leads to a discussion of barriers to entry, which are connected to the opportunity, not the entrepreneur, idea, or organization, and which affect the demand side of the entrepreneurial equation. Barriers to entry can exist before the entrepreneur acts; they are discovered during the entrepreneur's effort to crack the status quo; or they appear as the status quo fights back. After all, the status quo exists in part because it benefits strong interests, not just because of unintended market failures. When these powerful interests face the loss of privileges gained through marginalization, the interests do not accept the

54. Baumgartner, Green-Pederson, and Jones (2006, p. 32).
55. Baumgartner, Green-Pederson, and Jones (2006, p. 28).
56. Drayton (2002, p. 123).

challenge lightly. One way it remains the prevailing wisdom is to quash challenges, whether by acquiring and killing an idea or, one would hope, by adopting it as a new feature of its repertoire. To the extent it does the former, the individual entrepreneur fails; to the extent that it absorbs the idea, the entrepreneur has succeeded, albeit often without credit or gain.

Barriers to entry are one way for the equilibrium to perpetuate itself, and they have generated a great deal of research. Silicon Valley has long been viewed as having an open, independent, democratic, and pioneering spirit, while other technology corridors have a well-deserved reputation for being closed, hierarchical, and conventional. Similarly, some areas of the social equilibrium have been long associated with innovation, low-levels of government regulation, less competitiveness between organizations, and an inviting culture. Similarly, as James Hayton, Gerard George, and Shaker Zahra argued in 2002, some societies encourage innovation and change, while others are dominated by convention and even corruption. All of these characteristics would matter to the ease of entry for new entrepreneurs, whether in exploiting an existing opportunity or creating a new opening for change. They would also matter to what Austin, Stevenson, and Wei-Skillern identified as context, which they separate from opportunity as an independent variable in creating social value. "In the social sector," Austin and his two colleagues wrote, "factors such as interest rates, macroeconomic activity, government regulations, industry activity, labor markets, and the sociopolitical environment can be equally as important as in the commercial sector. Every organization faces competition for resources and for the goodwill of its employees and clientele."[57]

Special Vision

This focus on the nature of opportunities invariably leads into a discussion of the entrepreneur and the role of alertness in shaping recognition and action. Much of this work is well anchored in Kirzner's 1997 argument that alertness involves a clear break with Austrian economists such as Schumpeter who tend to view action as a "mechanical response" to an available opportunity.

ALERTNESS. According to Kirzner, not only does this assumption rob "human choice of its essentially open-ended character in which imagination and boldness must inevitably play central roles," it ignores a key

---

57. Austin, Stevenson, and Wei-Skillern (2006, p. 8).

element of entrepreneurship: "What has occurred is that one has discovered one's previous (utterly unknown) ignorance. What distinguishes *discovery* (relevant to hitherto unknown profit opportunities) from *successful search* (relevant to the deliberate production of information which one knew one had lacked) is that the former (unlike the latter) involves that *surprise* which accompanies the realization that one had overlooked something in fact readily available." Or, as Kirzner put it, "It was under my very nose!"[58]

Writing only two years later in 1999, Kirzner wrote of the key attributes of social entrepreneurs as uniquely qualified to uncover opportunities:

> In order to make a discovery, in this world, it is simply not sufficient to be somehow more prescient than others; it requires that that "abstract" prescience be supported by psychological qualities that encourage one to ignore conventional wisdom, to dismiss the jeers of those deriding what they see as the self-deluded visionary, to disrupt what others have come to see as the comfortable familiarity of the old-fashioned ways of doing things, to ruin rudely and even cruelly the confident expectations of those whose somnolence has led them to expect to continue to make their living as they have for years past.[59]

In short, sight is not the only key to success. Success requires a much deeper set of skills and thinking patterns that are rarely found but can be encouraged and occasionally taught.

CORE CHARACTERISTICS. These skills and patterns have been linked to a variety of core characteristics of the entrepreneur that are well summarized in Daniel Forbes's literature review of 1999:

—At the imagination, discovery, and invention stage of a venture's life, Forbes found articles dealing with self-efficacy, perceived desirability and feasibility of an idea, entrepreneurial experience, deviance, personal control, and the use of decision shortcuts such as generalizing from relatively small samples, and perceptions of greater chances of success.

—At the launch and scaling-up stages, Forbes found articles addressing optimism, desirability, and feasibility again, persistence, growth-oriented intentions, the willingness to confront uncomfortable realities, a lack of second-guessing, a belief that one controls his or her own destiny, ability to process information quickly, and the use of metaphors to convey ideas.

---

58. Kirzner (1997, p. 84).
59. Kirzner (1999, pp. 12–13).

—At the diffusion, sustaining, and navigating stages, Forbes found articles focusing on search intensity, alertness, experience, the use of information cues, tolerance for ambiguity, the lack of regrets, decision speed, the use of mental models to imagine the future, pacing, investment acumen, intelligence, access to capital and other resources, "equivocality," and strategy.

Again, as Martin and Osberg argued in 2007 in their definition of social entrepreneurship, other high achievers such as artists and filmmakers share many of these characteristics and biases. Moreover, Baron argued in 1998 that most readers will recognize "the general tendency of all persons, not simply entrepreneurs to overestimate how much they can accomplish in a given period of time, or, turning the question around, to underestimate how long it will take them to complete a specific project. Examples of this effect, which is known as the planning fallacy, abound. Large-scale public projects generally take a much longer time to complete, and cost far more."[60]

In theory, investors would never give a potential entrepreneur a fellowship based on cognitive blind spots, the lack of counterfactual thinking, or the lack of regret. Nevertheless, such biases may be essential for ultimate success. Indeed, the readiness to persevere in the absence of enough resources is generally seen as essential for taking a new idea forward through the intense opposition that the status quo often exerts.

CONNECTING THE DOTS. Recognizing opportunities is no accident. According to the latest research, it involves a unique ability to see the relationships between what Baron called "seemingly unrelated events or trends."

This ability to connect the dots is not some deeply embedded personality trait, but it is a set of learned skills and assets that entrepreneurs use in scanning the environment. As Baron argued in 2006, the patterns that entrepreneurs see suggest ideas for new products or services, and this skill can be taught. He summarized the two propositions leading to this conclusion as follows:

—"Opportunities emerge from a complex pattern of changing conditions—changes in technology and in economic, political, social, and demographic conditions. They come into existence at a given point in time because of a juxtaposition or confluence of conditions that did not exist previously but is now present."[61]

60. Baron (1998, p. 286).
61. Baron (2006, p. 107).

—"Recognition of opportunities depends, in part, on cognitive structures possessed by individuals—frameworks developed through their
previous life experiences. These frameworks, which serve to organize
information stored in memory in ways useful for the persons who possess them, serve as templates that enable specific individuals to perceive
connections between seeming unrelated changes or events."[62]

Baron concluded his detailed review of the evidence for this connect-
the-dots perspective by quoting Danish philosopher Søren Kierkegaard:
"If I were to wish for anything, I should not wish for wealth and power,
but for the passionate sense of the potential, for the eye which, ever
young and ardent, sees the possible. . . . What wine is so sparkling, what
so fragrant, what so intoxicating as possibility?"[63]

ORGANIZATIONS

The organization is often taken for granted in the study of business and
social entrepreneurship, in part because other research priorities take
precedence in what is a growing, but still relatively small, research community. Beyond assuming that entrepreneurial organizations usually
start from scratch, which is not necessarily true, most researchers have
generally assumed that the organization takes care of itself, at least until
scale-up.

Introducing the Organization

Readers actually need no introduction to the evidence, given the discussion of corporate entrepreneurship in chapter two and success factors
in chapter three. Organization has always been part of the conversation
about business and social entrepreneurship, albeit with a general suspicion of big organizations as a source of change.

This suspicion has led inevitably to a focus on new ventures as the
antidote to bureaucracy. However, it is important to note that the vast
majority of new ventures simply do not, or cannot, grow. As Aldrich and
Martinez argued in 2001, most businesses not only start small but also
change little, if at all; most firms never add more employees; most new
entrepreneurs draw on their own savings to get started; and most fail.

It would be shocking if social entrepreneurship was somehow different. However, the field of social entrepreneurship almost never discusses

62. Baron (2006, p. 108).
63. Baron (2006, p. 117).

these simple facts of organizational life. Instead, the central worry appears to be less about giving nascent entrepreneurs help getting started, which is the central mission of Echoing Green, and more about picking winners among the handful of survivors.

There is also a general discomfort with creating the management systems that might allow survivors to prosper. Entrepreneurs are inevitably called to account for their actions and must develop the systems to ensure their organizations are both efficient and productive. As those systems grow, entrepreneurs are right to worry about the suppression of the risk-taking that led to their breakthroughs in the first place. This is not an insoluble problem, however, as the literature on corporate entrepreneurship suggests. Organizations can insulate themselves from aging and rejuvenate themselves. Although change is more difficult in existing organizations, there is little doubt that it occurs.

Starting from Scratch

This book has already made the case that existing organizations can generate socially entrepreneurial activity. The key question here is not so much whether innovation can occur in different kinds of organizations, however, but how to structure new and existing organizations to ensure that new combinations are tested, launched, and accelerated to impact.

The answer involves the search for the core characteristics of entrepreneurial organizations, especially in exemplars such as the Institute for OneWorld Health, Share Our Strength, and Teach For America that grow ever larger. Just as entrepreneurs have certain characteristics that make them more or less entrepreneurial, so do their organizations. But what actually makes entrepreneurial organizations different from their less entrepreneurial peers?

ORGANIZATIONAL ARCHITECTURE. Many of the answers involve the basic "architecture" of organizations. Assuming that organizations consist of hardware, that is anatomy (structure, reporting relationships, and so on); people—physiology (skills, leadership style, and so forth); and software—psychology (networks, values, for example), scholars such as Fariborz Damanpour have searched for links between a host of organizational characteristics that might increase innovativeness and the profits that go with them:

—Job specialization, which measures the degree to which jobs are narrow or broad

—Thickness, which measures the height and width of the organizational hierarchy

—Professionalism, which measures employee knowledge

—Complexity, which measures the degree to which organizational units operate in isolation or together

—Formalization, which measures the impact of roles and procedures in controlling behavior

—Centralization, which measures the degree to which authority is dispersed or concentrated

—Attitudes toward change, which measure leadership commitment to entrepreneurship

—Tenure, which measures employee length of service

—Access to knowledge, which measures the flow of information throughout the organization

—Administrative intensity, which measures the ratio of managers to employees as an indicator of autonomy

—Access to resources, which measures the amount of "organizational slack" for new ideas

—External communication, which measures the organization's connection to the environment and the opportunities therein

—Internal communication, which measures the movement of information across the units that produce entrepreneurship

Writing in 1991, Damanpour found that higher levels of specialization, thickness, professionalism, a positive attitude toward change, access to knowledge, administrative intensity, access to resources, and external and internal communications all contributed to greater innovativeness, while higher levels of centralization worked against innovativeness. He concluded, "The challenge for executives is to build congruent organizations both for today's work and tomorrow's innovation. Organizations need to have sufficient internal diversity in strategies, structures, people, and processes to facilitate different kinds of innovation and to enhance organizational learning."[64]

RADICAL DESIGN. The fields of social and business entrepreneurship are not just concerned with the basic structure of entrepreneurial hierarchies. They are also concerned about the capabilities for radical change. Damanpour may be the leading scholar here, too. Writing in 2006 with his colleague Daniel Wischnevsky, Damanpour argued that organizational characteristics vary greatly with the nature of the given innovation. Simply put, radical innovation requires a different kind of organization.

64. Damanpour (1991, p. 586).

TABLE 4-1. Innovation Makers and Innovation Adopters

Feature	Innovation Makers	Innovation Adopters
Definition of innovation	A new combination of existing products and services that disrupts the existing equilibrium	A product or process that is already part of the existing equilibrium
Process	Imagination, discovery, invention, launch, scale-up, sustaining momentum, diffusion, and navigation	Integration and scale-up
Key issue	Managing the project so that a new combination is created	Managing the assimilation of the product so it is accepted
Role of innovation	An end in itself	A means to an end
Managerial challenge	Matching organizational capabilities to opportunities	Matching organizational needs to an available innovation
Success factor	Generating an innovation	Generating productivity, economy, and efficiency

Creating such an organization involves a host of design decisions. Table 4-1 paraphrases the key differences between the two types of organizations according to Damanpour and Wischnevsky's work.

This work leads directly to the question of what capabilities are necessary for radical innovation. Assuming that opportunities for breakthroughs arise only on occasion and that they may not be predictable, organizations need certain capabilities in reserve and use other capabilities for ongoing work. As Andreas Herrmann, Oliver Gassmann, and Ulrich Eisert suggested in 2007, "In periods of relative stability and incremental innovation, it might be sufficient to possess the right resources and competencies to be aware of the known requirements of existing markets."[65]

However, as Herrmann and his colleagues continued, this deployment is not enough for successful radical innovation: "Now a dynamic approach is required: the resources and competencies, which laid the foundations for yesterday's success, might be insufficient or event restricting today. Thus, companies have to be able to adjust their resources and competencies and target the new requirements of future markets. This transformation includes the cannibalization of existing capabilities and markets in the sense of the Schumpeterian 'creative destruction.'"[66]

65. Herrmann, Gassmann, and Eisert (2007, p. 94).
66. Herrmann, Gassmann, and Eisert (2007, p. 94).

Aldrich and Martinez make a similar point in celebrating small, new organizations:

> Competence-destroying innovations require new knowledge, routines, and competencies in the development and production of a product/service. They fundamentally alter the set of relevant competencies required of an organization. Accordingly, they put existing organizations at a disadvantage, because such organizations are often not flexible enough to change. By contrast, because the main advantages of start-ups are their flexibility and the ability to change, they can easily overrun their slow and rigid "big sisters."[67]

The challenge for existing organizations is obvious—they must renew themselves even as they try to compete with their faster competitors, which is rather like building the plane while flying it.

THE PAUSE THAT RENEWS. Every socially entrepreneurial organization confronts the occasional pause, whether for capacity building, rest, or retooling. Learning and adaptation may put the organization on hold, leadership transitions may create a stall, and opposition may require a defensive stance.

As I argued in *Sustaining Innovation,* these kinds of pauses are part of keeping an innovating organization alive and innovating. My *Sustaining Innovation* organizations clearly knew when to say stop.

For roughly a third of the *Sustaining Innovation* organizations, the ultimate goal was to make their innovation the prevailing wisdom. At that point, the innovating would be over. For another third of the sample, the goal was to stay at the edge as long as possible. For the final third of the *Sustaining Innovation* organizations, single acts of innovation were designed to come and go with need. They innovated to the extent necessary and were often quite uncomfortable calling what they did innovation. The only reason they were seen as innovative, several complained, was that the outside world was so out of step with good practice.

Whatever the ultimate goal of the *Sustaining Innovation* organizations—whether to continue innovating as long as possible or eventually settle down as the new prevailing wisdom—almost all of the *Sustaining Innovation* leaders warned against innovating for innovation's sake. Some did so by refusing to label themselves or their work as innovative. "Are we innovative?" one of my innovators asked. "I think we are just

67. Aldrich and Martinez (2001, p. 44).

a bunch of people who work hard at what we do. We see a problem and work hard. I'd just as soon not label that innovation."

Generating Ideas

As organizations grow over time, they can easily become encrusted with needless bureaucracy that strangles innovation through rules and centralization. Hence, much of the literature on business entrepreneurship has focused on just what organizations can do to remain vibrant and innovative.

The answer is not to stay small and young forever, however. Indeed, as Damanpour and Wischnevsky argued, size and age are not particularly useful for predicting entrepreneurship. "In terms of organizational characteristics and the ability to innovate," they wrote in 2006, "the relatively autonomous, innovative unit within the established organization has more in common with the entrepreneurial organization than it does with the other units of its parent."[68] As they recommended, researchers should stop contrasting small with large and young with old, but instead they should compare fully entrepreneurial organizations with their moderately or not-too entrepreneurial peers, which is exactly what chapter seven of this book does.

Again, architecture plays a role in entrepreneurship. Social entrepreneurship will never be easy, if only because investors and investigators are equally impatient for success. But social entrepreneurship need not be so difficult. Even as we celebrate and admire the heroic leaders who struggle against the odds to create innovation in spite of their organizations, we can also aspire for a future in which innovation within the organization is less dependent on such acts of organizational defiance.

Staying entrepreneurial involves more than paying attention to the organizations' architecture. Although organizations can always reinvent themselves through large-scale remodeling in some distant future, they can quickly fall back to old habits. The leader exits, the board changes, new rules spread, the hierarchy thickens, and suddenly the organization is back to where it began. Such is the course of occasional bouts with "organizational rejuvenation," as it is sometimes labeled. Thus the most potent form of corporate entrepreneurship comes from "sustained regeneration," which is a constant process involving confrontations with the pernicious effects of growth and aging. Rather than waiting for an

68. Damanpour and Wischnevsky (2006, p. 276).

inevitable collapse, entrepreneurial organizations create a stream of new products and services, while exploring new markets. They also spin new ideas off of existing products, thereby expanding market share and profits. Jeffrey Covin and Morgan Miles wrote in 1999 that such firms tend to have the organizational culture and structures that support innovation: "They also tend to be learning organizations that embrace change and willingly challenge competitors in battles for market share. Moreover, at the same time they are introducing products and services for entering new markets, these firms will often be culling older products and services from their lines in an effort to improve overall competitiveness through product life cycle management techniques."[69]

These efforts vary greatly depending on whether one sees entrepreneurial activity as a linear or nonlinear process. Those who see the process as a straightforward progression from idea to impact (as presented in chapter two) might favor incubators and idea generators as devices for stimulating new ideas as part of alertness and idea development. But those who see the process as a nonlinear progression that moves back and forth from one step to another might favor informal processes for linking inventors to information to capital in often random order. They might also favor incubators and idea development, but rarely would they ask where a given idea is in the process. Much as the two approaches might agree that entrepreneurial activity involves a specific series of steps (again, as I do), the straight process approach offers fewer, but perhaps deeper, opportunities for stimulating invention.

Choosing a Sector

There is a growing consensus among researchers that socially entrepreneurial activity can flourish in a business, social benefit agency, or even a government bureaucracy. Although the field has long concentrated on social benefit organizations as a source of case studies and insights, Dees and Battle Anderson have argued that traditional boundaries between sectors are breaking down, creating "sector-bending" organizations and activities that embrace elements of the business and social sectors.

As Dees and Battle Anderson wrote in 2003, the choice of sector clearly has implications for organizational structure. Whereas for-profit organizations must distribute profits to their investors and shareholders,

---

69. Covin and Miles (1999, p. 51).

for example, social benefit organizations must push their profits back into the organization where they can be used for expansion. But whereas for-profits have ample access to raise capital and reward performance, social benefit organizations have only limited access to debt and no access to equity. And so it goes for the degree of market discipline, governance and control, culture and norms, and taxes.

Ironically, given our ongoing focus on social benefit organizations, past research has actually argued that these are much less comfortable places for social entrepreneurship. Writing of their sample of 145 randomly selected social benefit organizations, Michael Morris and his colleagues asked whether the innovativeness, risk-taking, and anticipation embedded in an entrepreneurial orientation are relevant and valuable concept in the social benefit context:

> Can one expect such organizations to take risks, invest in innovation, or engage in a process of creative destruction where current methods are obsolete? Some might be concerned that an emphasis on entrepreneurship could compromise the basic values, missions, and services of the non-profit. Further, where non-profit managers have less business-specific skills, the amount of time, resources, and effort involved with establishing and maintaining innovations can distract them from their core missions. Conversely, since non-profit leaders are heavily focused on their current missions, their ability to recognize new opportunities may be reduced.[70]

Morris and his colleagues were hardly alone in presenting a brief against the social benefit sector as a destination for socially entrepreneurial activity, although they eventually concluded that social benefit organizations are just as capable of entrepreneurship as businesses. Writing in 1996 from his perspective as a business scholar, Damanpour also highlighted the constraints facing social benefit organizations. But like Morris and his colleagues, Damanpour also found that the social benefit sector was no more or less likely to produce entrepreneurship. Social entrepreneurship simply does not belong in any one sector.

Ultimately, the choice of sector is just that, a choice. There are times when the social benefit sector is the right destination for social entrepreneurship, other times government must do the innovating, and still other times when business or sector-bending organizations should take the

70. Morris and others (2007, p. 15).

lead. The choice of sector needs to include more than business, social benefit, and hybrid organizations, however.

The choice must also include government. Government is not only a potential funder of social entrepreneurship, but it can be the source of breakthrough thinking as well. It might be difficult to find, but government does produce change. Indeed, Harvard University's Kennedy School of Government selects six to ten U.S. federal, state, and local governments each year for the Ford Foundation's Innovations in American Government Award. Looking at a similar prize administered by the Institute of Public Administration of Canada, Luc Bernier and Taïbe Hafsi wrote persuasively in 2007 about the drive for innovation across every province. Entrepreneurship has become a legitimate, indeed valued, activity and is increasingly integrated into the operations of individual organizations. Some of this entrepreneurship is driven by individual entrepreneurs, but much is driven by the institution.

Institutional entrepreneurship and individual entrepreneurship are very different, of course. Individuals tend to operate in young organizations, seek maximum growth, exercise moderate-to-high power, and have substantial resources. In contrast, institutions tend to be much larger and older, focus more on process innovation, operate with low-to-moderate government interest in their work, and are located in turbulent environments. In a sentence, individual entrepreneurs operate in much more visible, heavily resourced locations, while institutional entrepreneurs work under the radar. But whatever the difference, government is not just a target for external change; it is a source of socially entrepreneurial activity itself.

Insulation from Aging

Some of the most compelling work on socially entrepreneurial organizations involves the effort to balance incremental and radical innovation. Instead of juxtaposing one type of innovation against the other as different options for different conditions, this work argues that organizations should engage in both at the same time. Thus organizations are supposed to be simultaneously loose (meaning relatively autonomous units) but tight (that is, strong control from the top), big (extra money for good ideas) but little (everyone has a stake in the organization's success), young (a fresh supply of new people and new ideas) but experienced (stocked with seasoned professionals who know what they are doing), highly specialized (individual employees and units are given narrow pieces of the organization's overall job) but unified (everyone shares the same vision of the future). As Richard Adams, John Bessant, and Robert Phelps wrote in 2006, such organizations have high levels of the same polychronicity as that of polar explorers, while Michael Tushman and Charles O'Reilly argued that these organizations are ambidextrous.

This notion of dual innovation (as opposed to Daft's dual-core innovation of administration and program innovation) argues that organizations evolve over time as they invent new products and protect existing businesses. Writing of different types of innovation in 1996, Tushman and O'Reilly concluded that organizations go through relatively long periods of incremental change punctuated by opportunities for change. Because of the frequent focus on Apple as the great innovation, Tushman and O'Reilly use Apple as their example of the ambidextrous organization and the appointment of John Sculley as Steve Jobs's replacement as their example of the need to protect the existing business:

> Notice how Apple evolved over a 20-year period. Incremental or evolutionary change was punctuated by discontinuous or revolutionary change as the firm moved the three stages of growth in the product class: innovation, differentiation, and maturity. Each of these stages required different competencies, strategies, structures, cultures, and leadership skills. These changes are what drive performance. But while absolutely necessary for short-term success, incremental change is not sufficient for long-term success. It is not by chance that Steve Jobs was successful at Apple until the market became more differentiated and demanded the skills of John Sculley.[71]

Writing about their concept almost ten years later, however, the authors did not mention Apple at all, no doubt because Sculley gave too much attention to operations and not enough to innovation. In a sense, Apple moved from an innovation maker to an innovation adopter as it developed new systems for managing its breakthroughs. As such, the return of Steve Jobs signaled a commitment to the ambidextrous organization. Drawing in part on some of the operational successes forged during Sculley's brief tenure, Jobs took his organization through a desperately needed renewal. At some point, of course, he will leave again, just as Bill Gates has retired from Microsoft. The challenge then moves back to the radical design discussed above.

71. Tushman and O'Reilly (1996, p. 15).

Yet ambidexterity does not involve incremental *or* radical innovation, or incremental *to* radical. Rather, it focuses on incremental *and* radical. Indeed, in 2004 O'Reilly and Tushman argued that ambidextrous organizations actually master three types of innovation: incremental innovations, meaning "the small improvements in their existing products and operations that let them operate more efficiently and deliver ever greater value to customers"; architectural innovations, meaning "technology or process advances to fundamentally change some component or element of their business"; and discontinuous innovations, meaning "radical advances like digital photography that profoundly alter the basis for competition in an industry, often rendering old products or ways of working obsolete."[72]

The Order of Things Again

As I argued in my book *Sustaining Innovation,* there is no shortage of advice on how entrepreneurial organizations can increase their innovativeness. To the contrary, the problem is not too little advice, but too much. There are changes out there for every temperament, from reorganization to self-managed teams, new measurement systems to transformational leadership, and tighter controls to greater freedom. If organizations do not like the current fashion in organizational reform, the next one will come along soon enough, driven forward by a change industry of consultants that can only persevere by reinventing inventing, reengineering engineering, and reenvisioning visioning.

The real shortage of advice falls on the starting point of change. Asked where their organizations began the journey to natural innovation, respondents from my twenty-six organizations portrayed in *Sustaining Innovation* gave remarkably similar answers. First, they all started with vision. Without exception, the *Sustaining Innovation* organizations centered on their vision of the future—they talked about whom they served, why they existed, how to know when they were succeeding. They could measure outcomes, for example, because they knew what the valued outcomes were. They could celebrate success because they knew when it occurred. Without a strong sense of mission, nonprofit and governmental organizations cannot sustain innovativeness for a long period. They will have no basis on which to say yes or no as ideas bubble up. Second, they focused on management. Entrepreneurs cannot take advantage of

---

72. O'Reilly and Tushman (2004, p. 76).

the market, invest in promising ideas, or give permission to make mistakes *until* they create the management systems needed to track and control its financial and organizational future. There is no substitute for good management systems as a precursor for high performance and innovativeness. Organizations cannot sense the market, manage the market, or change the market if they do not have the management systems to help them see and exploit the market.

It is important to remember that the organization's mission is much more than a set of written words. It is a spirit, a focus, a sense; it is more something to be felt rather than to read. Thus mission need not be painted on an outside wall, drawn onto a blueprint, or enshrined in legislation to have meaning. Indeed, drafting a mission statement may be exactly the wrong thing to do in starting the journey toward innovativeness, particularly if that statement becomes some kind of sacred text that can never be questioned or changed. My *Sustaining Innovation* organizations did not always have the right answers, but they never wavered in challenging themselves to ask why they existed and whom they served. They always reserved the right to ask the core questions. If that meant penciling in a few new words here or there on the mission statement, so be it. If that meant erasing it entirely, so be that, too.

Third, these organizations emphasized the need for idea generators. Even as an organization builds a strong management system and harnesses the market, it can take a few simple steps to increase the odds that acts of innovation will occur, endure, and recur. Lowering the barriers to external and internal collaboration, providing the space to experiment, and issuing the call for ideas are all simple steps toward innovativeness. My *Sustaining Innovation* organizations also did exceptionally well with innovation investment funds.

Fourth, they believed in the possible. After listening to dozens of stories about failure and success, I came to believe that organizations cannot overestimate the importance of faith as a core value for sustaining innovativeness. There is simply no way to persevere in the face of the stress and uncertainty associated with true innovation without faith in something larger than oneself. Faith gives organizations the ability to forgive, endure, and imagine, and it is an essential ingredient for sustaining innovativeness over time. Faith provides the extra element that keeps an innovating organization vibrant even as it confronts the ordinary disappointments that are a result of challenging the prevailing wisdom.

CONCLUSION

The rapidly growing literatures on business and social entrepreneurship help winnow the true and false assumptions that I made at the start of this project. But the literature is not enough to be entirely confident in making preliminary calls. Ideally, the evidence should come from studies that compare successful with failed social entrepreneurship, thereby allowing researchers to sort out what does and does not matter most in producing actual impact.

As with many studies of organizational performance, including some of my own, these lists often urge organizations to copy Mary Poppins, who described herself as perfect in every way. Absent comparisons between different levels of socially entrepreneurial activity, transparently defined and measured, researchers will be unable to provide the kind of insights that might actually help social entrepreneurs succeed. This is not to argue that the literature is devoid of insights on the entrepreneurs, ideas, opportunities, and organizations that shape socially entrepreneurial efforts. To the contrary, the literature offers important insights on most of the underlying assumptions that shape the search for social entrepreneurship.

On the nature of the entrepreneur, the literature clearly supports those who believe social entrepreneurs have distinctive thinking and leadership skills, for example, even as it encourages researchers to focus more tightly on the links between these skills and actual choices. The literature also confirms that socially entrepreneurial activity can involve partners, teams, networks, and so forth. It implies that social entrepreneurs must often struggle to succeed as the social equilibrium fights back against change and strongly suggests that entrepreneurs rarely rest as they seek to avoid the high mortality rates of new ventures.

On the nature of the idea, the literature supports those who believe that socially entrepreneurial ideas must involve innovative efforts to change the prevailing social equilibrium as well as those who argue that innovative ideas can provoke the kind of intense backlash that demands some level of advocacy. The literature also suggests that entrepreneurial ideas are difficult to design, particularly given the need for both novelty and familiarity.

On the nature of the opportunity, the literature supports those who see opportunities for social entrepreneurship as nearly infinite, even as it seems to confirm the notion that such opportunities precede action, open and close quickly as the social equilibrium defends itself, and demand constant vigilance or alertness to exploit. The literature does not refute those who argue that there are many more entrepreneurial opportunities in the social sector than in the business sector and that these opportunities often come in broad packages driven by social movements.

Finally, on the nature of the organization, the literature emphatically rejects the notion that social entrepreneurship belongs in one sector only, even as it seems to confirm the idea that organizations occasionally pause in the entrepreneurial process for repairs and renewal and often become more bureaucratic over time, thereby creating barriers to future entrepreneurship. It also embraces the notion that high performance is a necessary, if not sufficient, requirement for sustainable social entrepreneurship, while generally rejecting those who argue that socially entrepreneurial organizations must generate their own revenues. Doing so may be wise counsel, but it appears to be a preference not a requirement.

These and other findings from the literature contribute to a deeper understanding of social entrepreneurship, but they demand further verification through evidence-based research. With notable exceptions, the literatures on business and social entrepreneurship have focused more on the development of meaningful hypotheses about behavior than on analysis of enough real-world cases to draw statistically meaningful conclusions that might improve the odds that social entrepreneurship will succeed. The next chapter summarizes at least one method for doing so.

CHAPTER FIVE

SELECTING CASES

The field of social entrepreneurship has spent much of the past decade telling success stories designed to celebrate, inspire, and teach. Few can read the stories without wondering how they might change the world too, nor can they miss the hopeful lessons learned: harvest exceptional ideas, embrace surprise, adapt and learn, recruit the right people, and above all persevere.

David Bornstein's *How to Change the World: Social Entrepreneurs and the Power of New Ideas* is a best-selling example of the genre. "The purpose of this book is not to exalt a few men or women," he began, "but to call attention to the role of a particular type of actor who propels social change."[1] Bornstein's website is even more direct in its social value proposition:

> *How to Change the World* tells the stories of people who have both changed their lives and found ways to change the world. It tell stories of people who have discovered how to use their talents and energy to advance deeply meaningful changes—defiant people who refuse to accept the status quo, who simply cannot sit still in the face of injustice, suffering or wastefulness. The book shows (and analyzes) how innovators advance new models to solve social and economic problems—how they make headway against the odds.

1. Bornstein (2004, p. 1).

Full of hope and energy, pragmatic solutions and compelling characters, this book will be practical and inspiring reading for individuals who seek to understand the fast growing field of "social entrepreneurship" and discover opportunities to enrich their work and their lives.[2]

There is nothing wrong with celebrating, inspiring, and teaching social entrepreneurs. The world needs all the social change it can get. If even one potential entrepreneur is moved toward change, the stories may be well worth the investment, especially if that one entrepreneur happens to be another Nobel Peace Prize winner. However, there is something wrong with drawing lessons from relatively small, if inspiring, samples of successes without matched samples of near successes and outright failures. Lacking a comparison group against which to compare success, would-be entrepreneurs have to scour each success story for common lessons that might help them succeed. Some will be led to use all six practices of Leslie Crutchfield and Heather Grant's *Forces for Good*, for example, while others will wonder which of the best practices actually matter in their ecosystem. Whereas the literature on business entrepreneurship is littered with research on near misses and outright disasters, the social entrepreneurship literature is mostly driven by research on heroic achievement.

MAKING LISTS

This is not to argue that the business literature is impeccably rigorous. For every best-selling book such as *Good to Great,* which is based on matched groups of great and merely good businesses, there are dozens of books built solely on success stories. Who wants to read a book about failure?

But the weakness in using single samples of successes or even failures remains nonetheless. Consider the frustrations in actually using the list of recommendations described in Tom Peters and Robert Waterman's 1983 best seller, *In Search of Excellence.* According to my New York University colleague George Downs and his co-author Patrick Larkey, the absence of a comparison group makes the list virtually unusable:

2. (http://howtochangetheworld.org/).

Since they do not make strong use of comparison groups, (i.e., they fail to include bad as well as good companies) in identifying the factors contributing to success, it is not clear from their study if there are unsuccessful companies with all or some of the eight "attributes." They do not describe their interview procedures very satisfactorily, raising the possibility that they elicited just the results for which they were looking. They emphasize intangible, unmeasurable factors; it is hard to imagine how one would go about devising measurable variables for the eight attributes. . . . Finally, the support the authors offer for their findings is largely anecdotal, an approach that increases the psychological impact of the findings on popular audiences but leaves the weight of evidence in scientific terms ambiguous.[3]

Yet, as the two authors acknowledge, "one cannot read the book without believing that the 'eight basics' contain a lot of wisdom about how to manage a large business successfully or at least what some of the characteristics of companies are after they become successful." If only organizations had the capacity to do them all at the same time.

Truthfully, I have been just as guilty of providing impossibly long lists of recommendations as any researcher. *Sustaining Innovation* was built entirely on 26 success stories of innovating organizations. Absent comparable samples of less-innovative organizations, the best I could offer readers was a long list of "preferred states of organizational being," a kind of Zen-like approach for inferring lessons from the success stories. All things being equal, for example, high-performing organizations might prefer really smart, passionate leaders who inspire excellence, innovation, and employee commitment. Alas, all things are rarely equal. Whereas *Forces for Good* had just six practices of high performers, my study produced 31 preferred states of being shared by all or most of my cases:

Five of these preferred states existed in all 26 organizations:
—The organization worries about its mission.
—Employees and the board identify with the mission.
—Employees receive adequate the training to do their jobs.
—The organization learns from its mistakes.
—The organization is disciplined about governance.

3. Downs and Larkey (1986, p. 54).

Another 12 of the preferred states existed in at least 23 organizations:
—There is external political support for innovation.
—The organization scans the environment for new funding.
—The organization maintains informal lines of communication.
—Leaders communicate decisions clearly.
—Leaders give permission to make mistakes.
—Employees enjoy their work.
—New ideas are harvested throughout the organization.
—The organization selects new ideas because they fit with mission.
—New ideas fit organizational capacity.
—The organization is disciplined about internal financial controls.
—The organization is disciplined about personnel systems.
—The organization is disciplined about its budget systems.
A final 14 of the preferred states existed in at least 20 organizations:
—The market provides incentives for innovation.
—The organization collaborates with other organizations in its field.
—The organization uses volunteers.
—Employees work across bureaucratic boundaries.
—The organization provides resources for idea development and launch.
—A single executive, not a committee, heads the organization.
—There is clarity about who makes what decisions.
—Leaders encourage innovative behavior.
—Leaders encourage participation.
—The organization pays attention to its audience, customers, or clients.
—The organization evaluates its programs.
—There a role for intuition and judgment in measuring success.
—The organization trusts its employees.
—New board members receive an orientation.
I have no doubt that many of these practices are essential for social change. But lacking a comparison group of less innovative organizations, I cannot be sure.

The field of social entrepreneurship faces a number of challenges in solving this methodological problem. There is little agreement on just what constitutes success, for example, nor is there a thoroughly vetted inventory of potential predictors. In research terms, there is little agreement on either the dependent or independent variable. Moreover, even where there have been useful comparisons such as Moshe Sharir and

Miri Lerner's 2006 study of Israeli social ventures, the sample sizes are often too small to generate enough statistical muscle for drawing strong conclusions.

Nevertheless, evidence-based analysis of successes, near successes, and outright failures is quite feasible. Indeed, there is more than enough social entrepreneurship in the world to generate at least some measure of differential impact, say, between levels of socially entrepreneurial activity. And there are at least some ways to measure inputs that might reveal patterns in this activity. At least for now, the field cannot let the perfect become the enemy of the good. Assuming that levels of socially entrepreneurial activity have some relationship to socially entrepreneurial success, measuring these levels can produce enough variation to start sorting advice.

Moving forward from the previous chapter's literature review, this chapter and the next present a limited comparison group study of socially entrepreneurial activity. Based on the consensus definition of social entrepreneurship as a pattern-breaking effort to create social value, the study was designed to examine differences between a sample of reputed high-performing social benefit organizations that exhibited different levels of socially entrepreneurial activity. Simply put, all high-performing organizations are not socially entrepreneurial, although I could easily argue that all socially entrepreneurial organizations must be high performing.

Indeed, analysis of my high-performing social benefit organizations suggests that highly entrepreneurial organizations are not markedly different from their less-entrepreneurial peers. However, the highly entrepreneurial social benefit organizations did exhibit certain strengths such as a greater focus on vision, challenges such as significantly greater rates of budget and program growth, and what some might view as occasional vulnerabilities such as less diversification, minimal employee involvement, relatively weak board governance, and a lack of access to independent revenues.

STUDYING SOCIALLY ENTREPRENEURIAL ACTIVITY

Much as researchers long for large samples and comparison groups, most research designs are limited in some way. After all, it is one thing to call for greater transparency in definitions and assumptions and quite another to develop nuanced methods for applying a definition and its assumptions to a real-world sample of cases.

This study is no different. Although it is built on a comparison of highly, moderately, and not-too socially entrepreneurial organizations, it also carries biases that limit its relevance to social entrepreneurship in general. As a general rule, therefore, readers should approach the following discussion as part of an exploratory study, not as any kind of final or near-final word on how socially entrepreneurial activity does or does not flourish. So noted, the study is based on a rigorous sampling method that involved a three-step, or "snowball," survey process in which the first survey rolled into the second and the second into the third.

The First Snowball, 2001

The first survey was conducted by Princeton Survey Research Associates on my behalf in the first months of 2001 using telephone interviews with a sample of 250 randomly selected members of the Alliance for Nonprofit Management, Grantmakers for Effective Organizations (GEO), and the Association for Research on Nonprofit Organizations and Voluntary Action (ARNOVA). Respondents were asked about the high-performing social benefit organizations they knew well and were given an opportunity to nominate up to three of these organizations for the second snowball survey.

The Second Snowball, 2001

The second survey was conducted by Princeton Survey Research Associates on my behalf in the summer months of 2001 using telephone interviews with senior executives at 250 of the organizations nominated as high performers by the Alliance, GEO, and ARNOVA sample. These 250 respondents were asked about their basic philosophies of leadership and management, their organization's relationship with the external environment, internal structure, leadership, and management systems. They were also asked about management reforms and tools for improving performance.

The second survey clearly showed that the 250 high performers took organizational excellence seriously: "It is tempting to conclude that the journey toward high performance begins with but a single step," I wrote in *Pathways to Nonprofit Excellence*. "However, the reality is much more complicated. Achieving and sustaining high performance is hard work and involves the same tenacity, endurance, risk taking, trial and error, and stubbornness that produce innovation and program success."[4]

The Third Snowball

The third survey was conducted by Princeton Survey Research Associates on my behalf in 2006 using Internet interviews with senior executives at 131 of the 250 high performers surveyed in the second snowball survey. This group of respondents was contacted by e-mail, given a link to a password-protected survey website, and asked again for their opinions about the characteristics of their organizations. This survey also included a battery of questions about the definition and amount of social entrepreneurship in each respondent's organization. With responses from executives in 131 of the 250 organizations, this third survey had a response rate of 53 percent, which produced a margin of error of plus or minus 9 percent.[5] Readers should note that there is no way to know whether the senior executives in the third survey were the same as the ones interviewed in the second.

Biases

Despite the relatively high response rate in 2006, the results discussed below are based on a relatively small number of respondents. Given the small sample sizes, readers cannot assume that the surveys of senior executives at the reputational high performers apply to other social benefit organizations generally or to high performers specifically.

Readers should remember that my 2001 and 2006 samples of high-performing organizations were only high performers by reputation. Lacking a fully valid and reliable measure of performance, readers cannot know whether the organizations in my samples were actually high performers or simply bore the mark of good advertising and media coverage. Nevertheless, the sample did come from 250 Alliance, GEO, and ARNOVA members who were familiar with the social benefit sector and had strong opinions about what constituted high performance.

As a result, my two surveys of senior executives have biases that can be traced back to the first survey—biases that are inherent in any effort to identify exemplars. Some respondents clearly had a self-interest in

4. Light (2003, p. 108).
5. This error rate means that the answer to any given question could be off by 9 percent in one direction or the other.

nominating their favorite social benefit organizations, perhaps because their favorites were grantees or clients; for others, almost certainly reputations produced nominations, with respondents basing their nominations on what they knew about their favorite social benefit organizations from a distance; and still others might have been guessing about high performance according to the size of the budget or the number of clients served. Without discounting it, this study is built on a sample that has clear faults.

DEFINING TERMS

Even before my third survey reached the 250 organizations, my research team discovered that three were no longer operating. With these three off the list, my research team began searching for evidence of socially entrepreneurial activity in the remaining 247 organizations. The search focused on a series of simple conclusions about what constituted socially entrepreneurial activity—for example, missions had to center on changing the social equilibrium; programs had to push beyond services to solutions; evaluations had to show a link between vision and impact; and financial statements had to show evidence of commitment to change.

The search also involved as much independent evidence as possible to buttress initial cuts: organizational biographies, annual reports, newspaper stories and magazine articles, teaching cases, award lists, my own site visits, other studies and books, profiles from Echoing Green and Ashoka, even Wikipedia entries.

As the team soon discovered, many of the 247 described innovation, decisiveness, risk-taking, and entrepreneurship as essential components of high performance. Asked in 2001 what a poorly performing organization should do to improve its performance, some respondents focused on programs, others emphasized management, but the vast majority said the two were connected. This emphasis on interactions between the dual cores (technical and administrative) of innovation supports Roger Martin and Sally Osberg's notion that charitable organizations can be doing very noble work without pursuing sustainable changes in the social equilibrium. As such, it is quite possible that all successful social entrepreneurship involves high performance, even as all high performance innovation does not produce successful social entrepreneurship, if it produces any social entrepreneurship at all.

Coding Socially Entrepreneurial Activity

The first and arguably most important step in this study of social entrepreneurship involved an effort to assign a level of social entrepreneurship to each of the 247 high-performing social benefit organizations. Such an effort required tough judgments about just what constitutes a high, moderate, or lower level of socially entrepreneurial activity, especially when many organizations might argue that the mere presence of at least some entrepreneurial activity confirms their full commitment to challenging the social equilibrium. Absent such coding, however, it is impossible to compare organizations in searching for the characteristics that matter most for socially entrepreneurial activity. Simply defined, therefore, organizations that put 80 to 100 percent of their budgets, time, personnel, and overall effort toward pattern-breaking change were coded as highly socially entrepreneurial, while organizations that gave roughly 20 to 80 percent of their energy to pattern-breaking change were coded as moderately socially entrepreneurial, and organizations that gave less than 20 percent of their energy to pattern-breaking change were coded as not-too socially entrepreneurial. Table 5-1 provides a short description of the three levels and an example of each. Appendix A provides the final list of 247 highly, moderately, and not-too socially entrepreneurial organizations.

Judging the level of socially entrepreneurial activity was hardly an exact science, however. Coders simply had to make a general conclusion about the degree of engagement visible through their objective assessment, while using the percentages as a rough guide to their decisions. To every extent possible, my team focused on actual activity, not mere words in the mission statement, when coding each of the 247 organizations.

As my research team found, some of the high performers such as ACCION International, the Center on Budget and Policy Priorities, Civic Ventures, Environmental Defense, and Share Our Strength had been celebrated repeatedly over the years as exemplars of social entrepreneurship, while others were virtual unknowns. In turn, some of the high performers were well-established existing organizations such as Bread for the World, CARE, Institute for Agriculture and Trade Policy, and the Ms. Foundation for Women that had existed for decades before being identified by my research team as socially entrepreneurial, while others were recent start-ups. But whether celebrated or invisible, existing organization

TABLE 5-1. Examples of Socially Entrepreneurial Activity

Level	Definition	Example
Highly socially entrepreneurial	The organization shows clear and consistent evidence (80–100 percent of its energy) that it seeks to create social change through innovative and pattern-breaking methods and ideas. Nearly all of the organization is focused on addressing significant social problems through its programs, process, or applications.	**ACCION International** With a mission to end poverty, ACCION uses microfinancing and training to help individuals become self-sufficient: "Our goal is to bring microfinance to tens of millions of people—enough to truly change the world." ACCION's ultimate goal is to end an intractable social problem, and it has been frequently cited as an example of a socially entrepreneurial organization.
Moderately socially entrepreneurial	The organization shows moderate evidence (20–80 percent of its energy) of an effort to pursue pattern-breaking change. These moderately entrepreneurial organizations tend to have a single department or section of the organization that is pursuing pattern-breaking change, while the rest of the organization focuses on service-delivery or other standard organizational activities.	**Heartland Alliance** With almost seventy programs, housing centers, and health care units, Chicago's Heartland Alliance is a comprehensive, complicated social benefit organization. However, because there are so many programs and activities, it is difficult for Heartland Alliance to focus all of its attention on innovation. As a result, it has a few distinct programs that pursue pattern-breaking ideas, such as Enlaces América that "coordinates leadership development within immigrant communities and leads advocacy efforts relating to migration, trade and economic development."
Not-too socially entrepreneurial	The organization shows the least evidence (less than 20 percent of its energy) of an effort to create social change. While the organization does provide needed services to society, it is more focused on effective service delivery than on developing innovative programs.	**Volunteers of America of Minnesota** As a high-performing chapter of a high-performing national federation, VOA of Minnesota provides what it calls "a wide variety of human service programs and opportunities for individual and community involvement." The focus of the organization is on providing effective services that improve the community.

or start-up, the 247 social benefit organizations were either pursuing pattern-breaking change at some level or were not.

Pattern-breaking change is very much in the eye of the beholder. What might look like pattern-breaking change to one team member might have been ordinary, good practice to another. Thus every organization was coded twice to determine the level of intercoder reliability, which is one measure of the validity of a given framework. Looking at the same evidence, the two coders agreed on 224 of the 247 decisions about socially entrepreneurial activity, a 91 percent reliability rate. The remaining 23 disagreements were resolved through consensus within the research team.

It is important to note that even the not-too entrepreneurial organizations listed in appendix A often exhibit elements of entrepreneurial action. This is certainly the case for Lakefront SRO in Chicago, which clearly aims to move residents of its single-room occupancy housing into jobs and independent housing. This is also the case for the Manchester Neighborhood Housing Services (now called NeighborWorks® Greater Manchester), which is redeveloping a poor neighborhood; Open Hand Chicago, which has expanded and innovated to keep pace with the changing nature of the AIDS crisis; and even the Pacific Repertory Theatre, which pushes the artistic envelope with an expanding list of breakthrough plays. Indeed, one could easily argue that virtually all of the organizations on my list show at least some level of entrepreneurial instinct—the challenge is more to grow it and disseminate it than to create the initial spark.

Caveats

This coding scheme has several vulnerabilities that may limit its ultimate validity. Although it was studiously independent of the surveys of the high-performing organizations, the coding was nonetheless affected by potential biases.

First, the coding was based on open sources and reports, which were themselves influenced by an organization's reputation. My team could have given higher ratings to organizations they already knew well or to those that had significant visibility through past awards, fellowships, and grants. Like the information collected from the three surveys, the coding for this study was ultimately based on perceptions. In turn, these perceptions could have been influenced by what a given coder or respondent saw in the world around him or her and inevitably is influenced by biases that each coder or respondent brought into the process.

Second, the 247 high-performing organizations were nominated by Alliance, GEO, and ARNOVA members who work closely with these organizations. However, many of these respondents must have used other sources to make their nominations. After all, they attend conferences where they talk with senior executives of reputed high-performing organizations, read news articles and brochures about award winners, talk with each other about which organizations are up or down. They may have even made grants or contributions to some of their nominees.

Third, and perhaps most important, the coding process focused on a sample of high-performing organizations. If high performance is essential for innovation and vice versa, then this sample would tend to contain a higher percentage of socially entrepreneurial organizations. Unfortunately, there is no available evidence on the percentage of high-performing social benefit organizations among social benefit organizations as a population and thus no way to know whether and how the results discussed in this chapter and the next might apply to either high-performing social benefit organizations in general or the social benefit sector as a whole.

WHEN DOES SOCIALLY ENTREPRENEURIAL ACTIVITY BECOME SOCIAL ENTREPRENEURSHIP?

There is considerable debate among social entrepreneurship researchers about when socially entrepreneurial activity actually becomes social entrepreneurship. Roger Martin and Sally Osberg applied a very strict standard in 2007, using business entrepreneurship as their example:

> Interestingly, we don't call someone who exhibits all of the personal characteristics of an entrepreneur—opportunity sensing, out-of-the-box thinking, and determination—yet who failed miserably in his or her venture an entrepreneur; we call him or her a business failure. Even someone like Bob Young, of Red Hat Software fame, is called a "serial entrepreneur" only after his first success; i.e., all of his prior failures are dubbed the work of a serial entrepreneur only after the occurrence of his first success. The problem with *ex post* definitions is that they tend to be ill defined. It's simply harder to get your arms around what's unproven. An entrepreneur can certainly claim to be one, but without at least one notch on the belt, the self-proclaimed will have a tough time persuading investors to place bets. Those investors, in turn, must be willing to assume greater risk as they assess the credibility of would-be entrepreneurs and the potential impact of formative ventures.[6]

6. Martin and Osberg (2007, p. 30).

The challenge is to set the bar for successful entrepreneurship high enough to focus on important, difficult, and successful efforts, but not so high as to exclude efforts that have produced the proof of concept that warrants further investment. Consider Martin and Osberg's interpretation of Schumpeter's 1934 definition of entrepreneurship: "Successful entrepreneurship . . . . sets off a chain reaction, encouraging other entrepreneurs to iterate upon and ultimately propagate the innovation to the point of 'creative destruction,' a state at which the new venture and all its related ventures effectively render existing products, services, and business models obsolete."[7] Defined as such, social entrepreneurship only exists in success, not in activity. At least for this study, my research team could not and did not make any judgments about actual transformation. All they coded was level of socially entrepreneurial activity even among organizations that appeared to have achieved success in changing the social equilibrium to some degree.

The Institute for OneWorld Health

The Institute for OneWorld Health is a perfect example of the difficulty in distinguishing between socially entrepreneurial activity and social entrepreneurship. Founded in 2000 by Victoria Hale to identify and develop new medicines that are particularly effective in reducing disease in poor countries, OneWorld Health calls itself "the first U.S. nonprofit pharmaceutical company." OneWorld Health also builds partnerships for the distribution of its low-cost drugs. Driven to combat life-threatening diseases such as malaria, OneWorld Health clearly wants to alter the social equilibrium surrounding the distribution of medicines.

Martin and Osberg expressed no reservation in describing Hale as a social entrepreneur, meaning that she was engaged in socially entrepreneurial activity: "First, Hale has identified a stable but unjust equilibrium in the pharmaceutical industry; second, she has seen and seized the opportunity to intervene, applying inspiration, creativity, direct action, and courage in launching a new venture to provide options for a disadvantaged population; and third, she is demonstrating fortitude in proving the potential of her model with an early success."[8]

But Martin and Osberg also concluded that Hale had not produced enough change by 2007 to create a new social equilibrium. She might have been close, but she had not crossed the line:

7. Martin and Osberg (2007, p. 31).
8. Martin and Osberg (2007, p. 36).

Hale's venture has now moved beyond the proof-of-concept stage. It successfully developed, tested, and secured Indian government regulatory approval for its first drug, paromomycin, which provides a cost-effective cure for visceral leishmaniasis, a disease that kills more than 200,000 people each year. . . . Time will tell whether Hale's innovation inspires others to replicate her efforts, or whether the Institute for OneWorld Health itself achieves the scale necessary to bring about that permanent equilibrium shift. But the signs are promising.[9]

Extrapolating from Martin and Osberg's argument, the number of *social entrepreneurs* might be very high at any given time, but the amount of *social entrepreneurship* they produce might be very low.

Those who use a more inclusive definition might argue that Hale crossed the line into social entrepreneurship when she achieved proof of concept. Or they might argue that she crossed the boundary when she won approval for paromomycin. The question remains when social entrepreneurship actually occurs—it is certainly not when an entrepreneur begins to imagine a new equilibrium, nor when a new idea emerges and is launched. But is social entrepreneurship achieved when an idea passes the tipping point for change, when it is diffused to a certain percentage of communities, or only when the equilibrium collapses?

Social entrepreneurs may not care about the distinction at all. They whittle down problems like chopping wood, moving forward without much rest. At least for this book, however, it is best to think about socially entrepreneurial activity. I made no effort to determine whether and by how much each socially entrepreneurial organization had changed the environment, a judgment that may be very much in the eye of the beholder or beneficiary.

An Update

The signs continue to be promising for OneWorld Health. A year after the Martin and Osberg article went to press, OneWorld Health was listed as the lead organization in producing and disseminating a semi-synthetic version of Artemisinin, which is one of the most powerful drugs for treating malaria. With funding from the Bill and Melinda Gates Foundation, OneWorld Health is about to break through its second pharmacological equilibrium. Artemisinin will not only be made widely

9. Martin and Osberg (2007, p. 36).

available, but it will cost $1 for an adult cure and just half that for a child's cure.

Meanwhile, OneWorld Health's effort to work with for-profit drug makers to manufacture low-cost drugs continues to be copied by other organizations. At least six other organizations have replicated the OneWorld Health model, the most recent being a new social benefit organization located in New Haven, Connecticut, called Developing World Cures. Spun off in early 2008 from Connecticut United for Research Excellence (CURE), a for-profit biotechnology firm, Developing World Cures is modeled on OneWorld Health and is focusing on many of the same diseases.

OneWorld Health also cracked the regulatory equilibrium in Washington, D.C. On September 27, 2007, Congress passed the Food and Drug Administration Amendments Act, which contained a provision encouraging the development of treatments for tropical diseases. The provision gives a "tropical disease product application" priority status in the Food and Drug Administration review process. Under the provision, pharmaceutical companies receive a voucher for priority review that can be redeemed or traded to other firms. Although OneWorld Health did not lobby for the legislation, its success with the distribution of new drugs to the so-called bottom of the pyramid proved that the pharmaceutical industry could do well while doing good.

The greatest test of Victoria Hale's entrepreneurship in OneWorld Health lies ahead, however. Having worked tirelessly for eight years to move from socially entrepreneurial activity to social entrepreneurship, she retired as chief executive officer in late 2007. Although she was not worn out per se, she clearly needed a break. So do many social entrepreneurs as they battle the prevailing equilibrium. The challenge lies in building an organization that can continue with its socially entrepreneurial activity when the original entrepreneur pauses or leaves.

INITIAL COUNTS

While acknowledging these caveats, my research team made every effort to stand back from other definitions and influences in their final decisions. Although the coding involved considerable judgment, the intercoder reliability is high enough to suggest that the decisions were consistently based on the best objective evidence possible. After all, it is one thing to provide a tighter definition of social entrepreneurship and quite another to make it work as a tool for sorting organizations among the categories of highly, moderately, and not-too entrepreneurial.

Despite the inherent difficulty in making these judgments, evidence based and conservative though they were, the results suggest that there is more socially entrepreneurial activity than the conventional wisdom suggests. Of the 247 organizations examined in advance of the third snowball survey, 46 (19 percent) were coded as having high levels of socially entrepreneurial activity, another 83 (34 percent) were described as having moderate, or partial, levels of socially entrepreneurial activity, and 118 (48 percent) were seen as having little or no socially entrepreneurial activity at all.

These numbers and percentages were not particularly different among the 131 high performers that participated in the 2006 survey. Among the 131 respondents in the third survey, 34 (26 percent) were coded highly socially entrepreneurial, 44 (34 percent) were in the moderately socially entrepreneurial category, and 53 (40 percent) were in the not-too socially entrepreneurial category. Readers can find a complete list of the mission and purpose statements of the 131 organizations in appendix A.

The fact that more than half of the high performers in both surveys showed at least some level of entrepreneurial activity provides limited support for my hypothesis that existing organizations have the capacity to engage in pattern-breaking change and the innovation that goes with it. As already noted, however, some of the organizations such as ACCION, Share Our Strength, and Doctors Without Borders started life with high levels of socially entrepreneurial activity, while others, such as CARE, had existed for decades before changing their missions toward solving an intractable problem. Among the 131 high performers that participated in the 2006 survey, just 24 percent of the highly socially entrepreneurial organizations had been operating less than twenty years, another 74 percent were between twenty- and forty-nine-years-old, and just 3 percent were older than fifty. In turn, 41 percent of the highly socially entrepreneurial organizations had budgets under $1 million, 26 percent had budgets between $1 million and $5 million, and 32 percent had budgets of more than $5 million. Although table 5-2 shows that the three groups of organizations did not differ significantly in budget, they were most certainly different in age. The highly socially entrepreneurial organizations were much younger on average than their less socially entrepreneurial peers, a pattern that fits with the image of socially entrepreneurial organizations.

TABLE 5-2. Age and Size of the 131 Organizations Surveyed in 2006[a]
Percent

Variable	Highly socially entrepreneurial	Moderately socially entrepreneurial	Not-too socially entrepreneurial
Age of organization (years)			
Less than 20	24	27	19
20–49	74	45	47
50 or more	3	27	34
Budget (in dollars)			
Less than 1 million	41	30	38
1 million to 4.99 million	26	23	32
5 million or greater	32	48	30

a. Percentages may not add to 100 because of respondents who gave no response or because of rounding.

This is not to suggest that the level of socially entrepreneurial activity was unrelated to age and size of the organization, however. Based on objective data collected from each of the 131 respondents, the highly socially entrepreneurial organizations were much less likely to be older than fifty (just 3 percent compared with 34 percent of the not-too socially entrepreneurial organizations) and slightly more likely to have smaller budgets with faster growth. As shown later, the organizations that were coded as highly socially entrepreneurial reported much higher levels of growth in their programs and in their budgets.

The counts of highly, moderately, and not-too socially entrepreneurial high performers may be the most important contribution from this study. It certainly consumed the most research time as my coders collected and then sifted through the evidence. But this coding also goes to the heart of my basic questions about the number of social entrepreneurs, the nature of ideas, the amount of opportunity, and key characteristics of a socially entrepreneurial organization. At the very least, the coding suggests that there may be considerable capacity for pattern-breaking change, not to mention a possible relationship between high performance and socially entrepreneurial activity. It certainly suggests that there may be more socially entrepreneurial activity under way than is often assumed, especially if moderately socially entrepreneurial organizations that do not focus exclusively on changing the social equilibrium are allowed into the tent. Like corporate entrepreneurship that occurs through incubators and businesses-within-businesses, existing organizations can be simultaneously traditional, in blending highly structured services, and socially entrepreneurial, in seeking an end to the problems that they see every day.

IN THE REAL WORLD

Alongside the objective coding of socially entrepreneurial activity, the 2006 survey of 131 high-performing organizations asked two questions about the definition of social entrepreneurship and each organization's level of socially entrepreneurial activity. As the responses show, the many assumptions now coursing through the field simply have not penetrated deeply into the lexicon of social benefit organizations.

What Words Mean

The 2006 survey of 131 senior executives at the high performing organizations revealed considerable confusion about what social entre-preneurship is. Asked late in the survey what the words "social entre-preneurship" meant to them, and given the opportunity to write as much as they wanted in the open-ended box, respondents gave a long list of answers that divided into three broad categories:

—Thirty-six percent defined social entrepreneurship as some kind of business-like activity, whether it is used for performing more efficient operations or for generating revenue. "It's taking the blinders off the pro-vision of service opportunities and making the back room more business-like," a respondent from a medium-sized chapter of a national health and human services organization said. "I use social entrepreneurship in the context of developing unrestricted revenue from sources other than our program fees and revenues, to be the fourth leg of funding," said a respondent at a children and family services organization. "We look at shared profits as an incentive for all concerned."

—Thirty-one percent defined social entrepreneurship as a form of innovation. "Jay walking—not standing and waiting for the light to change," said a respondent from a national hunger alleviation organiza-tion. Or as a respondent from a national affordable housing organization said, social entrepreneurship is "an orientation of being innovative and creative to improve the lives and organizations of other people rather than focusing on creating a monetary profit."

—Twenty percent defined social entrepreneurship as a form of social change. "Identify social problems and attempt to solve them by changing the system; spreading the solutions and persuading communities, societies, and the world to adopt the solutions," said a respondent from a national watchdog group. "Programs or activities that bring social value," said another respondent at a New York City arts organization in combining the business-like and social change definition à la J. Gregory Dees and

Beth Battle Anderson, "and that improve a community and its members, but that do not have adequate earned revenues to stand alone as a viable commercial/profit business model."

In addition, 12 percent said social entrepreneurship either had no meaning to them or did not answer the question at all.[10] According to a respondent from an arts organization, social entrepreneurship was "an absurd phrase that has been so over used I am hoping against all hope that it will go away." Another respondent from a history center said it meant "absolutely nothing."

It is important to note that many of the 131 respondents gave more than one response to the question. Respondents who started their definition with a reference to innovation of some kind were the most likely to add a secondary response—although 31 percent focused entirely on innovation, five percent added a secondary reference to business-like activity such as paying attention to the bottom line, while 63 percent paired innovation with social change such as making a large-scale impact on their communities or society as a whole. When the primary and secondary definitions are added up, just 23 percent of the 131 answers fit the contemporary definitions of socially entrepreneurial activity discussed earlier in this book. Although many of the respondents touched on parts of the whole, the vast majority of respondents simply did not focus on solving intractable social problems, and almost none (just 6 responses total) discussed leadership of any kind.

Despite this overall confusion, several respondents did come close to the prevailing definition of social entrepreneurship as an effort to create social value, systemic change, a new social equilibrium, or pattern-breaking change, including at least one respondent from a national foundation who defined social entrepreneurship as "the pursuit of innovative solutions to some of society's hardest problems." Substitute a word here or there, and ignore the lack of reference to the social entrepreneur, and the definition almost surely would be as comfortable to Dees, Bill Drayton, and Martin and Osberg as it is to me.

It is useful to note that the definitions varied across respondents from the organizations that were coded as highly, moderately, and not-too socially entrepreneurial. Respondents from the highly socially entrepreneurial organizations were less likely to mention business-like activities

10. The percentages do not sum to 100 because of "Don't know" answers or no responses and rounding.

than were their peers, for example, but more likely to mention innovation, while respondents from the not-too socially entrepreneurial organizations were the most likely to mention business-like activities and the least likely to use innovation. Overall, the lack of definition clarity helps explain the self-reported levels of socially entrepreneurial activity discussed below. Lacking a clear sense of what the term means, it is no surprise that so many respondents would say their organizations were socially entrepreneurial. Simply put, the lack of an agreed-upon definition has created a very inclusive tent.

This does not mean the field should invest scarce resources in an education campaign across the sectors, however. Rather, the lack of definition clarity even among high-performing social benefit organizations confirms the need for continued efforts to explain the concept of social entrepreneurship in the context of actual progress made. It also suggests that research on just what constitutes social entrepreneurship may help the field distinguish innovation directed at efforts to change the status quo from the vast amount of innovation that takes place among social benefit organizations. Reading through the list of 131 self-reported definitions, there also appears to be good reason for more debate on innovation. At least according to these definitions, there are places where innovation is the central tool in changing the social equilibrium and others where its role is tightly focused on ordinary good practice.

How Words Apply

There is good reason for such a debate, especially given the estimates of activity reported by respondents from the 131 organizations surveyed in 2006. Readers are warned that respondents were only asked about the amount of socially entrepreneurial activity in their own organizations after they had given their own definition of social entrepreneurship, which may have pushed the estimated level of activity upward.

At the same time, readers should note that the estimates were based on a prompt that gave respondents a tighter definition of the term. Asked first to think of social entrepreneurship as "an effort to address significant problems through pattern-breaking approaches," respondents were then asked how well the words "social entrepreneurship" described their own organizations. Of the 131 respondents, 27 percent answered that the term described their own organizations "very well," another 49 percent said "somewhat well," and 22 percent said "not too well" or "not well at all." The remaining 2 percent gave no response.

Although these statistics suggest that there is considerable socially entrepreneurial activity in the social benefit sector, the answers did not fit the objective coding. Of the organizations coded as highly socially entrepreneurial, for example, only 26 percent said that the words "social entrepreneurship" described their organizations very well, another 47 percent said somewhat well, 24 percent said not too well or not well at all, and 2 percent gave no response. In turn, respondents from the organizations that were coded as moderately or not-too socially entrepreneurial also described their organizations as very or somewhat socially entrepreneurial. Thus 36 percent of respondents in organizations that were coded as moderately socially entrepreneurial said the words "social entrepreneurship" described their organizations very well, while 21 percent of those in organizations that were coded as not-too socially entrepreneurial said the same. At least according to these self-reports, more than half of the 131 respondents saw at least some socially entrepreneurial activity in their midst, which created relatively low matches between the coding and the self-report measures. The lack of consistency raises the question about the most accurate measure of pattern-breaking change, while suggesting the need for more precise definitions. Table 5-3 shows a comparison of the reported levels of social entrepreneurship with the coded levels of socially entrepreneurial activity.

The question is whether the estimates are accurate. For the organizations that were coded as not-too socially entrepreneurial, it could be the allure of the term, which is so prominent today. It could also reflect the ongoing effort to wrap old programs in a revenue-producing idea—the notion being that one way to generate grants is to use the most popular language available, which appears to be *social entrepreneurship*. It could be the influx of new executives who have encountered versions of the term as they have become more professionalized in their work. Finally, it could be that these respondents *want* to be more socially entrepreneurial in their work but may not know exactly how to make the shift.

The second part of the accuracy question is why the organizations that were coded as highly socially entrepreneurial were no more likely than their moderately and not-too socially entrepreneurial peers to declare themselves as socially entrepreneurial. On the one hand, respondents in the organizations that were coded as somewhat or not-too socially entrepreneurial would seem to have every incentive to report social entrepreneurship wherever possible in an effort to improve their funding base. On the other hand, respondents in highly socially entrepreneurial

TABLE 5-3. Levels of Reported Social Entrepreneurship[a]

Percent

Respondents' reporting how well social entrepreneurship describes the organization	Coded levels of socially entrepreneurial activity		
	Highly socially entrepreneurial	Moderately socially entrepreneurial	Not-too socially entrepreneurial
Very well	26	36	21
Somewhat well	47	45	53
Not too well	12	11	19
Not well at all	12	2	6
N = 131			

a. Percentages do not add to 100 because some respondents did not answer.

organizations might be more likely to minimize their activity because they worry about defining themselves out of potential funding from traditional foundations—the tall poppy syndrome again. Given my overall confidence in the coding of socially entrepreneurial activity, the rest of this book will focus on the criteria outlined in table 5-1.

STRATEGIC SWARMING

Assume for a moment that the coding of socially entrepreneurial activity among my 131 organizations approximates the amount of such activity across the sectors generally. The question is whether the surprisingly reported high levels are a sign of great progress or misplaced enthusiasm. Bluntly asked, should the field support more socially entrepreneurial activity?

On the one hand, social investors might be cautious about growth because resources are still scarce and demand for funding is soaring as nascent social entrepreneurs emerge from fellowship programs and professional schools—investors already have enough trouble making choices. Current social entrepreneurs might also be cautious—many of the ideas that will change the world are just emerging and need time to develop without further crowding. Finally, the prevailing wisdom would almost certainly resist further growth—prevailing wisdom has enough to do fighting the social entrepreneurs who are already pushing for change. On the other hand, nascent social entrepreneurs would favor expansion—let competition do the winnowing, and the best idea will emerge. Social service agencies might also favor growth—they want to change the world too and have essential insights about the problems that drive social entrepreneurship. The activist's answer might favor an environment of the many too—punctuations involve a combination of movements and organizations that appear to come together for a moment in time to reshuffle the world.

The concept of "swarming" may provide the best strategy for combining caution with enthusiasm. As John Arquilla and David Ronfeldt defined the term in 1998, swarming involves a "deliberately structured, coordinated, strategic way to strike from all directions at the same time."[11] It works best, they argued, when designed around the use of myriad, small, dispersed, networked pods organized in clusters to carry out their attacks. Developed by the RAND Corporation as a new tactic for warfighting, swarming has actually had its greatest impact in social change.

Humans are hardly the only living things to swarm—bees, wolves, mosquitoes, and viruses all use swarming behavior to conquer their adversaries. Armies are not the only organizations to swarm, either—businesses, social activists, drug cartels, and even football teams also use swarming to overwhelm small and large opponents alike by "flooding the zone" with pressure.

Although wars will still involve massed forces, swarming is becoming the preferred method for creating social and military success. From 1994 to 1998, for example, Zapatista rebels in Mexico used swarming to mount a revolution in the southern state of Chiapas. Although their revolution started on January 1, 1994, as a traditional military contest between relatively large units (500–700 fighters) on each side, the Zapatista forces were no match for the Mexican army. Having failed to provoke a national uprising through massed battle, the rebels soon dispersed to squads of 12–16 fighters for what became widely dispersed skirmishes that could have lasted for decades in the dense rain forests of Chiapas. The rebels also opened a second, virtual front in the war by calling upon a loose network of human rights groups such as Amnesty International, Physicians for Human Rights, the Jesuit Refugee Service, and Food First to join an Internet-based movement. What began as a war of bullets soon became a war of e-mails, faxes, and telephone calls that produced international attention, divided the Mexican government against itself, panicked investors and creditors alike, and rallied public support. Although

11. Arquilla and Ronfeldt (1998 p. 7).

the Mexican army could have continued fighting, the information "net-war," as Arquilla and Ronfeldt called it, brought the government to the negotiating table only twelve days into the conflict and back again each time when the war flared back up.

The problem is that swarming can only occur with coordination. It is not enough to plant a thousand flowers and hope that they will somehow come together by accident. The socially entrepreneurial activity must be supported by an infrastructure that calls the strongest organizations to attack the prevailing wisdom. This infrastructure must also invest in the most promising social entrepreneurs, ideas, and organizations and pick the right opportunities. The high rates of socially entrepreneurial activity might be very important to identifying the strongest entrepreneurs and so forth, but they may undermine successful swarming once the equilibrium begins to buckle.

CONCLUSION

The presence of so much socially entrepreneurial activity among my sample of social benefit organizations begs the question of success. There may be a great deal of effort but little real impact. Some organizations might not have the organizational skills to move much beyond launch; others might be unable to scale up their efforts to the tipping point for impact, while still others might dabble in change more as an occasional distraction or hobby than as a true cause. The challenge is to design a system for measuring progress at each stage of the socially entrepreneurial process, whether it is viewed as linear or nonlinear. Doing so would not only create new and early investment points for social value angels, it would promote better theories of change and more testing. After all, learning and adaptation may be less expensive early in the socially entrepreneurial process than late, especially in the production of products that are subject to regulation and recall.

Lacking a better measurement system, investors have little choice but to make their most significant commitments at the proof of concept stage, which occurs too late for imagination and launch but much too early for sustainable success. Investors can hardly be faulted for holding back until the formal launch of an idea if they have no tools for measuring progress at earlier points in time, however. As a result, the lack of measurement creates an unintended version of the hit television series "Survivor" in which nascent social entrepreneurs must prove their worth by winning a number of beauty contests that may have nothing to do with actual impact.

Developing measures of socially entrepreneurial progress involves a hard confrontation with failures. As noted at several earlier points in this book, researchers have been more interested in studying success than failure, in part because success has been defined as simple survival, while failure has been hard to find. Yet the bias against failure runs deeper than methodology. It also involves a vested interest in showing that business and social entrepreneurship actually matter to important issues such as profits and social value. We want so badly to believe in the potential solutions to intractable problems that we sometimes neglect the probability of failure. But failure also produces benefits, especially in the comparisons that can be made with success. As Rita Gunther McGrath wrote in 1999, failure remains a powerful teacher:

> By carefully analyzing failures instead of focusing only on successes, scholars can begin to make systematic progress on better analytical models of entrepreneurial value creation. Indeed, just as a clearer understanding of the nature of volatility and risk has spawned an explosion of instruments and product for managing their effects better, so, too, a direct and unflinching look at the downside of entrepreneurship will create considerable opportunities. Perhaps, in entrepreneurial scholarship to come, intelligent failures will even be celebrated.[12]

Socially entrepreneurial endeavors can fail for many reasons—a courageous social entrepreneur, good idea, ripe opportunity, and ambidextrous organization may not be enough. But researchers simply do not know enough about failure to help them move beyond hunches about the six practices of this or the four pillars of that. If the field is to develop better investment tools, it simply must look at failed investments.

12. McGrath (1999, p. 28).

CHAPTER SIX

COMPARING ACTIVITY

Investing in social entrepreneurship will always rely on instinct—no matter how precise the plan, investors and entrepreneurs both must make leaps of faith as they move forward. They can produce and evaluate reams of data, but the eventual decision to launch involves a fundamental belief that the new combination has promise. The leap of faith may be informed, but it is still a leap.

Letting go of rules, taking risks, and trusting others involve a leap of faith. Faith can be deeply grounded in rigorous analysis and tightly linked to past experience, but sooner or later, every innovation involves a decision to take the organization beyond the realm of known experience. If that organization has been disciplined about its work, it should be ready for the uncertainty ahead. Having done everything possible to anticipate the risks, however, some highly socially entrepreneurial organizations will take the leap only to find themselves standing at the edge of the canyon. It helps enormously if they have packed a parachute at the start of their journey.

Luckily, entrepreneurs do not need to be great prophets to create change, though some might argue that Muhammad Yunus is just that. But entrepreneurs do need to have faith that the prevailing wisdom can be changed. No matter how much cost-benefit analysis the organization pours into its decision, no matter how many evaluators and auditors it brings to the task, it must eventually make a leap of faith. It is part of the entrepreneurial quality.

169

Unfortunately, it is impossible to measure the hopeful imagination that underpins social entrepreneurship. The best one can do is to identify the conditions that make leaps of faith possible, which was the ultimate purpose of my survey of the high-performing organizations. By searching for statistically significant differences between levels of socially entrepreneurial activity, I hoped to disprove the hypothesis that there is no difference between the three groups—that highly socially entrepreneurial organizations are, indeed, different from their less socially entrepreneurial peers.

The search for differences is based primarily on the 2006 survey of the 131 high-performing social benefit organizations. In addition, the 2001 survey of the 250 high performing social benefit organizations provides at least some additional insights on the assumptions embedded in the definition of social entrepreneurship. A comparison of major findings from the 131 social benefit organizations that participated in the 2001 and 2006 surveys can be found in appendix B, while the 2006 survey is included in its entirety with comparisons of the responses from the highly, moderately, and not-too socially entrepreneurial organizations in appendix C.

With responses from senior executives at 131 social benefit organizations, the 2006 sample dwarfs much of the research in a field that has generally focused on relatively small numbers of reasonably well-known cases. However, even a sample of 131 cases is still too small for the kind of sophisticated statistical analysis often found in larger surveys. Recall that the margin of error in the 2006 survey for comparisons among the organizations that were coded as highly, moderately, or not-too entrepreneurial is plus or minus 9 percent, meaning that any given answer could be 9 percentage points higher or lower than reported.

Such a high margin of error means that it is nearly impossible to make comparisons within the three subgroups—one cannot ask with any confidence, for example, whether the thirty-four organizations that were coded as highly socially entrepreneurial are different from each other on a host of key questions, such as the role of visionary leadership in achieving impact or the level of sophistication in management systems. Nevertheless, analysis of the 131 responses offers an opportunity to explore significant differences and tendencies among the reputed high-performing social benefit organizations. In turn, these results provide ample insights on what might be found in a larger sample of high performers and can help guide future comparative surveys of organizations engaged in high- and low-impact social change. Such a survey would not start with high performers but with impact, thereby identifying potential lever points that would help investors and practitioners alike identify opportunities for solving intractable problems. In this regard, there are similarities and differences among the three groups of organizations profiled below, in part because the sample itself was based on reputed high performers, which came in many shapes and sizes.

FINDING SIMILARITIES

All of the statistical comparisons across the 131 organizations did not produce differences. Although the organizations that were coded as highly socially entrepreneurial did show significant strengths and vulnerabilities when compared with their less socially entrepreneurial peers, the three groups of organizations were generally more alike than different.

It is not clear whether the similarities reflect the general characteristics shared by all high-performing social benefit organizations regardless of their level of socially entrepreneurial activity, or whether they confirm the commitment of highly socially entrepreneurial organizations to match the management excellence of their exemplary peers.

This is not to argue that highly socially entrepreneurial, high-performing organizations are paragons of management excellence. Nor is it to suggest that the pursuit of excellence is sufficient for impact. But there is ample evidence that poor management is often the source of failure—the entrepreneur may be highly motivated, the idea may be right, and opportunity ripe, but the organization must be configured for sustainability. After earlier debunking the straw man of perfect management, Grant and Crutchfield later provide a long list of management principles that are essential for sustainability: modest diversification of revenues, a broad individual donor base, competitive executive compensation, sophisticated information technology, and a willingness to invest in their own capacity. "Although none of these basic management practices alone leads to breakthrough impact," they wrote, "a solid organizational foundation is essential to sustaining impact over time."[1] Put another way, management excellence is necessary but not sufficient for socially entrepreneurial activity.

1. Grant and Crutchfield (2007, p. 40).

TABLE 6-1. Levels of Performance, 2006[a]
Percent

Reported level	Highly socially entrepreneurial	Moderately socially entrepreneurial	Not-too socially entrepreneurial
Very high	62	68	36
Somewhat high	29	27	55
Average	9	0	9
Somewhat poor	0	0	0
Very poor	0	0	0
N = 131			

a. Percentages may not add to 100 because some respondents gave no response or because of rounding errors.

High Performing . . .

At least for now, my survey and past case studies suggest that highly socially entrepreneurial organizations are just as highly performing, if not more so, as any other entity. They are able to recruit and retain entrepreneurs who are ready to pursue change, develop ideas that hold the promise of a new social equilibrium, identify or create opportunities that are waiting for action, and build organizations that can sustain change for the long term.

Indeed, 62 percent of the respondents at organizations that were coded as highly socially entrepreneurial also rated their organization as very high performing in achieving its mission compared with just 36 percent of the respondents at the not-too entrepreneurial organizations. It is interesting that 68 percent of the respondents at the moderately entrepreneurial organizations also rated their organization as very high performing, perhaps suggesting that high performance frees resources or energy for at least some innovation within an organization. The figures do not establish any causal link between high performance and high levels of socially entrepreneurial activity, however. It could be that high performance leads to high levels of socially entrepreneurial activity, or vice versa. Table 6-1 shows the result.

. . . Yet Vulnerable

Vulnerability comes in many shapes and sizes and involves exposure to both internal and external conditions. On internal vulnerability, respondents at the highly socially entrepreneurial organizations were no more likely than their moderately and not-too-entrepreneurial peers to report high levels of internal vulnerability to challenges such as staff turnover and technology problems. Just 6 percent of respondents at the highly socially entrepreneurial organizations said their organizations were very vulnerable to internal challenges compared with 5 percent and 8 percent of the respondents at the moderately and not-too entrepreneurial organizations, respectively. This is not to argue that the 131 organizations were invulnerable, however. Indeed, 56 percent of the respondents at the highly socially entrepreneurial organizations reported that their organizations were at least somewhat vulnerable to internal challenges, as did 52 percent and 53 percent of their less socially entrepreneurial peers, respectively.

Vulnerability never goes away it seems, in spite of the fact that all three types of organizations had engaged in at least some capacity building during the five years before the 2006 survey. According to the survey, 62 percent of the respondents at the highly socially entrepreneurial organizations said their organizations had engaged in capacity building, as did 57 percent and 68 percent of the respondents at the moderately and not-too entrepreneurial organizations, respectively.

Thus even as the highly socially entrepreneurial organizations show significant strengths, they also show other vulnerabilities. Respondents in the organizations that were coded as highly socially entrepreneurial reported that the commitment to vision was the most important contributor to their socially entrepreneurial activity, for example, but they reported greater vulnerabilities in board governance. In addition, these respondents reported that their organizations had less difficulty recruiting leaders than their peers had but also said that access to information technology and staff training was less important to achieving their organization's mission. And these respondents were much more likely to describe their organizations as high performers.

Before turning to the search for similarities and differences within the four components of social entrepreneurship, readers are reminded that the sample size in this study was very small, which limits the statistical significance of the differences among highly, moderately, and not-too entrepreneurial organizations. Therefore, much of the following discussion involves tendencies in the data that can only be validated by much larger sample sizes. Nevertheless, these tendencies provide a starting point for pinpointing degrees of socially entrepreneurial activity related to the entrepreneur, the idea, the opportunity, and the organization.

ENTREPRENEURS

Given the lack of clarity in defining social entrepreneurship among the 131 respondents, it would be no surprise to find some confusion in defining the term *social entrepreneur*. Is an entrepreneur someone who generates revenue, innovation, and social change? Or is an entrepreneur simply another kind of leader? Concerns about misinterpretations led me to avoid the term altogether by focusing on *leader* instead.

This does not mean entrepreneurs were absent from the survey. Rather, the entrepreneur was almost certainly present in the general discussion of leaders and leadership. As one of the six respondents who did use *leadership* in defining social entrepreneurship said, "Social entrepreneurship is leadership by people working together to solve large problems, social or environmental, without waiting for government or the private sector to lead the way or find them." Many other respondents may have simply assumed that leadership was part of the equation, whether they were explicit about it or not.

Working Alone?

Apropos of the earlier assumption that *entrepreneur* is not necessarily singular, respondents at the highly socially entrepreneurial organizations were slightly more likely to say their entrepreneurial activity came from a group or unit within the organization: 48 percent of the respondents at the highly socially entrepreneurial organizations said their self-reported socially entrepreneurial activity came from such a group or unit; 44 percent and 38 percent, respectively, of the respondents of moderately and not-too entrepreneurial organizations said the same. In turn, the less socially entrepreneurial organizations were somewhat more likely to focus on the individual leader such as a founder or executive director as a source of their entrepreneurial activity. Although 20 percent of the respondents at the highly socially entrepreneurial organizations said that their self-reported socially entrepreneurial activity came from an individual leader, 28 percent and 31 percent of their peers at moderately and not-too entrepreneurial organizations said their organizations had relied on just such individual leadership for their self-reported activity (table 6-2).

Much as respondents may have been confused by the term social entrepreneur, this analysis nonetheless suggests that visionary leadership

TABLE 6-2. Sources of Reported Social Entrepreneurship, 2006[a]
Percent

Primary source	Highly socially entrepreneurial	Moderately socially entrepreneurial	Not-too socially entrepreneurial
An individual leader	20	28	31
A group or unit within the organization	48	44	38
Clients and or other stakeholders	12	6	13
Funders and contributors	4	0	3
$N = 100$[b]			

a. Percentages may not add to 100 because some respondents gave no response or because of rounding errors.

b. Only respondents who described their organizations as "very" or "somewhat" socially entrepreneurial were asked this question.

is the most important characteristic of the leaders of highly socially entrepreneurial organizations. Analysis of the 2001 survey also suggests that highly socially entrepreneurial organizations focus first and foremost on program impacts, not management excellence. They may have achieved excellent management, as noted above, but it is not their first priority. According to the 2001 survey of the high-performing social benefit organizations interviewed again in 2006, 47 percent of the respondents in highly socially entrepreneurial organizations said an organization could be very well managed and still not achieve its program goals, while only 32 percent of their peers at not-too entrepreneurial organizations agreed. And 41 percent of the respondents at highly socially entrepreneurial organizations said that organizations should first improve their programs as a path toward greater impact, while only 17 percent of their colleagues at not-too entrepreneurial organizations agreed.

These findings can be used in the search for the core characteristics that lead to visionary leadership. To the extent that inspiration, direct action, creativity, courage, and fortitude are intimately related to visionary leadership, Roger Martin and Sally Osberg's list of key leadership traits is right on target; to the extent that recognition and relentlessness, adaptation and learning, and bold action without a limitation of resources currently in hand are intimately linked to visionary leadership, J. Gregory Dees's list is also on target. And to the extent that ethical fiber is intimately linked to visionary leadership, Bill Drayton's focus is also on target.

TABLE 6-3. Founder Engagement, 2006[a]

Percent

Status of founder	Highly socially entrepreneurial	Moderately socially entrepreneurial	Not-too socially entrepreneurial
Founder running the organization			
Yes	21	16	11
No	79	83	89
Founder still actively involved in the organization			
Yes	37	30	19
No	63	68	81
N =131			

a. Percentages may not add to 100 because some respondents gave no response or because of rounding errors.

Holding Fast

Whatever they are called, the senior executives of the highly socially entrepreneurial organizations who responded to the 2006 survey were somewhat more likely to be the founders of their organizations—21 percent of the highly socially entrepreneurial organizations were headed by the founders compared with 16 percent and 11 percent of their moderately and not-too entrepreneurial peer organizations, respectively.

More significant, 37 percent of respondents at the highly socially entrepreneurial organizations said their founders were still actively involved in some way, whether as chief executives, board members, consultants, and so forth compared with 30 percent of the respondents at their moderately entrepreneurial and just 19 percent of respondents at their not-too entrepreneurial peers (table 6-3). Acknowledging that some of the highly socially entrepreneurial organizations were founded decades before this survey, it seems reasonable to argue that their founders were much more likely than their peers at the less socially entrepreneurial organizations to stay involved in their organizations for the long term.

Founders are obviously more likely to work at younger rather than at older organizations. Not surprising, none of the organizations that were older than fifty years had a founder still actively involved, while almost half of the organizations younger than twenty years did. But while acknowledging the small sample sizes involved (just 21 organizations were younger than twenty-years-old), the highly socially entrepreneurial organizations within this set were more likely to hold their founders.

Thinking Differently

The 2001 survey showed few other differences across the 131 organizations that also responded to the 2006 survey. Interviewed in 2001 and asked about the elements of organizational high performance, respondents at the organizations that were coded in 2006 as highly socially entrepreneurial were neither significantly more nor significantly less likely to say that such leadership characteristics as decisiveness, honesty, charisma, and faithfulness were very important *separately* from high performance.

Moreover, when asked in the 2001 survey which of these leadership characteristics was more important for leaders of a high-performing organization, there were no statistically significant differences among the answers from what would be later coded as highly socially entrepreneurial and less socially entrepreneurial organizations. The only characteristic that came close to significance was the "need to be trusting," which 18 percent of the respondents at highly socially entrepreneurial organizations rated as most important compared with 7 percent and 8 percent of respondents at the moderately and not-too entrepreneurial organizations, respectively. The 2001 survey also revealed no differences among respondents on the need for a leader to be a good fundraiser, encourage risk-taking, or know how to motivate people. At least by these measures, there are questions about whether the leaders of highly socially entrepreneurial organizations think differently from their peers.

Despite these similarities, the 2001 survey also suggests that the leaders of highly socially entrepreneurial organizations put a greater emphasis on a mission even to the exclusion of new ideas that might take their organizations in different directions. On the one hand, respondents at highly socially entrepreneurial organizations were less likely to report that their organizations encouraged risk-taking in the development of new ideas, largely because taking risk was inherent in their mission. According to the 2001 survey, 50 percent of respondents at the highly socially entrepreneurial organizations reported this support for risk-taking compared with 61 percent and 66 percent of their peers at less socially entrepreneurial organizations, respectively. On the other hand, respondents at the highly socially entrepreneurial organizations were slightly more likely to report that their organizations encouraged employees to participate in key decisions, with 82 percent of these respondents stating that such participation was very important to their

TABLE 6-4. Support for Risk-Taking and Participation, 2006[a]
Percent

Importance of leadership category	Highly socially entrepreneurial	Moderately socially entrepreneurial	Not-too socially entrepreneurial
Risk-taking			
Very important	50	61	66
Somewhat important	41	32	32
Not too important	9	5	0
Not important at all	0	0	2
Asking employees to participate in key decisions			
Very important	82	61	74
Somewhat important	15	34	25
Not too important	2	3	2
Not important at all	0	0	2
N =131			

a. Percentages may not add to 100 because some respondents gave no response or because of rounding errors.

organization's mission; 61 percent and 74 percent of their peers at the moderately and not-too entrepreneurial organizations agreed, respectively. Table 6-4 shows these results.

These results may be more about the less socially entrepreneurial organizations in the sample than about the highly socially entrepreneurial set. It could be, for example, that not-too entrepreneurial organizations need to encourage risk-taking actively, as a stimulus to entrepreneurship and innovation. It could also be that moderately entrepreneurial organizations are less likely to include their employees in key decisions because their organizations are divided by the presence of competing missions.

Similar results emerged from the 2006 survey. Asked about the elements of high performance again, respondents at the highly socially entrepreneurial organizations were neither significantly more nor significantly less likely to say that having visionary leadership, being innovative, being well managed, and having unrestricted revenues were each very important to achieving their organization's mission. Nor were they more or less likely to say that having visionary leadership, being innovative, being well managed, and having unrestricted revenues were very important to engaging in high levels of socially entrepreneurial activity.

Common Histories

Whether they were founders or not, the chief executives at the organizations that were coded highly socially entrepreneurial were somewhat less likely to have spent as much time in the social benefit sector as their peers at the less socially entrepreneurial organizations and more likely to have at least some for-profit experience. Again according to the 2006 survey, 57 percent of the chief executives at the highly socially entrepreneurial organizations had spent all or most of their careers in the social benefit sector compared with 72 percent and 70 percent of the chief executives at their moderately and not-too entrepreneurial peers, respectively. In turn, 25 percent of the chief executives at the highly socially entrepreneurial organizations had spent all or most of their careers in the for-profit sector compared with 14 percent and 11 percent of their less socially entrepreneurial peers, respectively.

Rare Breeds Again

This is not to argue that leadership is irrelevant to highly socially entrepreneurial activity. When asked in 2006 which of these same four characteristics was deemed to be the most important to achieving either the organization's mission or engaging in high levels of socially entrepreneurial activity, the respondents at the highly socially entrepreneurial organizations were more likely to put the emphasis on visionary leadership.

Asked first about achieving their organization's mission, 47 percent of respondents at highly socially entrepreneurial organizations said that having visionary leadership was the most important factor in achieving their organization's mission compared with 30 percent and 34 percent among respondents at the moderately and not-too entrepreneurial organizations, respectively. Asked later in the survey about successful socially entrepreneurial activity, 50 percent of respondents at highly socially entrepreneurial organizations put visionary leadership at the top of their list compared to 34 percent and 32 percent at the moderately and not-too socially entrepreneurial organizations, respectively (table 6-5). At least for the respondents at the highly socially entrepreneurial organizations, commitment to vision is the core organization resource, even when compared with being innovative. As the data suggest, having unrestricted revenue mattered much more for organizational performance (achieving the organization's mission) than it did for socially entrepreneurial activity, a

TABLE 6-5. Organizational Characteristics of High Performance and
Socially Entrepreneurial Activity, 2006[a]
Percent

Organizational characteristic	Highly socially entrepreneurial	Moderately socially entrepreneurial	Not-too socially entrepreneurial
Most important to achieving the organization's mission			
Having visionary leadership	47	30	34
Being innovative	21	30	19
Being well managed	30	30	40
Having unrestricted revenue	19	11	6
Most important to achieving successful socially entrepreneurial activity			
Having visionary leadership	50	34	32
Being innovative	32	41	36
Being well managed	9	14	21
Having unrestricted income	3	9	9
N = 131			

a. Percentages may not add to 100 because some respondents gave no response or because of rounding errors.

finding that suggests the high regard for vision as the linchpin of pattern-breaking change.

Given the long list of entrepreneurial traits and characteristics discussed in the business and social entrepreneurship literature, it is impossible to know whether visionary leadership is, in fact, the most important way to differentiate among levels of socially entrepreneurial activity. It could be, for example, that visionary leadership and the idea matter most at the launch of an organized effort to change the social equilibrium, while the strength of the social equilibrium matters more to the acceleration of the idea, and organization is most important during the scale-up to maximum impact. As suggested earlier in this book, however, it could also be that all four components of social entrepreneurship interact throughout the process.

IDEAS

The idea is at the centerpiece of most definitions of social entrepreneurship, and it was evident in the 2001 and 2006 surveys. For example, the 2001 survey found that highly socially entrepreneurial organizations were

TABLE 6-6. Types of Reported Socially Entrepreneurial Activity, 2008[a]

Percent

Activity	Highly socially entrepreneurial	Moderately socially entrepreneurial	Not-too socially entrepreneurial
Administrative and operating systems	4	6	8
Program design	48	28	21
Both	48	67	67
N =100[b]			

a. Percentages may not add to 100 because some respondents gave no response or because of rounding errors.

b. Only respondents who described their organizations as "very" or "somewhat" socially entrepreneurial were asked this question.

slightly more likely to be national in scope, but they showed no other major differences in their basic missions when compared with the other two groups of social benefit organizations.

Programs, Process, or Both

The three groups did differ in the kind of socially entrepreneurial activity they reported, however. Forty-eight percent of respondents at the organizations coded as highly socially entrepreneurial reported that their entrepreneurial activity involved program design; in contrast, 67 percent of the respondents at the moderately and not-too entrepreneurial organizations, respectively, reported that their activity involved administration and program design. Although the responses show the very high premium placed on program design among highly socially entrepreneurial organizations, there are still plenty of questions about the "how to do" innovation and "what kind of" innovation to do at these organizations as well. So noted, many highly socially entrepreneurial organizations might take a lesson from their not-too entrepreneurial peers regarding the need for simultaneous changes in program design and administration as an essential pathway to success. Table 6-6 shows the differences in the type of socially entrepreneurial activity.

PROGRAMS FIRST? Readers must be very cautious in interpreting these findings, particularly given the problems with the levels of self-reported social entrepreneurship discussed earlier in this chapter. Nevertheless, the responses do suggest that highly socially entrepreneurial organizations do focus quite heavily on their programs, which is no doubt part of the reason that they achieved growth in the demand for their services, but which is possibly a detriment to sustaining performance.

This focus on programmatic change also comes with a greater likelihood that highly socially entrepreneurial organizations have experienced an increase in fiscal pressure over the past five years, which suggests a lag between demand and funding as these organizations struggle to scale up, a greater need for innovative cost-saving systems and operations, or perhaps both. According to the survey, 26 percent of respondents at the highly socially entrepreneurial organizations reported rapid growth in fiscal pressure compared with 16 percent and 17 percent of the respondents at the less socially entrepreneurial organizations, respectively.

Finally, the focus on program design fits well with the lack of reported program diversification in each organization. Asked whether their programs were "very diversified," "somewhat diversified," "not too diversified," or "not diversified at all," only 18 percent of the respondents at the highly socially entrepreneurial organizations answered "very diversified," compared with 61 percent of respondents at the moderately entrepreneurial and 49 percent at their not-too entrepreneurial peer organizations.

FACING GROWTH. There were other significant differences across the three levels of socially entrepreneurial organizations, especially in reported demands for services and budgets, both of which are measures of the potential expansion of a given idea. The 2001 survey showed no differences on these measures; however, the 2006 survey found much higher rates of reported growth among the highly socially entrepreneurial organizations.

In 2006, for example, 50 percent of the respondents at the organizations that were coded as highly socially entrepreneurial reported rapid growth in program demand compared with just 23 percent and 26 percent of respondents at the moderately and not-too entrepreneurial organizations, respectively (table 6-7). In turn, 29 percent of these highly socially entrepreneurial respondents reported rapid growth in their organization's budget compared with 7 percent of the respondents at the moderately and 13 percent of the respondents at the not-too entrepreneurial organizations. Conversely, only 9 percent of the respondents at the highly socially entrepreneurial organizations reported little or no growth in program demand. Of their not-too entrepreneurial peers, 19 percent reported little or no growth or some level of contraction. Similarly, for a question concerning their organization's budget, just 21 percent of the respondents at the highly socially entrepreneurial organizations reported little or no growth or some level of contraction compared with 37 percent of respondents at the not-too entrepreneurial

TABLE 6-7. Growth in Program Demand and Budget during the Past Five Years, 2006[a]
Percent

Levels of growth	Highly socially entrepreneurial	Moderately socially entrepreneurial	Not-too socially entrepreneurial
Program demand			
Rapid	50	23	26
Steady	41	70	55
Little or no growth	9	5	17
Steady contraction	0	0	2
Rapid contraction	0	0	0
Budget			
Rapid	29	7	13
Steady	50	66	47
Little or no growth	12	20	26
Steady contraction	6	0	11
Rapid contraction	3	2	0
N = 131			

a. Percentages may not add to 100 because some respondents gave no response or because of rounding errors.

organizations. The moderately entrepreneurial organizations were simultaneously the least likely to report rapid growth or little or no growth. For the most part, they were growing at a steady pace, while the highly socially entrepreneurial organizations were skyrocketing and the not-too entrepreneurial organizations appeared to be stagnating somewhat.

These are all reasonable illustrations of the potential impact of a given idea, but these findings need to be supplemented by more refined measures of the size and scope of the idea and its novelty, uniqueness, familiarity, and so forth. Although such measures could be collected through objective means by coding the actual program activity of each organization, this task would involve an enormous amount of effort.

OPPORTUNITIES

Despite its role in many of the prevailing definitions of social entrepreneurship, the opportunity for change remains a mystery. Where does it come from, how is it recognized, can it be created, and why are some opportunities answered and others not? Much as the questions matter greatly to the social equilibrium, the 2001 and 2006 surveys contained

only a handful of questions that are directly concerned with the opportunity for change.

Degrees of Difficulty

This study used the word *environment* as a surrogate for *opportunity,*
assuming that respondents would be more likely to understand the first
term rather than the second. But whatever the term, respondents at the
highly socially entrepreneurial organizations clearly saw a different environment than what their peers at the less socially entrepreneurial organizations saw. In 2001, for example, all respondents were asked about the
nature of their environment, which is a reasonable term for describing
the place where opportunities reside. According to the survey, respondents at the organizations that were later coded as highly socially entrepreneurial were significantly less likely to describe their environments as
not particularly competitive or heavily regulated. Specifically, 52 percent
and 82 percent of the respondents at the organizations that were coded
as highly socially entrepreneurial said the words *competitive* and *heavily
regulated* did not describe their organizations well, respectively, compared with just 31 percent and 55 percent of the respondents at the
organizations that were coded as moderately or not-too entrepreneurial,
respectively. Reading between the lines, socially entrepreneurial organizations seem to "go where they ain't," meaning that they pick opportunities with ample room for action.

EXTERNAL CHALLENGES. Moreover, the 2006 survey found significant differences among the three groups regarding the kinds of external, or environmental, challenges they faced. Just 9 percent of respondents at the
highly socially entrepreneurial organizations said their organizations were
very vulnerable to external challenges, such as competition or access to
funding, as opposed to 23 percent and 28 percent of the respondents at
the moderately and not-too socially entrepreneurial organizations, respectively (table 6-8).

Highly socially entrepreneurial organizations do seem to operate
where there is less competition, perhaps explaining the lack of diversification discussed below. Why diversify when funding is relatively open to
single organizations?

As for managing the environment, respondents at the three types of
organizations were in rough agreement that having a clear mission,
collaborating with other organizations, and measuring results were
very important in achieving their missions. There is clearly room for

TABLE 6-8. Vulnerability to External Challenges, 2006[a]
Percent

Level of vulnerability	Highly socially entrepreneurial	Moderately socially entrepreneurial	Not-too socially entrepreneurial
Very	9	23	28
Somewhat	65	59	53
Not very	26	18	19
Not at all	0	0	0
N = 131			

a. Answers may not sum to 100 because some respondents gave no response or because of rounding errors.

improvement in the latter, however; 59 percent of respondents at the highly socially entrepreneurial organizations said measuring results was very important to the mission. This may be a higher mark than some critics might suggest—the image of the single-minded, highly focused, idea-driven entrepreneurial organization is so pervasive that it is a wonder that they would measure results at all.

Although all three groups of organizations were equally likely to have clear missions, collaborate, and measure results, the highly socially entrepreneurial organizations were less likely to use strategic planning to manage into the future: 41 percent of the respondents at highly socially entrepreneurial organizations said that a strategic plan was very important to achieving their mission, and 59 percent and 58 percent of their moderately and not-too entrepreneurial peers said the same, respectively.

ISOLATION. Alongside the lack of strategic planning, the highly socially entrepreneurial organizations appear to exist in relative isolation from the rest of the social benefit world. This isolation involves at least some distance from traditional sources of help and encouragement. At least according to the 2001 survey, respondents at highly entrepreneurial organizations were less likely than their peers at not-too entrepreneurial organizations to say that government, graduate schools, management support organizations, external rating organizations, and social benefit associations had helped improve the performance of their organizations.

Highly socially entrepreneurial organizations were most connected in 2001 to foundations and providers of technical assistance. As already noted, these connections not only provide needed resources but produce the relatively high levels of organizational capacity building mentioned earlier in this chapter. Organizations cannot improve their performance

TABLE 6-9. Sources and Interventions for Performance, 2001[a]
Percent

Source creating a great deal or fair amount of improvement	Highly socially entrepreneurial	Moderately socially entrepreneurial	Not-too socially entrepreneurial
Foundations	70	66	68
Government	24	25	26
Graduate schools	18	27	21
Management support organizations	24	22	41
External rating organizations	12	21	34
Providers of technical assistance	65	48	66
Associations of nonprofits	35	49	70
N =131			

a. Multiple answers were allowed.

without at least some help, and highly socially entrepreneurial organizations appear to have been just as likely as their peers to seek it. Table 6-9 shows the patterns from the 2001 survey.

It is always possible that respondents did not seek as much help across the wide spectrum of potential support because that help was irrelevant to their mission. After all, highly socially entrepreneurial organizations may need different kinds of help, such as capacity building and management assistance, that are directly related to changing the social equilibrium. They may also need their own associations, management support organizations, consultants, and so forth and already have a mixed set of graduate schools that generate support, most notably the burgeoning number of business schools that have met growing student demand for more courses on social entrepreneurship.

MANAGEMENT REFORMS. However, respondents at the highly socially entrepreneurial organizations were less likely to report much impact that was due to past management reforms in their environments, including leadership training, management standards, strategic planning, collaboration, reduced duplication, and so forth. At least in 2001, respondents at the organizations later coded as highly socially entrepreneurial were less likely than their peers to endorse leadership tenure, public transparency, and standard business tools. Although the lack of enthusiasm for these three reforms suggest potential vulnerabilities, the unwillingness or inability to adopt standard business tools is perhaps most problematic. This finding is clear among the executives at the 131 organizations that participated in the 2001 and 2006 surveys:

—Just 32 percent of the respondents at the highly socially entrepreneurial organizations interviewed in 2001 said that using business tools had improved their organization's performance a great deal compared with 48 percent and 51 percent of respondents at their moderately and not-too socially entrepreneurial peer organizations, respectively.

—And just 18 percent of respondents at the highly socially entrepreneurial organizations contacted again in 2006 said they used business tools to a great extent to improve their performance compared with 32 percent at moderately entrepreneurial and 38 percent at not-too entrepreneurial organizations.

At the same time, the highly socially entrepreneurial organizations were only slightly more likely to have received a great deal of capacity building over the course of the five years before the survey in 2006.

Thus the lack of connection to traditional sources of help and the unwillingness to adopt contemporary management reforms may reflect the perceived irrelevance of these interventions to socially entrepreneurial activity. Meeting the need of highly socially entrepreneurial organizations for specialized assistance may require new associations, specialized consultants alongside business consultants who work for the social benefit sector pro bono, or more practitioner-oriented learning resources and conferences such as the Skoll World Forum and the Ashoka gatherings. The demand appears to exist.

At the same time again, the lack of connection may reflect some of the cognitive biases that make social entrepreneurs more entrepreneurial. Their optimism, risk-taking, belief in the basic power of ideas, and reduced interest in challenging their own assumptions about the future may lead them to reject traditional sources and forms of help. This may be to their advantage in persevering against the odds—better not to know what might stop them, for example. But it may undermine their success in scaling up to greater impact.

ORGANIZATIONS

The highly socially entrepreneurial organizations profiled in the two surveys of 2001 and 2006 shared the high performance of their peers. According to the 2001 survey, all three sets of organizations—highly, moderately, and not-too socially entrepreneurial—were equally likely to have flat organizations, give their employees authority to make routine decisions on their own, and encourage their employees to work in teams.

And according to the 2006 survey, these organizations were just as likely as their peers to report a strong preference for working in teams and low vulnerability to internal challenges such as staff turnover or technology problems. In short, they shared many of the attributes of high performance.

This support for the default hypothesis lends confidence to the idea that socially entrepreneurial organizations can be just as high performing as any social benefit organization. Although every organization has vulnerabilities of one kind or another, there is nothing in the 2001 and 2006 surveys that leads to great worries about the overall effectiveness of the socially entrepreneurial entities. And there is certainly nothing that gives respondents at the highly socially entrepreneurial organizations pause.

None of this is to argue that highly socially entrepreneurial organizations are perfect, of course. Indeed, the 2001 and 2006 surveys show vulnerabilities that may be well rooted in the commitment to vision. Driven to accomplish great goals, highly socially entrepreneurial organizations may not invest in basic systems, encourage their staffs to take risks in developing new ideas, or actively engage their boards.

Resources for Change

The greatest vulnerabilities within the highly socially entrepreneurial organizations involve resources for basic capacity, which may reflect the lack of unrestricted and diversified revenues. According to the survey, the respondents at the organizations that were coded as highly socially entrepreneurial were less likely to report that their organizations generated a great deal of unrestricted revenue. Thus, just 15 percent of these respondents reported that their organizations had very diversified sources of funding compared with 39 percent of their moderately and 26 percent of their not-too entrepreneurial peers. And only 15 percent reported that their highly socially entrepreneurial organizations generated a great deal of unrestricted revenue compared with 27 percent and 25 percent of their moderately and not-too socially entrepreneurial peers, respectively (table 6-10).

The highly socially entrepreneurial organizations were hardly struggling for revenues, however—a majority of these organizations were at least somewhat diversified and generated a fair amount of unrestricted revenues. Nevertheless, respondents at the highly socially entrepreneurial organizations reported a greater dependency on grants and contributions than did their not-too entrepreneurial peers, creating at least some future vulnerability as program priorities and donor interests change.

TABLE 6-10. Sources and Amounts of Revenue, 2006[a]

Percent

Revenue	Highly socially entrepreneurial	Moderately socially entrepreneurial	Not-too socially entrepreneurial
Amount of unrestricted revenue generated			
Great deal	15	27	25
Fair amount	62	43	53
Not too much	24	30	23
Not at all	0	0	0
Degree of diversification of funding			
Very diversified	15	39	26
Somewhat diversified	65	45	49
Not too diversified	21	16	25
Not diversified at all	0	0	0
Sources of unrestricted revenue			
Grants and contributions	88	93	89
Fees for services	47	68	68
Earned revenue from a nonprofit business activity	24	48	45
$N = 131$			

a. Multiple answers were allowed.

NEEDS AND WANTS. Just because respondents at the highly socially entrepreneurial organizations reported less unrestricted or diversified revenue than their less socially entrepreneurial peers reported does not mean that they did not want it. Asked whether unrestricted revenue was important to achieving their organization's mission, 59 percent of the respondents at highly socially entrepreneurial organizations said such revenue was very important compared with what 52 percent and 68 percent of their moderately and not-too socially entrepreneurial peers said, respectively.

However, it is also important to note that diversification carries its own risks, not the least of which is the tendency to drift as funders ask for different programs. Organizations that draw from different revenue streams may also soon find that they must build extra capacity to manage the different expectations of each investor, not to mention the administrative costs of servicing each grant. Past research on the growth of nonprofits suggests that diversification across funding streams is not essential for nonprofits to scale up. Even so, most high-growth nonprofits still seek diversification within their single revenue stream. Diversification across streams may not be essential for growth, but it does appear to be a cornerstone of risk management.

The disparities between the three groups of organizations were particularly significant on access to unrestricted revenue, perhaps suggesting that highly socially entrepreneurial organizations may not know how to raise unrestricted revenue or may not have the time. Twenty-six percent of the respondents at highly socially entrepreneurial organizations and 67 percent and 79 percent of respondents at moderately and not-too entrepreneurial organizations, respectively, said their organizations generated a great deal or fair amount of unrestricted revenue. To the extent that unrestricted, diversified revenues provide opportunities for innovation and organizational capacity building, the highly socially entrepreneurial organizations might make the case for more of each.

Even as the lack of unrestricted, diversified revenue confirms the determination of entrepreneurial organizations and their leaders to persevere despite the odds, it also exposes a significant threat to survival and capacity building. As goes a single program in a focused portfolio, so goes the entrepreneur and organization. Although there is no evidence here that highly socially entrepreneurial organizations choose dependency deliberately, it may be a natural by-product of their raison d'être.

ORGANIZATIONAL RESOURCES. This disconnection between growth and capacity may reveal itself in attitudes toward key organizational resources. Although all three groups of organizations said that having enough employees was very important to achieving their mission, respondents at the highly socially entrepreneurial organizations were less likely than their peers to say that providing enough information technology and training were also very important.

According to the survey, 52 percent and 64 percent of respondents at the moderately and not-too entrepreneurial organizations, respectively, said that it was very important to provide enough training to achieve their organization's mission; only 38 percent of the respondents at the highly socially entrepreneurial organizations agreed. And 66 percent and 62 percent of the less socially entrepreneurial organizations, respectively, said that providing enough information technology is very important to achieving their organization's mission compared with 47 percent of the respondents at the highly socially entrepreneurial organizations (table 6-11). It could be that these findings simply reflect the lack of access to *relevant* training and the presence of state-of-the-art information technology already, but the findings may also reveal vulnerabilities that might undermine the drive forward.

TABLE 6-11. Importance of Providing Resources for Socially Entrepreneurial Activity, 2006[a]

Percent

Level of importance	Highly socially entrepreneurial	Moderately socially entrepreneurial	Not-too socially entrepreneurial
Providing enough information technology			
Very important	47	66	62
Somewhat important	47	32	36
Not too important	6	2	2
Not at all important	0	0	0
Providing enough training			
Very important	38	52	64
Somewhat important	47	45	30
Not too important	15	2	6
Not at all important	0	0	0
N =131			

a. Percentages may not add to 100 because some respondents gave no response or because of rounding errors.

Again, these findings may reflect the overwhelming focus on the underlying idea that drives highly socially entrepreneurial organizations forward. As I have argued in the past, innovative organizations make their management systems serve the mission, not vice versa. In doing so, they ensure that the basic thrust of the organization remains tightly focused on the end, not the means. At the same time, they also create the potential for the kinds of management problems that may undermine the very impact they seek. Nevertheless, the lack of importance assigned to information technology is particularly puzzling in organizations that are often portrayed as cutting-edge. It could be that respondents at the organizations coded as highly performing may have been rating the importance of state-of-the-art technology. But a plain reading of the question suggests that they either had problems purchasing needed technology or simply did not see such technology as an essential element of impact.

Time and funding for developing new ideas also provide resources for growth. But at least according to the 2006 survey, access to time and resources is a potential problem at highly socially entrepreneurial organizations. Just 44 percent of the respondents at the highly socially entrepreneurial organizations said that these two resources were very important to their organization's mission, while 59 percent and 57 percent of the

TABLE 6-12. Importance of Time and Resources for Developing New Ideas, 2006[a]
Percent

Level of importance	Highly socially entrepreneurial	Moderately socially entrepreneurial	Not-too socially entrepreneurial
Very important	44	59	57
Somewhat important	56	39	42
Not too important	0	2	0
Not at all important	0	0	0
N =131			

a. Percentages may not add to 100 because some respondents gave no response or because of rounding errors.

respondents at the moderately and not-too entrepreneurial organizations, respectively, agreed (table 6-12).

The lack of independent resources may involve the rapid growth of highly socially entrepreneurial organization, which leaves little time for market development. It may also reflect the intense focus on the original vision and the lack of management systems for tracking independent resources. At least according to the 2001 survey, 63 percent of the respondents from the organizations later coded as highly socially entrepreneurial said their accounting systems provided timely access to information compared with 77 percent and 83 percent of respondents at the moderately and not-too entrepreneurial organizations, respectively. Whatever the reason, the lack of readiness or willingness or both to invest becomes a particularly significant vulnerability as entrepreneurial organizations start thinking about new ideas for achieving their missions.

BOARD ENGAGEMENT. The underlying focus on the idea may also explain the 2001 findings regarding board governance, which suggest that social entrepreneurs may view active boards as a possible hindrance to their vision. Although the respondents at the highly socially entrepreneurial organizations were just as likely as their peers to say that their boards understood their general responsibilities and duties as a board, they were less likely to say that their boards understood their role in setting policy and overseeing performance.

At least according to the 2001 survey, they were also much less likely to report relatively frequent board meetings. Of the respondents at the moderately and not-too entrepreneurial organizations, 30 percent and 36 percent, respectively, said that their boards met nine or more times a year, respectively; only 12 percent of the respondents at the highly socially entrepreneurial organizations reported such a heavy workload. Instead, 29 percent reported that their boards met less than four times a year, and just 9 percent and 2 percent of their moderately and not-too entrepreneurial peers gave a similar response.

These lower levels of board engagement may give highly socially entrepreneurial organizations more freedom to maneuver, not to mention more time and resources to invest in their ideas. After all, board meetings demand a great deal of organizational commitment, too. Nevertheless, the lack of board engagement is a troubling vulnerability. Highly socially entrepreneurial organizations must be as accountable to their boards and to the external world as any other organization. Indeed, they may need even more board governance than their less socially entrepreneurial peers need. At a minimum, they cannot give the prevailing social equilibrium any excuse for questioning their performance. Moreover, given the recent congressional focus on board governance at the American Red Cross, highly socially entrepreneurial organizations must be especially careful about creating the impression that their board governance does not meet the contemporary demand for stronger board involvement.

MODERATELY SOCIALLY ENTREPRENEURIAL ORGANIZATIONS

Before ending this discussion of the surveys, it is important to note the potential role of moderately entrepreneurial organizations in stimulating social change. The moderately entrepreneurial organization most certainly has the capacity for at least some socially entrepreneurial activity, yet it also has some of the bureaucratic weight that makes such activity more difficult.

Thus there were times in the analysis when the moderately entrepreneurial organizations looked more like highly socially entrepreneurial organizations compared with their not-too entrepreneurial peers—for example, respondents at the moderately entrepreneurial organizations reported much higher levels of founder involvement, higher overall performance, and a somewhat lower commitment to being well managed than their not-too entrepreneurial peers reported. There were other times, however, when the moderately entrepreneurial organizations looked exactly like their not-too entrepreneurial peers—for example, respondents at the moderately entrepreneurial organizations reported the same modest growth in program demand and budget, higher vulnerability to external challenges, and higher importance of providing information technology and training as respondents at the not-too entrepreneurial organizations reported. At the same time, there was also a clear indication that organizations sometimes need to stop "entrepreneuring" so that they can rebalance for further growth or manage an unexpected crisis. Asked whether there had been periods during the past five years when their organization had not been as socially entrepreneurial or when socially entrepreneurial activities had to be put on hold, very high percentages of respondents at the three groups of organizations answered yes. Although the question was restricted to respondents who had said that the words *social entrepreneurship* described their organizations very or somewhat well, the results suggest that organizations either took breaks along the way to social change or had started their efforts during the past five years. Either way, the finding hints at the possibility that socially entrepreneurial activity is not always a 24/7 activity.

Finally, there were times when the moderately entrepreneurial organizations looked very different from the highly and the not-too entrepreneurial organizations—for example, respondents at the moderately entrepreneurial organizations reported the greatest diversification of programs and funding as well as the largest budgets among the three groups of social benefit organizations. (See appendix C for these results.) These organizations may not have been growing as fast as their highly socially entrepreneurial peers, but they were much more diversified.

It is this diversification that holds important insights for the moderately socially entrepreneurial organization. Although the survey did not ask whether this diversification was helpful per se, it is easy to argue that it generated the excess revenues needed for socially entrepreneurial activity among the moderately socially entrepreneurial organizations. Facing slower growth, though growth nonetheless, these moderately entrepreneurial organizations may have used the diversification to subsidize their pattern-breaking change.

It is not clear that every diversified organization has the potential for socially entrepreneurial activity, although there is at least some support for this notion in the 2006 survey. However, to be even moderately entrepreneurial, an organization would have to deal with the very real constraints that come with diversification itself—the drift in mission that comes from relying on too many funding streams, for example, not to mention the bureaucratization that comes as organizations age.

CONCLUSION

This study clearly shows the potential for exemplary performance among highly socially entrepreneurial organizations. At least in the two surveys, these organizations looked just as well managed on the whole as their less socially entrepreneurial peers, in part perhaps because they were already old and large enough to have created the assorted operating approaches and systems needed for high performance. Also, they are committed admirably to vision. If only all social benefit organizations put such a heavy emphasis on achieving their vision. Nevertheless, there is cause for at least some concern about sustainability, though there was no significant difference across the three groups of organizations on age. Yet what makes the highly socially entrepreneurial organizations so exciting also yields vulnerabilities, especially in the lack of diversified programs and funding.

This lack of diversification makes perfect sense in keeping the highly socially entrepreneurial organizations tightly focused on their missions, and efforts to diversify might bend their missions toward satisfying their investors, not their vision. Although this focused approach may yield the kind of high performance that the respondents at the highly socially entrepreneurial organizations reported, it also creates the conditions for crisis as these organizations confront the natural breakdowns that occur in organizational life. On the one hand, diversification can diffuse missions. On the other, it can provide a cushion against events that might stall a highly socially entrepreneurial organization.

This is not a brief for heavy investments in diversification, however. Rather, it suggests that highly socially entrepreneurial organizations need to pay attention to their vulnerabilities. Given their tremendous potential in creating pattern-breaking change, they should make every effort to protect against the risks embedded in their efforts to challenge the existing social equilibrium, including rainy day funds, diversification, strategic planning, and hedges against the loss of particularly significant supporters.

Preparing for inevitable pauses need not distract highly socially entrepreneurial organizations from their mission. Rather, it should be seen as a hedge against a potentially hostile world. In theory, the closer they get to success, the more threats they face as the social equilibrium defends itself. Hedging is not just good for successful business entrepreneurship, it may be essential for sustaining socially entrepreneurial activity in its battle to create a new equilibrium.

CHAPTER SEVEN

DRAWING CONCLUSIONS

This study challenges and confirms much of the conventional wisdom about socially entrepreneurial activity and social entrepreneurship. The study may be exploratory in nature, but it does yield strong insights about the nature of socially entrepreneurial activity, especially as it occurs among high-performing social benefit organizations.

As readers have been warned repeatedly, this study contains both biases and caveats. I cannot claim to have read the entire literature on either business or social entrepreneurship, for example, and clearly I missed important work that might have changed the discussion of the four components of social entrepreneurship, as well as the underlying assumptions embedded in the covering definition of social entrepreneurship. Nor can I claim that the surveys in 2001 and 2006 represent a valid sample of socially entrepreneurial organizations generally, or even high performing socially entrepreneurial organizations specifically.

The most I can claim is that the study reflects an effort to explore potential differences among the highly, moderately, and not-too entrepreneurial organizations that emerged from my sample of reputed high-performing social benefit organizations in 2001. This study does not deal with J. Gregory Dees and Beth Battle Anderson's notion of sector bending nor the growing amount of socially entrepreneurial activity that occurs among and between social benefit organizations, businesses, and governments.

Nevertheless, there is grist for further research embedded in this study, not the least of which is the relatively large amount of socially entrepreneurial activity that appears to exist among high-performing social benefit organizations. Given the limitations cited above, this study cannot prove that a quarter of all high-performing social benefit organizations are highly socially entrepreneurial, nor can it prove that another third are moderately so. But the study does suggest that there may be significant opportunities to expand socially entrepreneurial activity in the social benefit sector and that such activity can change the social equilibrium, given adequate resources. It can also ask whether this socially entrepreneurial activity might be enhanced through the spin-off of programs and units from their moderately entrepreneurial hosts or through scale-up to much greater organizational engagement.

However, the key question is not how much socially entrepreneurial activity exists, but how it can be expanded to maximum impact. Given the promise involved in the general movement toward altering a persistent and resistant social equilibrium, the field needs to be much more supportive in helping social entrepreneurs achieve their goals, whether it should be through organizational development, capacity-building infrastructure, more aggressive research and development, stronger networks of other social entrepreneurs and socially entrepreneurial organizations, or further encouragement and funding of management improvements. This help must involve careful research, however, not hunch.

FINDINGS

The key findings of this study rest on the interviews of senior executives at 131 high-performing social benefit organizations as well as a detailed literature review across the fields of business and social entrepreneurship. The survey respondents shared little common ground on the definition of social entrepreneurship, which in turn may have led to the very high estimates of the level of socially entrepreneurial activity in the organizations that were coded as less entrepreneurial by my research team. Nonetheless, the surveys do provide conditional insights on how highly socially entrepreneurial organizations differ from their less entrepreneurial peers, provided, of course, that the initial coding of the organizations was accurate. Although the surveys showed high levels of similarity among the different groups of organizations, thereby confirming the ability of highly socially entrepreneurial organizations to achieve and maintain high performance (or at least live up to their reputation thereof), it also revealed significant differences among the three groups of organizations.

Entrepreneurs

This study confirms the important role of entrepreneurs in stimulating socially entrepreneurial activity. Indeed, the most important difference in the 2006 survey may well involve the significant engagement of the original founders in their organizations. Fully one in five of the highly socially entrepreneurial organizations were still headed by their original founder, while another three out of five still engaged their founder in some meaningful way. One can only assume that they are holding fast to their mission, helping their organizations maintain a clear focus on social change.

This continued engagement may help explain the role of *commitment to vision* as the most important factor in both organization performance and socially entrepreneurial activity. Highly socially entrepreneurial organizations clearly put a greater emphasis on this commitment than on being well managed. They do not neglect management per se, at least according to respondents' ratings of their own organization's performance. But it is performance based on vision that appears to drive the ratings.

Given the fact that the highly socially entrepreneurial organizations were just as likely to be large and old as the moderately and not-too socially entrepreneurial comparison groups, this focus on vision emerges as a potentially critical characteristic of entrepreneurs. Logically it would exist somewhere in the middle layers of the pyramid of characteristics presented earlier in this book. Vision would certainly affect agility, for example, including tolerance for ambiguity and risk, and surely vision affects alertness. Although there is ample room for further research on the link between vision and other core characteristics, such research should focus clearly on core characteristics that link to vision. Bluntly put, if a core characteristic does not contribute to commitment to vision, it is not a core characteristic at all.

Ideas

The study clearly suggests that ideas matter to a variety of organizational indicators, most notably the remarkably high levels of growth in the demand for programs and the perceived level of budgetary growth. The highly socially entrepreneurial organizations either choose ideas with great potential for growth or the growth itself created the resources for socially entrepreneurial activity.

There is also good evidence that the highly socially entrepreneurial organizations prefer certain kinds of socially entrepreneurial activity. Given the biases embedded in the question about the organization's level of socially entrepreneurial activity, there appeared to be a clear preference by highly socially entrepreneurial organizations for ideas that might alter the basic structure of the social equilibrium. Again, this is not to argue that the organizations that were coded as highly socially entrepreneurial organizations did not care about management—indeed, almost half of the respondents at these highly socially entrepreneurial organizations said that their organizations were involved in program design and administrative systems.

This commitment to vision creates consequences for management nonetheless, indicated by the somewhat lower levels of enthusiasm among respondents at the highly socially entrepreneurial organizations toward providing resources such as time and funding for the development of new ideas. At the same time, these organizations were also more committed to asking employees to participate in key decisions that affect their missions. These organizations clearly believe in their vision and, by implication, their ideas for achieving it. They seem less interested in developing new ideas per se but quite committed to a strategy for driving that vision throughout the organization.

Opportunities

The study shows that highly socially entrepreneurial organizations have a preference for working in certain kinds of environments that may provide more opportunities to establish their presence and scale up toward challenging the prevailing social equilibrium. According to the 2006 survey, respondents at the organizations that were coded as highly socially entrepreneurial reported that their organizations worked in less competitive and regulated corners of their environments, a finding that was confirmed in the 2001 survey as well. As already noted, they seem to "go where they ain't," meaning that they focus on opportunities with the greatest room to challenge the prevailing wisdom.

Their external environment is hardly forgiving to such efforts, however. Despite their remarkable growth, the highly socially entrepreneurial organizations either do not operate in areas of the environment with the potential for revenue diversification or choose to avoid diversification as a potential deadweight on their vision. Although this lack of diversification does create vulnerabilities that might occur because of the eventual evaporation of support as seed grants expire, the organizations that were coded as highly socially entrepreneurial may simply view diversification as an obstacle to their vision. Hence, they may justifiably focus on single streams of revenue.

These organizations may have plenty of practical reasons for rejecting diversification, however. They may focus on single streams of revenue because of concerns regarding the administrative burdens of managing multiple streams. As past research suggests, each additional stream carries its own costs, whether in duplicative accounting streams, different deadlines for reporting, or new evaluation systems. It is one thing for these organizations to measure results about their programs, for example, and quite another to measure results using the many different languages of results management that currently burden social benefit organizations in general. Not only is focused funding a way to maintain the commitment to vision, it also may be a way to keep the highly socially entrepreneurial organizations as agile as possible in reacting to new opportunities.

Strategic planning is one way to manage the different kinds of uncertainties facing organizations created by external threats, few though they might be at highly socially entrepreneurial organizations. However, as the surveys show, these organizations assign less importance to strategic planning than their less entrepreneurial peers do. Once again, they may be worried about the administrative burdens involved in strategic planning—done well, it is a time-consuming task. But the lack of implied interest in strategic planning may also reflect the intense commitment to vision. These organizations may eschew planning because they already know where they want to go, which can be a strength or a vulnerability.

Organizations

Finally, the study shows that the highly socially entrepreneurial organizations share many of the attributes of their less socially entrepreneurial peers in most areas of organizational life:

—Except for assigning lower importance to strategic planning, they manage their external relations just as effectively, assigning the same level of importance to setting clear missions and measuring results.

—Except for lower confidence in their accounting systems (a finding from the 2001 survey), they also have similar internal management structures, operating with relatively flat hierarchies (another finding from the

2001 survey), while assigning the same level of importance to encouraging units within the organization to work together.

—Except for assigning lower importance to encouraging employees to take risks in developing new ideas, they have similar commitments to participatory leadership, assigning roughly the same levels of importance to having a shared vision for the organization's future and to encouraging employees to participate in key decisions as did their less entrepreneurial peers.

—Except for assigning lower importance to providing training and information technology and having less active boards (still another finding from the 2001 survey), they have similar commitments to providing enough resources to succeed, assigning the same importance to having enough staff.

The exceptions listed above raise questions about *sustaining* high performance as the highly socially entrepreneurial organizations continue to challenge the prevailing wisdom. Organizations cannot survive long without the firm direction that strategic planning provides, for example, or the accountability that strong board governance provides. Nor can they expect high performance from their employees if they neglect information technology and training.

This is not to argue that highly socially entrepreneurial organizations are poorly governed. Indeed, some research suggests that they use very different forms of governance than those used by their less entrepreneurial peers and that they have much more agile systems. Nevertheless, they must also pay attention to the vulnerabilities embedded in the exceptions cited above. If they are growing so fast that they do not have the resources for training and information technology, their investors should provide it. And if their governance does not meet contemporary demands for active engagement by the board and better understanding of the board's role in providing policy guidance, their investors should demand it.

It is impossible to know, of course, whether assigning lower importance to training and information technology means that the highly socially entrepreneurial organizations are actually providing less of these key resources. But the 2006 survey suggests potential vulnerabilities in basic operating capacity. There is simply no reason why socially entrepreneurial organizations should not be competitive on these kinds of resources, unless they are either so committed to vision that they neglect the basics or because their investors are so committed to vision that they are only willing to invest in the idea.

If the idea matters, so does management. To the extent management systems produce bureaucratic inertia, socially entrepreneurial organizations need to be deliberate about protecting their flexibility, through strategic planning, capacity building, training, or other interventions. But to the extent that management is essential for scale-up and impact, socially entrepreneurial organizations need to embrace it.

TRUE OR FALSE

This study hardly resolves the debate over definitions and assumptions, which is still central to the development of the field. To the contrary, the field is still some distance from even discussing the underlying assumptions that guide contemporary research, let alone determining which assumptions matter most in separating different forms of social entrepreneurship; shaping strategies for the launch, acceleration, and scale-up of actual interventions; or building an inventory of advice on how to increase the odds that the prevailing equilibrium will change.

Revisiting Assumptions

Despite all the caveats noted in previous pages, this study does provide a set of admittedly conditional findings that may help advance the search for social entrepreneurship. Building on the literature review and surveys discussed in this book, there is enough soft evidence to make speculative decisions on my forty assumptions as to whether they are true or false. Based on the evidence, box 7-1 compares my assumptions when I began this study in 2006 with my assumptions when I completed the various components of the study early in 2008. The arrows indicate assumptions that changed from false to true, or vice versa.

Recalling that *false* is the default position in the absence of at least some evidence to the contrary, this study led me to change twenty of my past assumptions, from false to true and just two from true to false, suggesting that social entrepreneurship is an uncommon but not impossible act.

Regarding entrepreneurs, the study suggests that social entrepreneurs (1) never rest as they move forward toward change; (2) think differently from other high achievers; (3) persevere against the odds; (4) share common histories, with occasional exceptions; and (5) continue to imagine, in part because they are high achievers. It is important to note that these assumptions need not always be true, nor do they necessarily limit the number of entrepreneurs. Socially entrepreneurial activity can become "natural" through organizational design, while the number of entrepreneurs can be increased by helping motivated individuals, teams, and networks learn how to think like an entrepreneur.

Regarding ideas, the study also suggests that socially entrepreneurial ideas are (6) designed to change the world and (7) must grow at least minimally to achieve success. Even as they surprise the social equilibrium, socially entrepreneurial ideas do not necessarily have to be absolutely new. Indeed, in the study of government innovation, there is a long history of using old stuff in new ways—that is, cobbling together a set of familiar ideas in an entirely new combination. Similarly, scaling to success does not necessarily require global scale. It can involve moving from one city block to an entire neighborhood, for example, or one neighborhood to a larger community. The key is to pay attention to the dissemination of the breakthrough, not to its visibility to the world. In a sense, modesty becomes social entrepreneurship, if only to lull the prevailing wisdom into complacency.

Regarding opportunities, the study suggests that socially entrepreneurial opportunities (8) are rare, though not so much so that they only arise once in a great while; (9) cannot be predicted; (10) tend to occur in great punctuations when the demand for change rises to a tipping point; (11) emerge where entry costs are low; (12) open and close quickly as entrepreneurs surge toward action; (13) favor competition over collaboration; and (14) appear to the special few. These last two assumptions are linked to the notion that entrepreneurs think differently from other high achievers—competition has tended to improve ideas across the equilibrium, while alertness to opportunity is one of the key characteristics of success. Once again, not all these assumptions are fixed into the future—investors can easily help entrepreneurs identify opportunities, while training and education can improve the quality of competition.

Regarding organizations, the study suggests that socially entrepreneurial organizations (15) tend to nurture a stream of new ideas as they move forward into conflict with the prevailing equilibrium, (16) rarely pause as they pursue change, (17) are constructed differently from other high-performing organizations, (18) need unrestricted revenue to invest in organizational capacity and research and development, (19) can use diversified revenue to protect against fluctuations in a single stream of revenue, and (20) do insulate themselves from aging. This last assumption takes us all the way back to the concept of corporate entrepreneurship, which argues that organizational rejuvenation is a central challenge for maintaining market position. Just as corporations must change or die, socially entrepreneurial organizations must blend their pursuit of managerial excellence with a constant vigilance against bureaucracy, which is exactly what Apple and so many other firms do.

Two assumptions regarding ideas and organizations changed from true to false. The study suggests that (1) socially entrepreneurial ideas involve both radical new combinations *and* dramatic expansions of existing ideas and that (2) socially entrepreneurial organizations maintain constant forward motion, even as they create their organizational infrastructure—put another way, they build the plane while flying it. Levels of socially entrepreneurial activity clearly varied greatly among my sample of high-performing social benefit organizations and appear to vary among businesses.

As Ebenezer Scrooge might put it, the question about these changes is whether they reflect the future that will be or one that might be. Lacking a strong infrastructure and solid research base, it may be that future social entrepreneurs will always have to work 24/7, persevere against the odds, and sacrifice themselves to succeed. But the field could make life so much easier with relatively small investments in capacity building. There is no need for social entrepreneurship to be so difficult and no proof whatsoever that hardship improves the quality of ideas and level of impact. Quite the contrary, socially entrepreneurial activity can be a natural product of life in agile, alert, adaptive, and aligned organizations, which can be built through deliberate action.

Together, these conversions create a more exclusive definition of social entrepreneurship than did the definition I used in 2006. Figure 7-1 shows the continuum.

Moving toward Exclusive . . .

The eighteen conversions clearly indicate convergence toward Roger Martin and Sally Osberg's definition of social entrepreneurship. Five of the eighteen reversed my inclusive assumptions about entrepreneurs, who appear to be more of a rare breed than I had thought; seven challenged my inclusive assumptions about opportunities, which appear to be more ephemeral than durable; and another six changed my more inclusive assumptions about organizations, which simultaneously emphasize the need for strong management within flexible organizations. Only my assumptions about ideas emerged mostly intact.

FIGURE 7-1. A Continuum of Assumptions Revisited

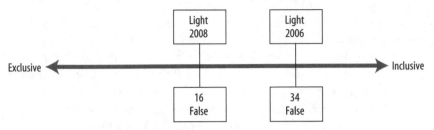

The change to a set of more exclusive assumptions does not mean that social entrepreneurs must be mythical heroes, even though their efforts may have heroic effects. But this change toward exclusivity does suggest that entrepreneurs play *the* central role in the change process. The field may not agree on just which characteristics are actually tied to success, but there is no question that some characteristics matter greatly. As such, this study suggests that Dees was on target in his 1998 description of social entrepreneurship as an exceptional act by exceptional people:

> Social entrepreneurship describes a set of behaviors that are exceptional. These behaviors should be encouraged and rewarded in those who have the capabilities and temperament for this kind of work. We could use many more of them. Should everyone aspire to be a social entrepreneur? No. Not every social sector leader is well suited to being entrepreneurial. . . . Social entrepreneurs are a special breed of leader, and they should be recognized as such. This definition preserves their distinctive status and assures that social entrepreneurship is not treated lightly.[1]

Viewed as a whole, my conversions suggest that social entrepreneurship is much more difficult than I originally believed. Although I still maintain that there is more socially entrepreneurial behavior across the sectors than previously imagined, success still involves a struggle against an entrenched equilibrium that often denies simple common sense. Indeed, if I had to pick one core characteristic of successful social entrepreneurs beyond commitment to vision, it would be perseverance against

1. Dees (1998, p. 5)

an array of obstacles, a point well made by Dees in arguing that social entrepreneurs act boldly without regard to resources in hand.

This is not to argue that business entrepreneurship is easy by comparison—witness the high failure rates of new businesses. But private markets provide significant incentives for new ideas, ample legal protection for inventions, and access to capital that simply does not exist for socially entrepreneurial activity. Thus many of the moderately entrepreneurial organizations in this study may be using subsidies from contracts, grants, and fees for service to subsidize their change efforts.

My conversions also emphasize the potential value of advocacy both in creating new opportunities for action and in defending new ideas from attack. If there is one lesson in case studies of social entrepreneurship, it is that many of the obstacles to success emerge from the prevailing social equilibrium. Although the literature of social entrepreneurship focuses almost exclusively on success, that success is not a foregone conclusion. At the very least, advocacy must remain part of the skill set that entrepreneurs bring to their task, whether as a primary component of the change effort or as a holstered weapon, so to speak, that must be brought to bear to achieve durable policy change. Advocacy is surely part of the policy impact that Ashoka uses to measure the success of its fellows, just as it is part of the defense against existing organizations that refuse to yield ground as a new idea emerges.

Finally, the conversions suggest the importance of paying attention to the organizational platform for socially entrepreneurial activity. New ventures face enormous pressure to become more bureaucratic over time and start their lives highly centralized around a specific idea. At the same time, existing organizations must shed their bureaucracies if they are to stimulate innovation within. Staying agile is not a foregone characteristic of social entrepreneurship, and it may require aggressive actions such as strategic planning, reorganization, and the use of business tools to maintain the acceleration that socially entrepreneurial organizations achieved early in the development process.

The conversions do not signal a new embrace of the garage theory of entrepreneurship, however. Indeed, entrepreneurs can actually be seen as organizational products—sometimes, they bolt their organizations in search of autonomy; other times, they find the encouragement to build from within. Viewed as such, social entrepreneurship has a dual meaning. It focuses on the social equilibrium, while being the product of social interactions. As Pino Audia and Christopher Rider argued from their own literature review, successful entrepreneurship involves a host of social networks inside and outside the endeavor. These networks are hard to build if the entrepreneur toils without contact with the outside world.

Nor do the conversions support the notion that the number of social entrepreneurs will be static far into the future. Bill Drayton may be quite right that the number of actual entrepreneurs is quite low today but may underestimate efforts to spur potential entrepreneurs into action through education and training. The federal government has a host of programs for increasing the number of business entrepreneurs, for example, not to mention whole departments and agencies, while the Ewing Marion Kauffman Foundation has embarked on an ambitious effort to strengthen entrepreneurship education at the nation's business schools. Perhaps a similar focus on potential social entrepreneurs might work just as well.

... while Remaining Inclusive

Notwithstanding my movement toward a more exclusive definition of social entrepreneurship, many of my original assumptions remain unchanged. Without saying *never*, the sixteen assumptions that I marked as false are likely to remain so, absent compelling empirical research to the contrary.

Building on the evidence in this study, for example, I am convinced that lonely entrepreneurs are not the only source of social entrepreneurship. There is more than enough evidence that socially entrepreneurial activity can come from more than one individual. The assumption that entrepreneurship belongs to the few may help narrow our vision in the search for promising investments and fellowships, but this clearly limits potential support for ideas that emerge from large dissemination networks such as CARE.

I am also convinced that socially entrepreneurial ideas do not have to grow to the maximum to succeed, though grow they must to some larger level of impact. Some entrepreneurs want to change the social equilibrium one small step at time, while others might seek replication by other organizations. Either path might produce global change, but entrepreneurs do not necessarily start with that ambition.

Although I did move toward a more exclusive stance on this assumption, I saw many examples of small ideas that stayed small and still had great impact. Moreover, in an age of high-speed knowledge transfer, it seems reasonable to argue that dissemination of system-changing ideas has never been easier, provided that someone is keeping watch. Although the ultimate impact of a given idea rests in its launch, scale-up, sustained momentum, and diffusion, the invention of a new idea can involve existing organizations. After all, the incandescent light was invented seventy-five years before Edison imagined a system for disrupting the status quo.

I also remain convinced that the social equilibrium can be nibbled away through multiple attacks. Moreover, a "thousand flowers" approach can create a healthy competition among ideas that produces stronger initiatives. This may mean that some ideas simply disappear over time, for example, while others may be elevated in prominence only to be acquired by organizations with greater access to capital. As in the microfinance case, private firms may even come to see the value of a profitable idea and establish their own presence in a market. The point is that ideas often evolve over time, switching sectors and winning new entrepreneurs along the way.

Finally, I am unalterably convinced that social entrepreneurship can emerge from existing organizations, especially if entrepreneurs have access to investment capital and protection as their ideas advance. The advantages of new ventures are clear: They focus their mission on a specific idea that has the novelty and familiarity to undermine the existing social equilibrium, and they tend to remain agile as they age. But just because existing organizations face extraordinary challenges in creating an entrepreneurial culture does not mean they are doomed to failure. To the contrary, entrepreneurial organizations have the resources to help new ideas scale up, provided that these organizations want to be part of a new equilibrium.

RESEARCHING ASSUMPTIONS

Even as box 7-1 provides some evidence of convergence toward a narrower definition of social entrepreneurship, it also suggests just how far research has to go to confirm the findings and settle continued controversies over the basic assumptions underpinning the evolution of the field.

—Researchers need to learn more about the core characteristics that link to the commitment to vision and the role of experience in forging what Drayton calls "entrepreneurial quality." When asking more questions about who the entrepreneur is, researchers must avoid the same frustrating search for deep personality characteristics that has distracted the study of business entrepreneurship over the years.

—Researchers also need to invest more heavily in understanding the socially entrepreneurial idea, including the role of growth, adaptation, advocacy, familiarity, and replication in the expansion of impact. While studying the life cycle of socially entrepreneurial ideas and the process that creates them, researchers must avoid the notion that social entrepreneurship must always be new to be accorded status.

—Researchers need to spend much more time on the socially entrepreneurial opportunity, including the number of opportunities, the impact of culture, and entrepreneurial skills in exploiting and creating entrepreneurial space. As researchers seek a better understanding of the opening and closing of opportunities for impact, they should also remain sensitive to the possibility that opportunities can be created through the same forms of advocacy that social entrepreneurs often use to defend their ideas from attack.

—Researchers need much greater information on the socially entrepreneurial organization, including the origins of the organization, its location, and its operations. Even as researchers pursue deeper knowledge of how socially entrepreneurial organizations age and grow without sacrificing the deep commitment to change, they must also examine the leverage points that lead to high performance more generally.

—Finally, researchers must pay attention to the crucial role of strategy in creating the combinations of entrepreneurs, ideas, opportunities, and organizations that underpin ultimate success. To the extent researchers are looking for the biggest opportunities to make a difference in the evolution of this field, strategy provides the greatest invitation. It is understudied, yet extremely important.

Some of the answers to these challenges will come from surveys of social entrepreneurs and their less entrepreneurial peers, others will come from pooled case studies of successes and failures, and still others will emerge as the field of business entrepreneurship continues to produce high-quality, evidence-based research. But assuming that research is essential to practice, whether in targeting funds or helping entrepreneurs succeed, there is still much to be done in resolving the core debates that the field faces. This research must involve more than rigorous methods. It must also be useful to all of us, which requires a commitment to applied knowledge beyond the edges of the research community. This means that the research should focus on key controversies in the field that might be of consequence to investors as well as to entrepreneurs, as they seek greater impact through their work. To the extent possible, the research should reach for insights that can be used to enhance the actual impact of social entrepreneurship.

The research must also involve an effort to sort what does and does not matter to impact. Such research should branch beyond success stories to include comparison groups that might distinguish between different groups of social entrepreneurship, most notably between high- and low-impact efforts. This research will not be easy—after all, one has to identify low-impact socially entrepreneurial activity, which requires hard definitions about the basic definitions of impact. As part of this effort, researchers should make their definitions of impact as objective as possible, as well as the measures that deal directly with performance.

Finally, the research must be timely. Research may be catching up to the substantial growth in the amount of investment in socially entrepreneurial activity, but it still needs to move more quickly. Researchers can increase timeliness by extending previous work on entrepreneurship, whatever the academic discipline. They can collaborate with other researchers who have collected case studies or conducted surveys. And they can increase timeliness by sharing their research designs and results with other scholars through forums such as Oxford University's 2007 Social Entrepreneurship Colloquium, in quick-turnaround journals such as *Innovation,* or through presentations at leading programs such as Harvard University's Social Entrepreneurship Collaboratory and the Catherine B. Reynolds Foundation Fellowships in Social Entrepreneurship at Harvard and Catherine B. Reynolds Foundation Program in Social Entrepreneurship at New York University.

The field bears a similar obligation to provide the resources for translation from research to practice, whether through intermediaries such as Ashoka's Global Academy for Social Entrepreneurship or competitions such as the World Bank's Development Marketplace. Together, researchers should work to develop integrated opportunities for knowledge sharing such as the Skoll World Forum, the Social Enterprise Alliance's annual conference, and other less formal gatherings.

The goal of this work involves a clear embrace of evidence as part of informed vision. Researchers must not be afraid to ask tough questions, nor should they be afraid to challenge the prevailing social equilibrium that exists within the field. But they must link their research to practice. Many already do just that, of course, but more needs to be done. The stakes that the field confronts are simply too great. Just as social entrepreneurs believe that intractable problems can be solved, researchers should accept the possibility that intractable questions can be answered, even if the answers come one study at a time.

RECOMMENDATIONS

Further research is not the only recommendation that emerges from this study. Investors and practitioners can also find evidence from the findings for a number of other recommendations.

Entrepreneurs

For those who care about assisting social entrepreneurs, the study suggests the need for further learning and recruitment opportunities through fellowship programs sponsored by such organizations as Ashoka and Echoing Green. There is simply too much isolation in the effort to create pattern-breaking change. If social entrepreneurs cannot find what they need from the usual sources of support, then this support needs to be built from the ground up. Social entrepreneurs may be intuitive thinkers, but they easily could avoid mistakes by talking with others. As much as such interaction may take time and energy from the vision, it is well worth the effort.

The study also suggests that entrepreneurs must create an appropriate balance between the single-minded pursuit of their vision and the need for high-performance management. Despite worries that management will somehow overwhelm vision, I believe the evidence suggests that entrepreneurs need management skills to succeed. Some might bring it with them as individual entrepreneurs, while pairs, teams, and networks may already contain it. But wherever it resides, entrepreneurs must accept the reality that management is essential to successful implementation. If they want evidence, they need only talk to their own employees—there is nothing more demoralizing than pursuing a strong vision without the resources to succeed. Working 24/7 without enough "stuff" to succeed is a recipe for turnover and pause. Either entrepreneurs must start talking about management, including governance, at the very beginning, or they will be addressing it in the midst of a crisis.

Working 24/7 can also be dangerous to one's health. Generally, social entrepreneurs are expected to persevere without pause, sometimes without a living wage to support them. It would be no surprise if they exhibited high rates of physical and emotional duress that go with pursuing their vision. If investors want to sustain high rates of engagement, they must be willing to invest in the entrepreneurs who provide it, which means the administrative support (including pension and health insurance) to continue the entrepreneurial chase.

Ideas

For those who care about designing socially entrepreneurial ideas that drive change, the study suggests the potential value of moderately entrepreneurial organizations as a source of pattern-breaking change. Investors and entrepreneurs should not ignore the potential contributions of these organizations as incubators of ideas and sources of potential spin-offs, and they should not underestimate the power of research and development for producing effective socially entrepreneurial ideas.

Nor should investors and entrepreneurs ignore the value of traditional research and development in producing the new combinations needed to disturb the social equilibrium. Currently, most social entrepreneurs must present a business plan to receive fellowships and venture capital. But there is virtually no source of funding for the core work needed to develop the "social value proposition" that drives these plans. Providing this support may be the single best investment for increasing the odds that entrepreneurs can move their ideas into the social marketplace faster.

It could well be, for example, that incubators and eventual spin-offs could become an important marketplace for matching entrepreneurial ideas to specific opportunities. Instead of excluding these organizations from the field, some investors might create intermediary organizations to harvest particularly promising ideas, while others might invest more heavily in ensuring that such ideas exist in welcoming environments with the resources necessary to achieve high impact.

The search for ideas could easily expand to small-scale efforts at the neighborhood and community level, too. Much of the contemporary conversation about socially entrepreneurial activity emphasizes broad geographic change; however, there are thousands of organizations that pursue pattern-breaking change through much more focused efforts. Such efforts might involve an effort to break a particularly vicious equilibrium in a specific setting, such as a crime-ridden city or beleaguered neighborhood. Replication of these ideas might be a much more efficient method of breaking similarly localized equilibriums in other regions, and replication should be considered frequently as part of the socially entrepreneurial skill set.

Opportunities

For those who care about identifying socially entrepreneurial opportunities, this study suggests ample room for building a search infrastructure to help entrepreneurs identify potential targets of change. Although alertness to opportunity appears to be a core characteristic of the social entrepreneur, some opportunities may appear for such a short time or in such a disguise that it goes unnoticed. Such an environmental scanning effort could also include support for the kind of hybrid organizations featured in Martin and Osberg's work, especially to the extent that these organizations use advocacy and activism to exploit or create wedges in the social equilibrium.

The search for opportunities could also involve innovative funding mechanisms that might allow social entrepreneurs to attack and navigate barriers to success. Without urging greater diversification for diversification's sake, investors could help entrepreneurs secure the needed capital and flexibility to survive the early threats to success. Such mechanisms already exist for investors, including the revolving loan fund operated by the Acumen Fund. But such funding may not be enough to provide the security to protect socially entrepreneurial organizations against the backlash created by a resilient social equilibrium. Without recommending government engagement on the level of the Bush administration's faith-based initiative per se, there may be ways to provide new streams of support that could provide needed diversification.

Organizations

For those concerned about building stronger socially entrepreneurial organizations, this study has been quite clear on the need for further investment in high-performance capacity. Alongside investments in the core idea, investors could easily support the research and capacity-building infrastructure needed to help these organizations build sustainable structures. Also, they could develop templates and other assessment tools for helping socially entrepreneurial organizations remain agile *and* accountable. The last thing the field needs today is a scandal that might give the social equilibrium the fodder to resist change.

High performance demands more than just occasional attention, however. It also involves the recruitment of committed managers. To those who argue that managers and leaders are fundamentally different and often incompatible, I suggest that leaders who cannot manage are high risks indeed. One reason so many business ventures involve teams is precisely to compensate for weaknesses in the single entrepreneur, particularly the weaknesses that undermine effective performance.

Social entrepreneurs and their investors must confront their own views of managers as little more than bureaucratic ciphers that do things right, not the right things. Nothing could be further from their role in high-performing organizations. If one accepts Joseph Schumpeter's distinction between inventors and innovators, managers could easily lay claim to the latter term.

This study also suggests social entrepreneurs and their investors must confront their long-standing belief that socially entrepreneurial activity simply cannot take place in existing organizations. Call it intrapreneurship or entrepreneurship, but whatever it is called, socially entrepreneurial activity appears to flourish in settings that provide the high performance needed for sustainable impact. This high performance can exist in many locations, including social benefit organizations, businesses, governments, and organizations in between. It can also exist in new organizations and old, small and large. The coding that underpins this study suggests that socially entrepreneurial activity is possible in existing organizations, including some with remarkably large dissemination systems that might provide the opportunity for much faster scale-up of promising ideas. The field simply cannot ignore such capacity by fiat.

CONCLUSION

Social entrepreneurship is evolving rapidly both as a concept and as a cause. Although the term has existed in good currency ever since Drayton founded Ashoka in the early 1980s, it is attracting increasing numbers of researchers as a topic for investigation and a legion of investors and social entrepreneurs as a rallying point for engagement.

As a concept, social entrepreneurship has captured interest across a wide range of academic disciplines. There is still considerable work to do in building a clear definition that will help researchers generate an integrated body of work and a long list of questions about entrepreneurs, ideas, opportunities, and organizations. But the field is coalescing around the notion that intractable social problems may not be as intractable as once believed. The number of case studies is increasing rapidly, even as researchers design new work that will distinguish social entrepreneurship as a distinctive field of endeavor.

As a cause, social entrepreneurship is attracting a new generation of change agents who have the core characteristics needed for sustainable change. Driven by commitment to their vision of sustainable success in addressing problems such as poverty, hunger, and disease and supported by an increasingly energetic community of investors, these change agents are moving rapidly to design and implement a broad mix of ideas for changing the social equilibrium. Although it is difficult to estimate just how many change efforts are currently under way, this study suggests that the number is certainly growing and includes new and old organizations alike.

The question facing the field is not whether a new generation of social entrepreneurs will accept the call to action—that much is clear from the remarkable increase in student interest in coursework on the topic. Rather, the question is how researchers can work together to increase the odds of success. Although failure is always an option for a business entrepreneur, it could not be more costly for a social entrepreneur. After all, every decision to support one idea involves an untold number of decisions to delay or deny others. The field of social entrepreneurship simply cannot tolerate the high failure rates found in business entrepreneurship. There is too much at stake, whether in sunk costs, missed opportunities, or needless sacrifice. Social entrepreneurs deserve more than respect; they also deserve the best odds possible.

BOX 7-1. Revisiting Assumptions

Assumption	Light 2006		Light 2008
Entrepreneurs			
1. Social entrepreneurs work alone.	False		False
2. Social entrepreneurs rarely rest.	False	→	True
3. Social entrepreneurs think differently from other high achievers.	False	→	True
4. Social entrepreneurs think alike among themselves.	False		False
5. Social entrepreneurs persevere against all odds.	False	→	True
6. Social entrepreneurs take greater risks.	True		True
7. Social entrepreneurs share common histories.	False	→	True
8. Social entrepreneurs are rare.	False		False
9. Social entrepreneurs stay involved.	False	→	True
10. Social entrepreneurs share "one best strategy" for success.	False		False
Ideas			
1. Socially entrepreneurial ideas try to change the world.	False	→	True
2. Socially entrepreneurial ideas always break with the past.	True	→	False
3. Socially entrepreneurial ideas are surprising.	False		False
4. Socially entrepreneurial ideas are complex.	False		False
5. Socially entrepreneurial ideas must grow to succeed.	False	→	True
6. Socially entrepreneurial ideas focus on programs, not process.	False		False
7. Socially entrepreneurial ideas rarely change from inception.	False		False
8. Socially entrepreneurial ideas are pure.	False		False
9. Socially entrepreneurial ideas provoke backlash.	True		True
10. Socially entrepreneurial ideas produce immediate results.	False		False
Opportunities			
1. Socially entrepreneurial opportunities are rare.	False	→	True
2. Socially entrepreneurial opportunities cannot be predicted.	False	→	True

Assumption	Light 2006		Light 2008
3. Socially entrepreneurial opportunities cannot be created.	False		False
4. Socially entrepreneurial opportunities occur in punctuations.	False	→	True
5. Socially entrepreneurial opportunities emerge in obvious places.	False	→	True
6. Socially entrepreneurial opportunities start the entrepreneurial process.	False		False
7. Socially entrepreneurial opportunities appear and disappear quickly.	False	→	True
8. Socially entrepreneurial opportunities carry degrees of difficulty.	True		True
9. Socially entrepreneurial opportunities favor competition over collaboration.	False	→	True
10. Socially entrepreneurial opportunities only appear to the special few.	False	→	True
Organizations			
1. Socially entrepreneurial organizations start from scratch.	False		False
2. Socially entrepreneurial organizations nurture a stream of new ideas.	False	→	True
3. Socially entrepreneurial organizations rarely pause.	False	→	True
4. Socially entrepreneurial organizations are constructed differently.	False	→	True
5. Socially entrepreneurial organizations must be totally entrepreneurial.	True	→	False
6. Socially entrepreneurial organizations belong in one sector.	False		False
7. Socially entrepreneurial organizations need unrestricted revenue.	False	→	True
8. Socially entrepreneurial organizations need diversified revenue.	False	→	True
9. Socially entrepreneurial organizations know how to fight.	True		True
10. Socially entrepreneurial organizations insulate themselves from aging.	False	→	True

APPENDIX A

MISSION AND PURPOSE STATEMENTS FROM THE SAMPLE OF HIGHLY, MODERATELY, AND NOT-TOO ENTREPRENEURIAL SOCIAL BENEFIT ORGANIZATIONS

Highly Entrepreneurial Organizations

1. **ACCION—New Mexico Chapter:** ACCION New Mexico is a non-profit organization that increases access to business credit, makes loans, and provides training, which enable emerging entrepreneurs to realize their dreams and be catalysts for positive economic and social change.

2. **ACCION International:** The mission of ACCION International is to give people the tools they need to work their way out of poverty. By providing "micro" loans and business training to poor women and men who start their own businesses, ACCION's partner lending organizations help people work their own way up the economic ladder, with dignity and pride.

3. **Arts and Business Council of Chicago:** A&BC-Chicago supports hundreds of non-profit arts groups by strengthening the management of their organizations through educational programs and business services, and by helping them build dynamic partnerships with the for-profit sector.

4. **Boston Plan for Excellence:** The Boston Plan plays two roles: to test new ideas that hold promise for accelerating improvements in schools and to press the district to look at its own policies and practices that slow reform. The Boston Plan for Excellence is the primary partner of the

Boston Public Schools in designing, piloting, refining, implementing, and institutionalizing elements of the district's reform initiative.

5. **Bread for the World:** Bread for the World is a nationwide Christian movement that seeks justice for the world's hungry people by lobbying our nation's decision makers. Bread for the World Institute seeks justice for hungry people by engaging in research and education on policies related to hunger and development.

6. **California Foundation for Independent Living Centers:** The mission of the California Foundation for Independent Living Centers is to advocate for barrier-free access and equal opportunity for people with disabilities to participate in community life by increasing the capacity of Independent Living Centers to achieve their missions. The entire focus of the Independent Living Movement is the realization that freedom to make choices and the ability to live in the community is a basic civil right that should be extended to all people, regardless of disability.

7. **CARE USA:** CARE is a leading humanitarian organization fighting global poverty. We place special focus on working alongside poor women because, equipped with the proper resources, women have the power to help whole families and entire communities escape poverty. Our mission is to serve individuals and families in the poorest communities in the world. Drawing strength from our global diversity, resources and experience, we promote innovative solutions and are advocates for global responsibility.

8. **Center for Public Justice:** We at the Center are committed to public service that responds to God's call to do justice in local, national, and international affairs. Our mission is to equip citizens, develop leaders, and shape policy in pursuit of our purpose to serve God, advance justice, and transform public life.

9. **Center on Budget and Policy Priorities:** The Center on Budget and Policy Priorities is one of the nation's premier policy organizations working at the federal and state levels on fiscal policy and public programs that affect low- and moderate-income families and individuals. The Center conducts research and analysis to inform public debates over proposed budget and tax policies and to help ensure that the needs of low-income families and individuals are considered in these debates. We also develop policy options to alleviate poverty, particularly among working families.

10. **Civic Ventures:** Civic Ventures is a think tank and an incubator, generating ideas and inventing programs to help society achieve the greatest

return on experience. Civic Ventures is reframing the debate about aging in America and redefining the second half of life as a source of social and individual renewal. Through programs and consulting, Civic Ventures brings together older adults with a passion for service and helps stimulate opportunities for using their talents to advance the greater good.

11. **Communities In Schools—Central Texas:** Communities In Schools is Central Texas' leading dropout prevention program. Through campus-based programs and special projects, Communities In Schools creates a network of volunteers, social services, businesses, and community resources that work together to break down barriers and help students succeed. And the formula works: last year, 99% of the students referred to Communities In Schools stayed in school.

12. **Community Alliance with Family Farmers (CAFF):** The Community Alliance with Family Farmers is building a movement of rural and urban people to foster family-scale agriculture that cares for the land, sustains local economies and promotes social justice.

13. **Doctors Without Borders:** Doctors Without Borders is an independent international medical humanitarian organization that delivers emergency aid to people affected by armed conflict, epidemics, natural or man-made disasters, or exclusion from health care in more than 70 countries.

14. **Environmental Defense:** Environmental Defense is dedicated to protecting the environmental rights of all people, including future generations. Among these rights are clean air, clean water, healthy food and flourishing ecosystems. We are guided by scientific evaluation of environmental problems, and the solutions we advocate will be based on science, even when it leads in unfamiliar directions. We work to create solutions that win lasting economic and social support because they are nonpartisan, cost-effective and fair.

15. **Focus: HOPE:** HOPE is a nationally recognized civil and human rights organization in Detroit, Michigan. Our mission is to use intelligent and practical action to fight racism, poverty and injustice.

16. **Grassroots Leadership:** We are a southern-based national organization that works to defend democracy, enhance the public good and stop the erosion of the public sphere. Grassroots Leadership's goal is to put an end to abuses of justice and the public trust by working to abolish for-profit private prisons.

17. **i.c.stars:** i.c.stars provides opportunities for inner-city young adults to harness the strength of technology for social and economic

leadership. By integrating technology training and leadership development, i.c.stars is shaping the next generation of technology leaders.

18. **Institute for Agriculture and Trade Policy:** The Institute for Agriculture and Trade Policy promotes resilient family farms, rural communities and ecosystems around the world through research and education, science and technology, and advocacy.

19. **Lawrence Alliance:** That we may continually eliminate discrimination in our city, and that we may move with purpose toward the day when tolerance and justice flourish unhindered within and beyond our city limits. The Lawrence Alliance will provide a listening ear in our community, making its presence known, gathering information, and providing information to the city's government and its citizens, advocating for the changes that must come.

20. **Liberty Hill Foundation:** The Liberty Hill Foundation partners with innovative and effective Los Angeles grassroots organizations to combat poverty and injustice, and help transform the "City of Angels" into a place that promises safety, equality and opportunity for everyone who lives here. Our motto is "Change, not Charity." Charity is important, but our dollars go the next step - organizing, advocating, creating change for the long term.

21. **Los Angeles Alliance for a New Economy (LAANE):** At LAANE, we are committed to building a new economy that restores the American dream of fair wages and benefits in return for hard work. We believe that jobs in growing industries which cannot be exported, including those in the fast-growing service sector, must serve as the foundation for rebuilding a strong and vibrant middle class. LAANE has created an exciting new model for improving the lives of working men and women and building healthy communities. Integrating policy, research, community organizing and communications, we have helped win living wages and better job opportunities for tens of thousands of workers and more sustainable communities for residents throughout the Los Angeles region.

22. **Ms. Foundation for Women:** The Ms. Foundation supports the efforts of women and girls to govern their own lives and influence the world around them. Through its leadership, expertise and financial support, the Foundation champions an equitable society by effecting change in public consciousness, law, philanthropy and social policy.

23. **Neighborhood Design Center:** NDC is a 30-year-old nonprofit organization founded in Baltimore City by volunteers dedicated to providing lower income communities with access to professional community

design services. NDC mobilizes volunteer professionals in support of community-sponsored initiatives to improve local neighborhood livability and viability. NDC teams from the design, planning, construction and development professions provide technical assistance to: Strengthen community participation in neighborhood development initiatives; Educate the public about the value of good design, planning and preservation as community revitalization tools; Increase investment in the sensitive rebuilding of neighborhoods. NDC empowers the work of neighborhood organizations with limited resources by providing access to a continuum of technical services, including predevelopment guidance, conceptual design and community planning.

24. **Npower:** NPower is a national network of local nonprofit organizations that provide high-quality, unbiased, affordable and appropriate technology assistance to other organizations. We know that these organizations perform some of society's most critical work, and that information technology can transform how they serve the people in their communities. We believe that organizations deserve the best technology resources, so that they can do their good work even better. Our vision is a thriving nonprofit sector in which all organizations have access to the best technology resources and assistance, and can apply them to help create healthy, vibrant communities.

25. **OMB Watch:** OMB Watch exists to increase government transparency and accountability; to ensure sound, equitable regulatory and budgetary processes and policies; and to protect and promote active citizen participation in our democracy.

26. **Openlands Project:** Openlands, founded in 1963, is an independent, non-profit organization dedicated to preserving and enhancing public open space in northeastern Illinois.

27. **Opportunity Finance Network:** Opportunity Finance Network is the leading network of private financial intermediaries identifying and investing in opportunities to benefit low-income and low-wealth people in the U.S. Our financing delivers both sound financial returns and real changes for people and communities. Our vision is a world where all people experience social, economic, and political justice and so have the opportunity to act in the best interests of their communities, themselves, and future generations. Our mission is to lead the opportunity finance system to scale through capital formation, policy, and capacity development.

28. **Pact:** Pact is a networked global organization that builds the capacity of local leaders and organizations to meet pressing social needs

in dozens of countries around the world. Our work is firmly rooted in the belief that local communities must be the driving force in ending poverty and injustice.

29. **Second Helpings:** At Second Helpings, we rescue prepared and perishable food, re-prepare it into nutritious meals, and distribute those meals to over 50 social services organizations that feed hungry people. We also use some of the food we rescue to train disadvantaged adults for careers in the culinary field, helping to eliminate hunger at its source.

30. **Share Our Strength:** Share Our Strength has helped guarantee that anyone hungry in America today has a place to go and get something to eat. Today, our priority is to end childhood hunger in America ensuring that the nearly 12 million American children facing hunger have access to the nutritious food they need to learn, grow and thrive.

31. **Southern Empowerment Project:** The Southern Empowerment Project is a multi-racial association of member-run, member-based organizations. SEP stands with the oppressed challenging racism and social injustice. SEP recruits and trains community leaders to become organizers to assist organizations in the South and Appalachia to solve community problems.

32. **Western Organization of Resource Councils:** WORC's mission is to advance the vision of a democratic, sustainable, and just society through community action. WORC is committed to building sustainable environmental and economic communities that balance economic growth with the health of people and stewardship of their land, water, and air resources.

33. **Youth In Action:** Youth In Action (YIA) is a non-profit youth development organization in Providence, Rhode Island. At YIA, high school youth gain the skills, resiliency, and determination to be success-ful adults. For almost 10 years, YIA has provided opportunities for more than 650 youth to exercise their highest level of leadership. YIA is at the forefront of youth leadership, receiving national recognition for its ground-breaking model in which youth compose the majority of YIA's Board of Directors and lead all of its programs. Not only do youth mas-ter important life-skills, but they also gain confidence in themselves and increase their academic achievement. YIA's model, which combines advanced leadership training with intensive individual support, empow-ers youth to become extraordinary leaders.

34. **Youth Villages:** Youth Villages is a private nonprofit organization dedicated to helping emotionally and behaviorally troubled children

and their families live successfully through innovative, research-based programs.

Moderately Entrepreneurial Organizations

1. **Amherst H. Wilder Foundation:** At the Wilder Foundation, we're here for people. Vulnerable people young and old, who are at an especially difficult point in their lives, whose needs might otherwise go unmet, whose situations require creative compassionate solutions. To promote the social welfare of persons resident or located in the greater Saint Paul metropolitan area by all appropriate means.

2. **Asian & Pacific Islander Wellness Center:** Our mission is to educate, support, empower and advocate for Asian and Pacific Islanders—particularly A&PIs living with, or at-risk for, HIV/AIDS.

3. **California Family Health Council:** CFHC carries out its mission by coordinating and supporting the delivery of health services in community-based organizations throughout California. The organization directs funding for providers of family health services, performs advanced research in reproductive health care and contraception, conducts education, training and community outreach efforts, and tests, implements and monitors effective programs. CFHC also acts as a catalyst for expanding health care services by building the capacity of community organizations and providing an informed public voice in support of family planning, reproductive health and high quality women's health care services.

4. **Center for Creative Leadership:** Center for Creative Leadership (CCL) is the leading nonprofit institution dedicated exclusively to leadership. CCL integrates cutting-edge research with innovative training, coaching, assessment and publishing to create proven impact for leaders and organizations around the world.

5. **Center for the Homeless:** By offering the best resources in our community to the people who need them the most, we provide our guests with the hope and the tools they need to break the cycle of homelessness and do miraculous things with their lives.

6. **Children's Express (Children's Pressline):** Children's PressLine uses an oral journalism process created by its predecessor, Children's Express. By relying on the spoken word rather than the written word, this methodology facilitates the participation of children of all ages and literacy levels. CPL enables kids to be trained quickly and easily, empowering them with their work and in the media.

7. **Charles River Watershed Association:** CRWA's mission is to use science, advocacy and the law to protect, preserve and enhance the Charles River and its watershed. Since its earliest days of advocacy, CRWA has figured prominently in major clean-up and watershed protection efforts, working with government officials and citizen groups from 35 Massachusetts watershed towns from Hopkinton to Boston. Initiatives over the last four decades have dramatically improved the quality of water in the watershed and approaches to water resource management.

8. **Chicago Foundation for Women:** One of the largest women's funds in the world, Chicago Foundation for Women believes that all women and girls should have the opportunity to achieve their potential and live in safe, just and healthy communities.

9. **Clearbrook Center:** Clearbrook, a Northern Illinois-based non-profit human service agency, is a leader, an innovator and an advocate in the field of developmental disabilities. By creating opportunities for children, adults and their families, we open up a whole new world to them one step at a time. After all, everyone is a star here at Clearbrook.

10. **Corner Health Center:** The Corner Health Center works to help young people make healthy choices which improve their lives now and in the future by offering a broad range of medical care, health education and support services to low-income, young people ages 12–21 and their children.

11. **Family Academy/Urban Education Exchange:** Urban Education Exchange (UEE) forms partnerships with urban elementary schools, providing them with comprehensive academic support. Through this unique approach, we have the potential to effect lasting change in our educational system, particularly in the under-served communities most desperately in need of education reform.

12. **FIRSTLINK:** FIRSTLINK's mission is to strengthen and enhance the quality of life in our community by mobilizing volunteers and connecting people to critical community resources.

13. **Five Rivers Community Development Corporation:** Five Rivers Community Development Corporation (FRCDC) develops affordable housing and fosters economic and leadership opportunities for Georgetown County residents.

14. **Friends of the Chicago River:** The mission of Friends of the Chicago River is to preserve, protect, and foster the vitality of the Chicago River for the human, plant, and animal communities within its watershed. Since 1979, Friends has been working to improve the health

of the Chicago River for the benefit of people and wildlife and by doing so, has laid the foundation for the river to be a beautiful, continuous, easily accessible corridor of open space in Metropolitan Chicago.

15. **Gennesaret Free Clinic:** We are health care professionals and other concerned individuals from Indianapolis, Indiana who have heard a calling to offer our talents and training to the homeless and indigent. Through our volunteer efforts, we endeavor to provide competent, accessible, and compassionate health care to the needy. Our faith moves us to show special respect and dignity to those who have been neglected for we realize that it is in such a healing encounter that we are all made whole by God.

16. **Girl Scouts—Penn Laurel Council:** Penn Laurel Girl Scout Council guides girls to develop their fullest potential by helping them learn to relate to others with understanding and respect. There are diverse opportunities for participation in Girl Scouting, from customized delivery systems to troops to individual Girl Scouts.

17. **Girl Scouts of the USA:** Girl Scouts of the USA is the world's preeminent organization dedicated solely to girls—all girls—where, in an accepting and nurturing environment, girls build character and skills for success in the real world. In partnership with committed adult volunteers, girls develop qualities that will serve them all their lives, like leadership, strong values, social conscience, and conviction about their own potential and self-worth.

18. **Grand Rapids Community Foundation:** Grand Rapids Community Foundation leads the community in making positive, sustainable change. Through our grantmaking and leadership initiatives we help build economic security, foster academic achievement, support human wellness, achieve ecological integrity, create vibrant neighborhoods and enrich the lives of the people here.

19. **Heartland Alliance:** Heartland Alliance is a service-based, human rights organization focused on investments in and solutions for the most poor and vulnerable men, women, and children in our society.

20. **Henry Street Settlement:** Henry Street Settlement delivers a wide range of social service and arts programming to more than 100,000 New Yorkers each year. Distinguished by a profound connection to its neighbors, a willingness to address new problems with swift and innovative solutions, and a strong record of accomplishment, Henry Street challenges the effects of urban poverty by helping families achieve better lives for themselves and their children.

21. **Housing Opportunities Made Equal (HOME):** Housing Opportunities Made Equal was founded in 1971 to fight discrimination in housing access. HOME endeavors to ensure equal access to housing for all people through the three housing centers, each of which focuses on a key area in the battle for equal housing access.

22. **Interfaith Refugee and Immigration Ministries:** For nearly 25 years, Interfaith Refugee and Immigration Ministries (IRIM) has provided a helping hand to Chicago's newcomers, giving them a chance at renewed hopes and dreams. Through our holistic array of programs and services, IRIM assists over 2,500 clients from all over the world each year. Along with community groups, congregations of faith, private and public funders, and neighbors like you, we are building communities of hope.

23. **Jane Addams Resource Corporation:** At Jane Addams Resource Corporation (JARC), we bridge community and market needs through adult education classes, job training programs, economic development services, and real estate initiatives to ensure that lower-income working adults achieve self-sufficiency and do not live in poverty. JARC's work helps to strengthen the local economy through the growth of neighborhood businesses.

24. **LifeWorks:** Our mission is to transition youth and families from crisis to safety and success. LifeWorks provides the most comprehensive network of services for youth and families in Austin. We offer a safety net of support to more than 10,000 youth and families every year. LifeWorks' services to runaway and homeless youth are a national model, providing a pathway from street life to self-sufficiency.

25. **Manna:** Since 1982 Manna has created and preserved over 800 units of affordable housing for low and moderate-income DC residents. In that time, our homeowners have accrued over $50 million in equity. And our financial literacy and homeowner training program has been replicated more than 200 times across the nation.

26. **Nature Conservancy:** The mission of The Nature Conservancy is to preserve the plants, animals and natural communities that represent the diversity of life on Earth by protecting the lands and waters they need to survive.

27. **New York Foundation for the Arts:** The New York Foundation for the Arts' (NYFA) mission is to serve individual artists, promote their freedom to develop and create, and provide the public with opportunities to experience and understand their work. NYFA accomplishes this by offering financial assistance and information to artists and organizations that

directly serve artists, by supporting arts programming in the community, and by building collaborative relationships with others who advocate for the arts in New York State and throughout the country.

28. **Northlight Theatre:** Northlight Theatre is dedicated to enhancing the cultural life of the North Shore and Chicago, presenting life-affirming theatrical works which reflect and challenge the values and beliefs of the community it serves, and engaging community members, young and old, in the theatrical experience.

29. **Penquis Community Action Program:** Penquis Community Action Program, incorporated in 1967, was created as a result of the Economic Opportunity Act of 1964 to bring locally developed solutions to the multifaceted problems faced by the poor. Its mission is to assist individuals and families in preventing, reducing, or eliminating poverty in their lives and, through partnerships, to engage the community in addressing economic and social needs.

30. **Pillsbury United Communities:** Our purpose is to help people out of poverty through developing strong relationships with individuals and their families. The foundation of our work originates with engaging and merging multiple constituencies: neighborhood residents, sister agencies, government bureaucracies, funding sources and anyone else who is interested in the health and viability of our communities.

31. **Planned Parenthood—Northern New England Chapter:** To provide, promote, and protect access to reproductive health care and sexuality education so that all people can make voluntary choices about their reproductive and sexual health. Planned Parenthood of Northern New England (PPNNE) is the largest reproductive health care and sexuality education provider and advocate in northern New England. PPNNE was founded in 1965 and now has 26 health centers across Vermont, New Hampshire, and southern Maine.

32. **Planned Parenthood—Rhode Island Chapter:** A private nonprofit agency, providing high quality, affordable and confidential family planning services. We provide reproductive health care, counseling and education to women and men of all ages. We encourage people to make healthy choices when considering their reproductive health.

33. **Project for Pride in Living:** PPL's mission is to assist lower-income individuals and families to work toward self-sufficiency by providing housing, jobs and training.

34. **Project Vida Health Center:** PVHC serves low-income families and is annually reviewed and evaluated by a Community Congress of

over 100 community residents. With clinic sites in East Central and Northeast El Paso, PVHC provides a full spectrum of primary care services. The area is a federally designated Medically Underserved Area and Health Personnel Shortage Area.

35. **Public Agenda:** Public Agenda's two-fold mission is to help: American leaders better understand the public's point of view, citizens know more about critical policy issues so they can make thoughtful, informed decisions.

36. **Rocky Mountain Youth Corps:** The Rocky Mountain Youth Corps recognizes and engages the strengths and potential of youth through team service in the communities, the schools, and the landscapes of northern New Mexico. RMYC is a stepping stone to new opportunities.

37. **Salesmanship Club Youth and Family Services:** The mission of Salesmanship Club Youth and Family Centers, Inc.: Helping transform children's futures by creating new possibilities for success. This mission is carried out in three ways: treatment for children who are experiencing emotional and behavioral difficulties and their families through our outpatient family therapy program, early intervention with children from less advantaged circumstances, and research, development, training and dissemination of innovative programs and practices. The J. Erik Jonsson Community School, a private school serving three-year-olds through sixth grade students, is our early intervention program. This work is carried out by our on-site research and evaluation team and individual therapists, teachers and administrative staff who publish articles in professional journals and present at conferences throughout the country.

38. **San Diego Opera:** Our passionate belief in our mission and our art form compels us to seek new audiences for opera, to enrich lives and stir the imaginations of all who open themselves to its uniquely magical allure. San Diego Opera will continue to explore every means of serving its audiences and community with the finest artistic and educational product it can offer. We are committed to both full participation in the civic and the cultural life of San Diego, and will endeavor always to do our part in realizing the evolving vision of "America's finest city."

39. **Second Harvest—Central Florida Chapter:** To fight hunger in Central Florida. This will be achieved by: providing access to food and other grocery products in order to meet the need, promoting and supporting the development of our partner agencies' ability to fulfill their missions, mobilizing leaders and communities by bringing visibility to

the invisible problem of hunger and poverty, and developing more holistic and County-specific solutions to hunger in the Central Florida region.

40. **Tree Musketeers:** Marcie the Marvelous Tree inspired third graders in 1987 to launch Tree Musketeers as the nation nation's first youth environmental organization—a nonprofit charity where kids are boss! While taking action to help the planet, kids teach other kids to become active citizens and community leaders. Neighborhood by neighborhood, kids can rescue Earth!

41. **University Settlement:** University Settlement sits at the heart of the Lower East Side, a beacon to the new immigrants and economically diverse families that live in this community. Every day, we strive to address their ever-changing needs, compassionately, holistically and precisely. Every year, we make a tangible difference in the lives of the 10,000 people that we serve.

42. **Visiting Nurse Association:** VNA programs span a lifetime—from prenatal care to care for young families to rehabilitation, long term care, adult day services and end-of-life care. We take pride in adhering to the highest quality standards and are accredited by the Joint Commission. The VNA is Medicare-certified and cares for 5000 individuals and families each year in Vermont's Chittenden and Grand Isle Counties.

43. **Women, Work, and Community:** Women, Work, and Community is committed to improving the economic lives of Maine women and their families. We work with women "where they are" and provide them with support, guidance, and the tools they need to take the next steps toward a more promising future.

44. **Woonsocket NDC:** Provides quality homes in quality neighborhoods for people with low and moderate incomes.

Not-Too Entrepreneurial Organizations

1. **Alban Institute:** Our continuing mission is to provide you with new research-based information and new ways to learn and minister more effectively within and outside your faith community. The Institute encourages dialogue with many traditions, people of diverse ethnicity, men and women, large and small congregations, and those in urban and rural settings.

2. **American Red Cross of Greater Chicago:** The American Red Cross, a humanitarian organization led by volunteers and guided by its Congressional Charter and the Fundamental Principles of the International

Red Cross Movement, will provide relief to victims of disasters and help people prevent, prepare for and respond to emergencies.

3. **American Red Cross of San Antonio Area:** The American Red Cross, a humanitarian organization led by volunteers and guided by its Congressional Charter and the Fundamental Principles of the International Red Cross Movement, will provide relief to victims of disasters and help people prevent, prepare for and respond to emergencies.

4. **Ancona School:** Welcome to The Ancona School, where children experience the power and joy of learning! A Montessori-based, independent school educating children from the preprimary to 8th grade, The Ancona School is located at the corner of 48th Street and Dorchester in Chicago's historic Hyde Park/Kenwood community. For over 40 years, our creative and experienced teachers have been helping children become confident risk-takers.

5. **ARTSBRIDGE:** ARTSBRIDGE is an arts council dedicated to improving the quality of life in the Mid-Ohio Valley by promoting and supporting the arts through financial and administrative support and arts education in our schools and community.

6. **Austin Recovery:** We offer medical detoxification and separate Men's and Women's Residential Programs designed to meet individual client needs. Our programs use a proven clinical model that balances the recovery principles of the 12 Steps with therapies specifically designed for the clients we serve. We are committed to providing an effective and affordable treatment alternative for working families seeking help for a loved one.

7. **Bayaud Industries:** Bayaud Industries is a community-based organization providing vocational rehabilitation and employment services to individuals with mental, emotional, physical, and economic challenges. Our mission is to create Hope, Opportunity and Choice, with work as the means through which people with disabilities and other barriers to employment can participate in the mainstream of life.

8. **Big Apple Circus:** The Big Apple Circus is more than just a circus. Our performance is rooted in tradition, but our commitment to kids and their families is a vision truly our own. In addition to its 325 circus performances each year, the Big Apple Circus administers four Community Programs aimed at making life better for disadvantaged, handicapped and hospitalized children.

9. **Big Brothers and Big Sisters of Central Arizona:** Big Brothers Big Sisters is a children's charity offering a mentorship program to youth

ages six to fifteen. The charity, non-profit organization, recruits, trains and supervises volunteers who are capable and dedicated mentors. These volunteers offer their time and guidance to children who are seeking a mentor; a positive role model in their lives.

10. **Boys & Girls Club of Greater Milwaukee:** The mission of the Boys & Girls Club of Greater Milwaukee is to inspire and empower all young people, especially those from disadvantaged circumstances, to realize their full potential as productive, responsible and caring citizens.

11. **Calvary Women's Services:** Calvary Women's Services is a non-profit organization in Washington, DC, that provides housing and support services to homeless women. Calvary's mission is two-fold: To provide homeless women with a place to live and basic services and to help educate and empower women for independent living. Calvary fulfills this mission by providing services that assist each woman with her personal goals to achieve stable housing, good health, recovery from substance abuse and employment.

12. **Care Alliance:** Care Alliance is a non-profit Federally Qualified Health Center (FQHC) whose mission is to provide high-quality health care, patient advocacy and related services to people who need them most, regardless of their ability to pay, in a manner that is cost-effective and that empowers people to improve their quality of life.

13. **Children, Inc.:** Children, Inc. provides developmental experiences for children in a variety of settings, partners with families to extend these developmental experiences and collaborates with the community to create opportunities that strengthen all families.

14. **Children's Museum of Indianapolis:** It is our vision to be recognized as the global leader among all museums and cultural institutions serving children and families. To create extraordinary learning experiences that have the power to transform the lives of children and families.

15. **Children's Village:** The mission of The Children's Village has been to provide safety and care to society's most vulnerable children. Today, we serve more than 700 children in residential programs, and provide programs and services in the community to approximately 3,000 children and 1,700 family members each year. All our programs are designed to give children the stability and nurturing they need to believe in themselves and to gain the skills and attitudes necessary to become productive, caring adults.

16. **Colorado Agency for Jewish Education:** The mission of CAJE is making Jewish life sacred through learning. CAJE shall identify and

endeavor to fill Jewish educational needs in the community, and shall provide centralized programs and services that individual institutions could not realize as effectively.

17. **CommuniCare Health Centers:** CommuniCare is a private, non-profit health care organization offering comprehensive medical and dental services, vision care, substance abuse treatment, health education and outreach services.

18. **Community Crisis Center:** To advocate for a healthy non-violent environment for all people providing information, resources, and support necessary to help individuals move through crisis to develop and pursue their own goals.

19. **Community Health Network:** Community has grown into an integrated health network guided by the mission of providing compassionate, quality, cost-effective health care services that help the residents of central Indiana get well and get back to what is important in their lives.

20. **Community Resource Exchange:** For over 25 years, Community Resource Exchange (CRE) has worked towards a more just, equitable and livable city for ALL New Yorkers. CRE provides strategic advice and technical services every year to over 350 community-based organizations that fight poverty and HIV/AIDS. CRE provides its clients with the information, skills and leadership training to make New York City stronger— one community group at a time.

21. **Community Services Planning Council:** To help people turn ideas into community action through information, planning, civic engagement and advocacy for human needs in the Sacramento Region. People in the Sacramento Region have information, resources and opportunities to improve the quality of life for themselves, their families and their communities.

22. **Community Support Programs, Inc.:** Community Support Programs, Inc. exists to serve the client/family and to enhance each person's opportunity to live successfully in the community. Through the provision of advocacy, direct and indirect service, housing, and coordination with other social service providers, Community Support Programs, Inc. offers unique and innovative programs.

23. **Creede Repertory Theatre:** For 42 years, the Creede Repertory Theatre has been contributing to Creede and its surrounding community—as a cultural hub in the San Luis Valley and as a friend to schools, businesses and nonprofits alike.

24. **Dallas Can! Academy:** To provide a second chance for at-risk youth and their families to achieve economic independence and hope for a better life through relationship-based education and training.

25. **Earth Share of Oregon:** Earth Share of Oregon (ESOR) is a federation of 68 leading local and national non-profit conservation groups that provides a convenient way for Oregonians to support conservation and healthy communities.

26. **Fan Free Clinic:** Fan Free Clinic provides medical treatment, health education, and social services to those in the Richmond area with limited access to care. We place special emphasis on welcoming the least served.

27. **Girl Scout Council of Greater Minneapolis:** Girl Scouting builds girls of courage, confidence, and character, who make the world a better place. In partnership with adult volunteers and the generous community, girls develop strong values, leadership skills, social conscience, and conviction about their own potential and self-worth that will serve them all their lives.

28. **Glendale Human Services Council (Quality of Life Community Services):** Bringing together people in need with agencies that care.

29. **Goodwill Industries of Northern Louisiana:** Improving people's lives through the power of work.

30. **Hands On Greater Portland:** Everyone can do something for the community. At Hands On Greater Portland, we develop this potential in volunteers. We connect them with opportunities to feed the hungry, teach our children, house the homeless, restore our environment and meet other important community needs.

31. **Jacob's Heart Children's Cancer Association:** Our mission is to improve the quality of life for children with cancer and support their families in the challenges they face.

32. **Jamestown Community Center:** The Jamestown Community Center provides 500 Mission District kids each year with the opportunity to learn, play, and grow through a range of after-school and summer programs—from art to theater, dance to soccer, and youth leadership to academic tutoring. Because of Jamestown, kids in this low-income neighborhood have the learning opportunities and support they need to reach their full potential.

33. **Lakefront SRO (Mercy Housing Lakefront):** To address the root causes of homelessness, Mercy Housing Lakefront staff and tenants advocate for increasing the supply of affordable housing and for policies that benefit the homeless.

34. **Lena Pope Home:** Lena Pope Home is committed to creating a future of hope for children and families through an effective continuum of behavioral healthcare services to strengthen families and develop resilient children.

35. **Manchester Neighborhood Housing Services:** Manchester Neighborhood Housing Services is a non-profit organization founded in 1992 by a partnership of residents, businesses and government leaders who wanted to rebuild Manchester's Center City through a plan for reinvestment and reinvigoration. With a population of more than 8,000 people, the Center City neighborhood, with borders from Elm to Maple and Bridge to Valley Streets, comprises the most densely populated region within Manchester. The neighborhood shows a high concentration of poverty.

36. **Merrimack River Watershed Council:** Our mission is to protect and promote the wise use of the Merrimack River Watershed.

37. **New Hampshire Historical Society:** Since 1823, the New Hampshire Historical Society has been preserving our state's past and telling its rich stories to each generation. Nowhere will you find a more extensive collection of objects and archives related to New Hampshire's history.

38. **Open Hand Chicago (Vital Bridges):** Vital Bridges helps people throughout metropolitan Chicago impacted by HIV and AIDS to improve their health and build self-sufficiency by providing food, nutrition, housing, case management and educational services.

39. **Pacific Repertory Theatre:** To present theatrical performances and special projects staged in various Monterey County locations. Artists use existing spaces operated by the organization for individual, studio and class use.

40. **Pact: An Adoption Alliance:** At Pact, we believe that in making an adoption plan, birth parents and adoptive parents enter into an agreement to recognize and protect the best interests of the child. Essential to that agreement is a lifelong commitment to recognize, respect and address the dual heritages - both personal and cultural - that are the child's birth right. Our goal is for every child to feel wanted, honored and loved, a cherished member of a strong family with proud connection to his or her rich heritages.

41. **Pittsburgh Center for the Arts:** Founded in 1945, Pittsburgh Center for the Arts is a non-profit community arts campus that offers arts education programs and contemporary art exhibitions, providing services and resources for individual artists throughout Western Pennsylvania.

The Center is where the community can create, see, support, and learn about visual arts.

42. **Proteus:** Proteus, Inc. is an ever-changing organization created to provide exceptional education, employment, training, and other services to the diverse population of Tulare, Kings, Fresno, and Kern counties. Founded in 1967, Proteus has become a leader at improving the quality of life of valley farmworkers and other special need populations; all the while, providing local employers with a well-trained pool of applicants.

43. **Richmond District Neighborhood Center:** The Richmond District Neighborhood Center (RDNC) is a hub for services in the Richmond District of San Francisco. RDNC directly implements programs for elementary, middle and high school youth. It serves as the site for other nonprofit programming and facilitates fruitful collaboration among agencies, schools, the faith community and other neighborhood organizations.

44. **Seniors Action Service, Inc.:** Seniors Action Service, Inc. is dedicated to enabling older individuals to maintain their highest level of independence, self-respect and dignity.

45. **United Cerebral Palsy of Metropolitan Dallas:** To Advance the Independence, Productivity, and Full Citizenship of Persons with Cerebral Palsy and Other Disabilities.

46. **United Way of America of Columbia-Willamette:** Helping people, changing lives, making every contribution count.

47. **United Way of America of Frederick County:** United Way of Frederick County is the caring force that brings our community together to focus on key human service issues for the greatest possible impact and results. The organization strengthens our community by its support of agencies that touch the lives of our citizens. Through its partnerships with employers, nonprofit agencies and volunteers, United Way plays an indispensable role in bringing together resources to address our most urgent social needs.

48. **Vista Community Clinic:** The mission of Vista Community Clinic is to provide quality health care and health education to the community focusing on those facing economic, social or cultural barriers.

49. **Volunteer! Baton Rouge:** Volunteer! Baton Rouge recognizes that volunteers need to be linked with the right kind of volunteer position to achieve successful, satisfying and productive involvement. As our community's resource center on volunteerism, we ensure that prospective volunteers have ongoing access to current information about volunteer

positions that most urgently require volunteers and service areas of highest priority in our community.

50. **Volunteer Center of Bergen County:** The Volunteer Center of Bergen County strengthens the community by connecting people with opportunities to serve, operating model volunteer programs, building capacity for effective volunteering, and participating in strategic partnerships that meet community needs.

51. **YMCA of Birmingham:** To put Judeo-Christian principles into practice through programs that build healthy spirit, mind and body for all.

52. **YMCA of Kansas City:** We build strong kids, strong families, and strong communities.

53. **YWCA of Central Massachusetts:** The YWCA of Central Massachusetts will strive to be an all-inclusive women's advocacy and resource center with a pro-active membership serving the diverse needs of women through leadership, service and support.

APPENDIX B

THE 2006 SURVEY QUESTIONNAIRE AND RESPONSES

Letters in columns show a significant difference at the 0.10 level between the identified columns. All figures are percentages.

Q1. First, we would like to ask you some background information about you and your organization. What is your position in the organization?

| | Base | Level of social entrepreneurship | | |
		High A	Moderate B	Not too C
Base	131	34	44	53
President/CEO/Executive Director	81	68	86 A	85 A
COO/CFO/Associate Executive Director/Executive Vice President	7	12	5	6
Vice President	2	0	0	4
Director/Co-Director/Manager	2	3	5	0
Assistant Director/Executive Assistant	1	3	0	0
Other (please specify)	6	12 B	2	6
No response	2	3	2	0

Q2. How many years have you been with the organization?

| | Level of social entrepreneurship | | | |
	Base	High A	Moderate B	Not too C
Base	131	34	44	53
Less than 5 years	29	26	18	40 B
5 to 10 years	16	26 C	14	11
More than 10 years	53	44	66 AC	49
Not sure	0	0	0	0
No response	2	3	2	0

Q3. How much of your professional career have you spent in the *non-profit* sector?

| | Level of social entrepreneurship | | | |
	Base	High A	Moderate B	Not too C
Base	131	34	44	53
All of your career	42	35	48	42
Most	36	38	34	36
Half	8	6	9	8
Less than half	13	18	7	15
None	0	0	0	0
Not sure	0	0	0	0
No response	2	3	2	0

Q4. And how much of your professional career have you spent in the *for-profit* sector?

| | Level of social entrepreneurship | | | |
	Base	High A	Moderate B	Not too C
Base	131	34	44	53
All of your career	1	0	0	2
Most	11	12	7	13
Half	5	0	7	8
Less than half	31	35	27	32
None	50	50	55	45
Not sure	0	0	0	0
No response	2	3	5	0

Q5. Are you the founder of your organization?

| | Level of social entrepreneurship | | | |
	Base	High A	Moderate B	Not too C
Base	131	34	44	53
Yes	14	21	14	9
No	85	79	84	91
No response	1	0	2	0

Q6. Is the founder still actively involved in your organization (such as, as a board member or consultant)?

Based on those who are not founders

| | Level of social entrepreneurship | | | |
	Base	High A	Moderate B	Not too C
Base	112	27	37	48
Yes	2/	37 C	30	19
No	72	63	68	81 A
Not sure	0	0	0	0
No response	1	0	3	0

Q7. Now we would like you to rate the *overall performance* of your organization. By high performance, we mean an organization's ability to achieve its mission whatever that mission might be. Is your organization very high performing, somewhat high performing, performing on average, somewhat poorly performing or very poorly performing?

| | Level of social entrepreneurship | | | |
	Base	High A	Moderate B	Not too C
Base	131	34	44	53
Very high performing	53	62 C	68 C	36
Somewhat high performing	39	29	27	55 AB
Performing on average	6	9 B	0	9 B
Somewhat poorly performing	0	0	0	0
Very poorly performing	0	0	0	0
No response	2	0	5	0

Q8A. How would you describe your organization's growth in program demand over the past five years?

	Level of social entrepreneurship			
	Base	High A	Moderate B	Not too C
Base	131	34	44	53
Rapid growth	31	50 BC	23	26
Steady growth	56	41	70 A	55
Little or no growth	11	9	5	17 B
Steady contraction	1	0	0	2
Rapid contraction	0	0	0	0
No response	1	0	2	0

Q8B. How would you describe your organization's growth in financial pressure over the past five years?

	Level of social entrepreneurship			
	Base	High A	Moderate B	Not too C
Base	131	34	44	53
Rapid growth	19	26	16	17
Steady growth	56	50	64	53
Little or no growth	14	18	14	11
Steady contraction	7	0	2	15 AB
Rapid contraction	1	3	0	0
No response	4	3	5	4

Q8C. How would you describe your organization's growth in budget over the past five years?

	Level of social entrepreneurship			
	Base	High A	Moderate B	Not too C
Base	131	34	44	53
Rapid growth	15	29 BC	7	13
Steady growth	54	50	66 C	47
Little or no growth	21	12	20	26
Steady contraction	6	6	0	11 B
Rapid contraction	2	3	2	0
No response	2	0	5	2

Q9A. How important is having visionary leadership to achieving your organization's mission?

| | Level of social entrepreneurship | | | |
	Base	High A	Moderate B	Not too C
Base	131	34	44	53
Very important	83	85	80	85
Somewhat important	15	15	16	13
Not too important	1	0	2	0
Not at all important	0	0	0	0
No response	2	0	2	2

Q9B. How important is being innovative to achieving your organization's mission?

| | Level of social entrepreneurship | | | |
	Base	High A	Moderate B	Not too C
Base	131	34	44	53
Very important	73	76	73	72
Somewhat important	25	24	25	26
Not too important	0	0	0	0
Not at all important	0	0	0	0
No response	2	0	2	2

Q9C. How important is being well managed to achieving your organization's mission?

| | Level of social entrepreneurship | | | |
	Base	High A	Moderate B	Not too C
Base	131	34	44	53
Very important	88	85	84	92
Somewhat important	11	15	14	6
Not too important	0	0	0	0
Not at all important	0	0	0	0
No response	2	0	2	2

Q9D. How important is having unrestricted revenue to achieving your organization's mission?

	Level of social entrepreneurship			
	Base	High A	Moderate B	Not too C
Base	131	34	44	53
Very important	60	59	52	68
Somewhat important	37	41	43	28
Not too important	2	0	2	2
Not at all important	0	0	0	0
No response	2	0	2	2

Q10. Which of these factors has been the *most important* to achieving your organization's mission?

	Level of social entrepreneurship			
	Base	High A	Moderate B	Not too C
Base	131	34	44	53
Having visionary leadership	36	47	30	34
Being innovative	23	21	30	19
Being well managed	32	24	30	40
Having unrestricted revenue	8	9	11	6
No response	1	0	0	2

Q11. Some experts say that high-performing nonprofits should seek more diversification of revenue, while others say that they should focus first on increasing unrestricted revenue. Which do you think is more important?

	Level of social entrepreneurship			
	Base	High A	Moderate B	Not too C
Base	131	34	44	53
Increase diversification of revenue	67	71	66	66
Increase unrestricted revenue	32	29	34	32
No response	1	0	0	2

Q12A. Now we would like to ask you a series of questions about how your organization deals with its external environment in achieving its mission. How important is having a clear mission?

| | Level of social entrepreneurship | | | |
	Base	High A	Moderate B	Not too C
Base	131	34	44	53
Very important	92	91	93	92
Somewhat important	8	9	7	8
Not too important	0	0	0	0
Not at all important	0	0	0	0
No response	0	0	0	0

Q12B. How important is collaborating with other organizations?

| | Level of social entrepreneurship | | | |
	Base	High A	Moderate B	Not too C
Base	131	34	44	53
Very important	60	56	61	60
Somewhat important	35	35	32	38
Not too important	5	6	7	2
Not at all important	1	3	0	0
No response	0	0	0	0

Q12C. How important is measuring results?

| | Level of social entrepreneurship | | | |
	Base	High A	Moderate B	Not too C
Base	131	34	44	53
Very important	66	59	73	66
Somewhat important	31	32	27	32
Not too important	3	9 B	0	2
Not at all important	0	0	0	0
No response	0	0	0	0

Q13. How important is your strategic plan for achieving your organization's mission?

	Level of social entrepreneurship			
	Base	High A	Moderate B	Not too C
Base	131	34	44	53
Very important	54	41	59	58
Somewhat important	37	44	30	38
Not too important	5	9 C	9 C	0
Not important at all	0	0	0	0
Do not have a strategic plan	3	3	2	4
No response	1	3	0	0

Q14A. How diversified is/are your organization's funding?

	Level of social entrepreneurship			
	Base	High A	Moderate B	Not too C
Base	131	34	44	53
Very diversified	27	15	39 A	26
Somewhat diversified	52	65 B	45	49
Not too diversified	21	21	16	25
Not diversified at all	0	0	0	0
No response	0	0	0	0

Q14B. How diversified is/are your organization's programs?

	Level of social entrepreneurship			
	Base	High A	Moderate B	Not too C
Base	131	34	44	53
Very diversified	45	18	61 A	49 A
Somewhat diversified	43	71 BC	30	36
Not too diversified	9	12	5	11
Not diversified at all	2	0	2	4
No response	1	0	2	0

Q15. Now we'd like to ask about your organization's *funding and external relationships*. How much unrestricted revenue does your organization generate?

	Level of social entrepreneurship			
	Base	High A	Moderate B	Not too C
Base	131	34	44	53
Great deal	23	15	27	25
Fair amount	52	62	43	53
Not too much	25	24	30	23
Not at all	0	0	0	0
No response	0	0	0	0

Q16. (Multiple mentions) What are your organization's sources of unrestricted revenue?

Based on those whose organization generates unrestricted revenue

	Level of social entrepreneurship			
	Base	High A	Moderate B	Not too C
Base	131	34	44	53
Grants and contributions	90	88	93	89
Fees for services	63	47	68	68
Earned income from a nonprofit business activity	41	24	48	45
Other (please specify)	26	35	25	21
No response	0	0	0	0

Q17. How much earned income from your nonprofit business activity does your organization generate?

Based on those whose organization's source of unrestricted revenue includes earned income from a nonprofit business activity

	Level of social entrepreneurship			
	Base	High A	Moderate B	Not too C
Base	53	8	21	24
Great Deal	26	13	24	33
Fair Amount	40	13	43	46
Not too Much	34	75 BC	33	21
No response	0	0	0	0

Q18. Please briefly describe what activities generate your organization's earned income (i.e., gift shop, fees for medical care, consulting, etc.)

Based on those whose organization generates unrestricted revenue

| | | Level of social entrepreneurship | | |
	Base	High A	Moderate B	Not too C
Base	131	34	44	53
Gave response	85	76	91 A	85
No response	15	24 B	9	15

Q19. How vulnerable is your organization to *external* challenges such as competition from other organizations or access to funding: very vulnerable, somewhat vulnerable, not very vulnerable, or not vulnerable at all?

| | | Level of social entrepreneurship | | |
	Base	High A	Moderate B	Not too C
Base	131	34	44	53
Very vulnerable	21	9	23	28 A
Somewhat vulnerable	58	65	59	53
Not very vulnerable	21	26	18	19
Not at all vulnerable	0	0	0	0
No response	0	0	0	0

Q20. How vulnerable is your organization to *internal* challenges such as staff turnover or technology problems: very vulnerable, somewhat vulnerable, not very vulnerable, or not vulnerable at all?

| | | Level of social entrepreneurship | | |
	Base	High A	Moderate B	Not too C
Base	131	34	44	53
Very vulnerable	6	6	5	8
Somewhat vulnerable	53	56	52	53
Not very vulnerable	36	32	39	36
Not at all vulnerable	5	6	5	4
No response	0	0	0	0

Q21A. And what about your organization's *internal management*. How important is giving employees authority to make routine decisions on their own to achieving your organization's mission?

| | | Level of social entrepreneurship | | |
	Base	High A	Moderate B	Not too C
Base	131	34	44	53
Very important	73	74	75	72
Somewhat important	24	24	20	28
Not too important	2	3	5	0
Not at all important	0	0	0	0
No response	0	0	0	0

Q21B. And what about your organization's *internal management*. How important is encouraging units within the organization to work together to achieving your organization's mission?

| | | Level of social entrepreneurship | | |
	Base	High A	Moderate B	Not too C
Base	131	34	44	53
Very important	73	71	73	75
Somewhat important	22	24	25	19
Not too important	2	3	0	4
Not at all important	2	3	2	2
No response	0	0	0	0

Q21C. And what about your organization's *internal management*. How important is providing resources such as time and funding for the development of new ideas to achieving your organization's mission?

| | | Level of social entrepreneurship | | |
	Base	High A	Moderate B	Not too C
Base	131	34	44	53
Very important	54	44	59	57
Somewhat important	44	56	39	42
Not too important	1	0	2	0
Not at all important	0	0	0	0
No response	1	0	0	2

Q22A. What about your organization's *senior employee leadership*. How important is asking employees to participate in key decisions to your senior leadership in achieving your organization's mission?

	Base	Level of social entrepreneurship		
		High A	Moderate B	Not too C
Base	131	34	44	53
Very important	72	82 B	61	74
Somewhat important	25	15	34 A	25
Not too important	2	3	2	0
Not at all important	1	0	0	2
No response	1	0	2	0

Q22B. What about your organization's *senior employee leadership*. How important is encouraging employees to take risks and try new ways of doing things to your senior leadership in achieving your organization's mission?

	Base	Level of social entrepreneurship		
		High A	Moderate B	Not too C
Base	131	34	44	53
Very important	60	50	61	66
Somewhat important	34	41	32	32
Not too important	4	9 C	5	0
Not at all important	1	0	0	2
No response	1	0	2	0

Q22C. What about your organization's *senior employee leadership*. How important is having a shared vision for the organization's future to your senior leadership in achieving your organization's mission?

	Base	Level of social entrepreneurship		
		High A	Moderate B	Not too C
Base	131	34	44	53
Very important	93	94	95	91
Somewhat important	6	6	2	9
Not too important	0	0	0	0
Not at all important	0	0	0	0
No response	1	0	2	0

Q23A. And what about your organization's *internal resources*. How important is providing enough information technology to achieving your organization's mission?

	Base	High A	Moderate B	Not too C
		Level of social entrepreneurship		
Base	131	34	44	53
Very important	60	47	66 A	62
Somewhat important	37	47	32	36
Not too important	3	6	2	2
Not at all important	0	0	0	0
No response	0	0	0	0

Q23B. And what about your organization's *internal resources*. How important is providing enough employees to achieving your organization's mission?

	Base	High A	Moderate B	Not too C
		Level of social entrepreneurship		
Base	131	34	44	53
Very important	85	82	89	85
Somewhat important	13	15	11	13
Not too important	2	3	0	2
Not at all important	0	0	0	0
No response	0	0	0	0

Q23C. And what about your organization's *internal resources*. How important is providing enough training to achieving your organization's mission?

	Base	High A	Moderate B	Not too C
		Level of social entrepreneurship		
Base	131	34	44	53
Very important	53	38	52	64 A
Somewhat important	40	47	45	30
Not too important	7	15 B	2	6
Not at all important	0	0	0	0
No response	0	0	0	0

Q24. To what extent does your organization use standard business tools or techniques to improve its performance?

| | Level of social entrepreneurship | | | |
	Base	High A	Moderate B	Not too C
Base	131	34	44	53
Great deal	31	18	32	38 A
Fair amount	53	53	57	51
Not too much	15	29 BC	11	9
None at all	1	0	0	2
No response	0	0	0	0

Q25. How much technical assistance/capacity building have you received in the past five years?

| | Level of social entrepreneurship | | | |
	Base	High A	Moderate B	Not too C
Base	131	34	44	53
Great deal	11	18 C	14	6
Fair amount	51	44	43	62 B
Not too much	33	32	36	30
None at all	5	6	7	2
No response	0	0	0	0

Q26. Words have different meanings to people. What do the words "social entrepreneurship" mean to you?

| | Level of social entrepreneurship | | | |
	Base	High A	Moderate B	Not too C
Base	131	34	44	53
Gave response	96	97	98	94
No response	4	3	2	6

Q27A. Defining social entrepreneurship as an effort to address significant problems through pattern-breaking approaches, how important is having visionary leadership to the performance of successful social entrepreneurship?

		Level of social entrepreneurship		
	Base	High A	Moderate B	Not too C
Base	131	34	44	53
Very important	82	79	82	85
Somewhat important	14	12	16	13
Not too important	1	3	0	0
Not at all important	0	0	0	0
No response	3	6	2	2

Q27B. Defining social entrepreneurship as an effort to address significant problems through pattern-breaking approaches, how important is being innovative to the performance of successful social entrepreneurship?

		Level of social entrepreneurship		
	Base	High A	Moderate B	Not too C
Base	131	34	44	53
Very important	82	82	86	79
Somewhat important	12	6	9	19 A
Not too important	2	6 C	2	0
Not at all important	0	0	0	0
No response	3	6	2	2

Q27C. Defining social entrepreneurship as an effort to address significant problems through pattern-breaking approaches, how important is being well managed to the performance of successful social entrepreneurship?

		Level of social entrepreneurship		
	Base	High A	Moderate B	Not too C
Base	131	34	44	53
Very important	75	68	70	83
Somewhat important	21	24	27	15
Not too important	1	3	0	0
Not at all important	0	0	0	0
No response	3	6	2	2

Q27D. Defining social entrepreneurship as an effort to address significant problems through pattern-breaking approaches, how important is having unrestricted revenue to the performance of successful social entrepreneurship?

		Level of social entrepreneurship		
	Base	High A	Moderate B	Not too C
Base	131	34	44	53
Very important	45	44	41	49
Somewhat important	46	50	43	45
Not too important	4	0	9 A	2
Not at all important	1	0	0	2
No response	5	6	7	2

Q28. In your opinion, which of the following words is the *most important* characteristic of successful social entrepreneurship?

		Level of social entrepreneurship		
	Base	High A	Moderate B	Not too C
Base	131	34	44	53
Having visionary leadership	37	50 C	34	32
Being innovative	37	32	41	36
Being well managed	15	9	14	21
Having unrestricted revenue	8	3	9	9
No response	3	6	2	2

Q29. How well do the words "social entrepreneurship" describe your organization?

		Level of social entrepreneurship		
	Base	High A	Moderate B	Not too C
Base	131	34	44	53
Very well	27	26	36 C	21
Somewhat well	49	47	45	53
Not too well	15	12	11	19
Not well at all	7	12	5	6
No response	2	3	2	2

Q30. Have there been periods of time over the last five years when your organization has not been as socially entrepreneurial or when socially entrepreneurial activities had to be put on hold?

Based on those who say "social entrepreneurship" describes their organization very or somewhat well

	Base	Level of social entrepreneurship		
		High A	Moderate B	Not too C
Base	100	25	36	39
Yes	68	72	61	72
No	31	28	36	28
No response	1	0	3	0

Q31. Who is the *primary* source of your organization's socially entrepreneurial activity?

Based on those who say "social entrepreneurship" describes their organization very or somewhat well

	Base	Level of social entrepreneurship		
		High A	Moderate B	Not too C
Base	100	25	36	39
An individual leader such as founder or executive director	27	20	28	31
A group or unit within the organization	43	48	44	38
Clients and/or other external stakeholders	10	12	6	13
Funders and contributors	2	4	0	3
Other (please specify)	16	16	19	13
No response	2	0	3	3

Q32. Does the socially entrepreneurial activity involve how your organization delivers its programs (e.g., its administrative and operating systems) or in what it delivers (e.g., its basic program design) or both?

Based on those who say "social entrepreneurship" describes their organization very or somewhat well

		Level of social entrepreneurship		
	Base	High A	Moderate B	Not too C
Base	100	25	36	39
Administrative and operating systems	6	4	6	8
Program design	30	48 C	28	21
Both	62	48	67	67
No response	2	0	0	5

D1. Finally, we would like to ask a few demographic questions. What is your gender?

		Level of social entrepreneurship		
	Base	High A	Moderate B	Not too C
Base	131	34	44	53
Male	51	50	52	51
Female	47	47	48	45
No response	2	3	0	4

D2. What is your age?

		Level of social entrepreneurship		
	Base	High A	Moderate B	Not too C
Base	131	34	44	53
18–29	0	0	0	0
30–39	9	12	7	9
40–49	21	24	16	25
50–59	45	44	50	42
60–69	22	18	27	21
70 or older	0	0	0	0
No response	2	3	0	4

D3. What is the highest level of education you have completed?

	Level of social entrepreneurship			
	Base	High A	Moderate B	Not too C
Base	131	34	44	53
Less than high school	0	0	0	0
High school graduate	2	0	2	4
College graduate	34	35	39	30
Master's degree	47	47	41	53
PhD	9	12	11	6
Other professional degree (please specify)	5	3	7	4
No response	2	3	0	4

D4. Which of these best describes your race and ethnicity?

	Level of social entrepreneurship			
	Base	High A	Moderate B	Not too C
Base	131	34	44	53
White	85	82	89	85
Black or African-American	6	9	5	6
Hispanic or Latino	2	3	2	2
Asian	3	3	2	4
Other	0	0	0	0
No response	3	3	2	4

APPENDIX C

DIFFERENCES BETWEEN HIGHLY AND NOT-TOO ENTREPRENEURIAL ORGANIZATIONS IN THE 2001 AND 2006 SURVEYS

The survey in 2001 interviewed 250 senior executives from organizations that were nominated as high-performing social benefit organizations. Only 131 are tracked from the 2001 survey to match the 131 organizations that responded to the survey in 2006.

Bold indicates that the stated difference is statistically significant at the 0.05 confidence level, which means that one can have at least 95 percent confidence that the relationship is not random; nonbold indicates that the difference indicates a nonsignificant trend within the data from the two surveys, which can be confirmed only with a larger sample size.

2001 Survey N = 131	2006 Survey N = 131
Entrepreneurs	*Entrepreneurs*

Highly socially entrepreneurial organizations are—

—Not different in identifying being decisive (76 percent among highly entrepreneurial compared with 85 percent among not-too entrepreneurial), honest (98 percent among both), charismatic (24 percent; 28 percent), faithful (81 percent; 88 percent), and trust (76 percent among both) as important characteristics of leadership

—Not different in identifying being a good fundraiser (70 percent; 77 percent), encouraging risk taking (65 percent among both), and motivating people (86 percent; 94 percent) as important leadership skills

—More likely (47 percent; 32 percent) to agree an organization can be very well managed and NOT achieve goals

—Equally likely (12 percent; 15 percent) to agree an organization can be very effective in achieving goals and NOT be well managed

—**More likely (41 percent; 17 percent) to say an organization should first work on program impacts in becoming high performing**

—Not different in saying that organization should improve its leadership (91 percent; 85 percent) and internal management systems (76 percent; 83 percent) to become high performing

—Less likely to say that organization should improve its internal structure (59 percent; 72 percent) and external relationships (56 percent; 66 percent) to become high performing

—Not different (50 percent; 57 percent) in encouraging discussion of issues before executive makes decisions

Highly socially entrepreneurial organizations are—

—More likely to have the founder as chief executive (21 percent highly entrepreneurial compared with 11 percent not-too entrepreneurial)

—**More likely (37 percent; 19 percent) to have the founder still actively involved in organization**

—Not different in saying that having visionary leadership (85 percent both), being innovative (76 percent; 72 percent), being well managed (85 percent; 92 percent) are important to achieving mission

—More likely (47 percent; 34 percent) to say that visionary leadership is most important to achieving mission

—Less likely (24 percent; 40 percent) to say being well managed is most important to achieving mission

—Less likely (50 percent; 66 percent) to say encouraging employees to take risks is very important to achieving mission

—Not different (94 percent; 91 percent) in saying that having a shared vision is important to achieving mission

—More likely (48 percent; 38 percent) to say that a group or unit within the organization is source of organization's socially entrepreneurial activity

—Less likely (20 percent; 31 percent) to say that an individual was the source of organization's socially entrepreneurial activity

—**Less likely (18 percent; 49 percent) to report diversified programs**

—Not different in saying that having visionary leadership (79 percent; 85 percent), being innovative (82 percent; 79 percent), and having unrestricted revenue (44 percent; 49 percent) are important to successful social entrepreneurship

—Less likely (68 percent; 83 percent) to say that being well managed is important to successful social entrepreneurship

—More likely (50 percent; 32 percent) to say that having visionary leadership is most important to successful social entrepreneurship

—Less likely (9 percent; 21 percent) to say that being well managed is most important to successful entrepreneurship

—More likely (48 percent; 21 percent) to say that organization's socially entrepreneurial activity involves programs, not process

2001 Survey N = *131*	*2006 Survey* N = *131*
Ideas	*Ideas*

Highly socially entrepreneurial organizations are—

—Are more likely to say that their organization is national in scope (15 percent among highly entrepreneurial compared with 6 percent among not-too entrepreneurial)

—Are more likely (12 percent; 6 percent) to say that "Other" is the organization's area of primary focus

—Not different (79 percent; 77 percent) in collaborating with other organizations

—Less likely (74 percent; 87 percent) to have experienced significant growth in demand for programs

Highly socially entrepreneurial organizations are—

—Not different (72 percent among both) in saying that their organization has put socially entrepreneurial activity on hold over past five years

—**More likely to report increase in program demand (50 percent among highly entrepreneurial compared with 26 percent among not-too-entrepreneurial)**

—More likely (29 percent; 13 percent) to report rapid growth in budget over the past five years

—More likely (26 percent; 17 percent) to report increase in fiscal pressure

Opportunities	*Opportunities*

Highly socially entrepreneurial organizations are—

—**More likely to use the Internet (97 percent among highly entrepreneurial compared with 74 percent among not-too entrepreneurial)**

—Not different (94 percent; 91 percent) in having a strategic plan

—Not different (47 percent; 44 percent) in having fresh strategic plan

—Not different (53 percent; 55 percent) in regularly surveying clients

—Not different in size of budget

—Not different (62 percent; 68 percent) in measuring results of what they do

—Not different (12 percent; 15 percent) in describing environment as turbulent

—**Less likely (26 percent; 9 percent) to describe environment as competitive ("not too well")**

—**Less likely (6 percent; 25 percent) to describe environment as somewhat heavily regulated**

—Less likely (47 percent; 64 percent) to have diversified funding base

—Less likely (44 percent; 58 percent) to have some unrestricted revenue

—Not different (18 percent; 11 percent) to have rainy day fund

Highly socially entrepreneurial organizations are—

—Less likely to say strategic plan is important to achieving mission (41 percent among highly entrepreneurial compared with 58 percent among not-too entrepreneurial)

—Not different (59 percent; 66 percent) in saying that measuring results is important to achieving mission

—Less likely (15 percent; 26 percent) to report diversified funding base

—Less likely (15 percent; 25 percent) to report great deal of unrestricted revenue

—**Less likely (24 percent; 45 percent) to report earned income ("great deal")**

—**Less likely (9 percent; 28 percent) to report being vulnerable to external threats**

—**Less likely (18 percent; 38 percent) to report that using business tools is important to improving performance**

2001 Survey N = 131	2006 Survey N = 131

Opportunities (continued)

Highly socially entrepreneurial organizations are—

—**Less likely to say management support organizations (24 percent; 41 percent), external rating organizations (12 percent; 34 percent), associations of nonprofits (3 percent; 23 percent) have contributed a great deal to improving performance**
—**More likely (12 percent; 0 percent) to say government has contributed a great deal to improving performance**
—Less likely to say that management standards (18 percent; 26 percent), collaborating with other nonprofits (29 percent; 38 percent), external rating organizations (3 percent; 9 percent), reducing duplication across sector (12 percent; 9 percent), encouraging strategic planning (47 percent; 58 percent), focusing on outcomes (29 percent; 36 percent), more transparency (15 percent; 23 percent), active donor involvement, **more leadership training (55 percent; 77 percent),** encouraging executive directors to stay longer (24 percent; 42 percent), and using standard business tools (32 percent; 51 percent) have improved performance
—More likely to say encouraging foundations to provide for capacity building (41 percent; 32 percent) and **management assistance grants (38 percent; 17 percent, "fair amount") had improved performance**

Organizations	*Organizations*

Highly socially entrepreneurial organizations are—

—Not different in having difficulty retaining staff or volunteers (3 percent among highly entrepreneurial compared with 2 percent among not-too entrepreneurial)
—**Less likely (62 percent; 36 percent) to have difficulty ("not difficult at all") in retaining leaders or board members (65 percent; 38 percent)**
—**More likely (21 percent; 4 percent) to be younger organization**
—**More likely (56 percent; 34 percent) to have fewer employees (less than 25)**

Highly socially entrepreneurial organizations are—

—**More likely to rate organization as high performing in achieving mission (62 percent among highly entrepreneurial compared with 36 percent among not-too entrepreneurial)**
—Not different (6 percent; 8 percent) in reporting high vulnerability to internal challenges
—Not different in giving employees authority to make routine decisions (74 percent; 72 percent) and encouraging units to work together (71 percent; 75 percent)

2001 Survey N = *131*	*2006 Survey* N = *131*
Organizations (continued)	*Organizations*

Highly socially entrepreneurial organizations are—	*Highly socially entrepreneurial organizations are—*

—More likely (38 percent; 13 percent) to have fewer volunteers (less than 25) but be more dependent on volunteers they have (47 percent; 38 percent)

—Not different (91 percent; 92 percent) in layers of management (less than 4)

—Not different (82 percent; 87 percent) in staff working in teams

—**More likely (29 percent; 2 percent) to hold fewer board meetings**

—Not different (56 percent; 58 percent) to say board understands its duties

—Less likely (62 percent; 79 percent) to say board understands its role in setting policy

—Less likely (56 percent; 68 percent) to say board understands its role in overseeing organization's performance

—Not different (94 percent; 92 percent) in internal communication being open and free-flowing

—Not different (21 percent; 23 percent) in linking pay to performance

—Not different (47 percent; 42 percent) in using data to make decisions

—Less likely (79 percent; 89 percent) to have position descriptions for staff

—**Less likely (65 percent; 83 percent) that accounting system provides easy access to accurate accounting of expenses and revenues**

—**Less likely (29 percent; 53 percent) to provide for staff training**

—Less likely (44 percent; 57 percent) to report that providing resources such as time and funding for new ideas is important

—Less likely (47 percent; 62 percent) to report that providing enough information technology is important to achieving mission

—Not different (82 percent; 85 percent) in reporting that having enough employees is important to achieving mission

—**Less likely (38 percent; 64 percent) to report that providing enough training is important to achieving mission**

—Not different (62 percent; 68 percent) in having received technical assistance and capacity building in past five years ("great deal" and "fair amount")

REFERENCES

Adams, Richard, John Bessant, and Robert Phelps. 2006. "Innovation Management Measurement: A Review." *International Journal of Management Reviews* 8: 21–47.

Ahuja, Gautam, and Curba Morris Lampert. 2001. "Entrepreneurship in the Large Corporation: A Longitudinal Study of How Established Firms Create Breakthrough Inventions." *Strategic Management Journal* 22: 521–43.

Aldrich, Howard E., and Martha Argelia Martinez. 2001. "Many Are Called, but Few Are Chosen: An Evolutionary Perspective for the Study of Entrepreneurship." *Entrepreneurship Theory and Practice* 25: 41–57.

Alvord, Sarah H., L. David Brown, and Christine W. Letts. 2004. "Social Entrepreneurship and Social Transformation: An Exploratory Study." *Journal of Applied Behavioral Science* 40, no. 3: 260–82.

Amabile, Teresa M., and others. 2005. "Affect and Creativity at Work." *Administrative Science Quarterly* 50: 367–403.

Andries, Petra, and Koenraad Debackere. 2006. "Adaptation in Technology-Based Ventures: Insights at the Company Level." *Journal of Management Reviews* 8: 91–112.

Antoncic, Bostijan, and Robert D. Hisrich. 2003. "Clarifying the Intrapreneurship Concept." *Journal of Small Business and Enterprise Development* 10: 7–24.

Arquilla, John, and David Ronfeldt. 1998. *The Zapatista Social Netwar in Mexico.* Santa Monica, Calif.: RAND Corporation.

Asterbro, Thomas, Scott A. Jeffrey, and Gordon K. Adomdza. 2007. "Inventor Perseverance after Being Told to Quit: The Role of Cognitive Biases." *Journal of Behavioral Decision Making* 20: 253–72.

Audia, Pino G., and Christopher I. Rider. 2005. "A Garage and an Idea: What More Does an Entrepreneur Need?" *California Management Review* 48, no. 1 (Fall): 6–28.

Austin, James, Howard Stevenson, and Jane Wei-Skillern. 2006. "Social and Commercial Entrepreneurship: Same, Different, of Both?" *Entrepreneurship Theory and Practice* 31, no. 1: 1–22.

Barendsen, Lynn, and Howard Gardner. 2004. "Is the Social Entrepreneur a New Type of Leader?" *Leader to Leader* 27: 43–50.

Baron, Robert A. 1998. "Cognitive Mechanisms in Entrepreneurship: Why and When Entrepreneurs Think Differently than Other People." *Journal of Business Venturing* 13: 275–94.

———. 2006. "Opportunity Recognition as Pattern Recognition: How Entrepreneurs 'Connect the Dots' to Identify New Business Opportunities." *Academy of Management Perspectives* 20, no. 1: 104–19.

Baum, J. Robert, and Edwin A. Locke. 2004. "The Relationship of Entrepreneurial Traits, Skill, and Motivation to Subsequent Venture Growth." *Journal of Applied Psychology* 89: 587–98.

Baumgartner, Frank R., Christopher Green-Pedersen, and Bryan D. Jones. 2006. "Comparative Studies of Policy Agendas." *Journal of European Public Policy* 13, no. 7: 959–74.

Baumol, William J. 2004. "Entrepreneurial Cultures and Countercultures." *Academy of Management Learning and Education* 3: 316–26.

———. 2005. "Entrepreneurship and Invention: Toward Their Microeconomic Value Theory." Paper 05-38. AEI-Brookings Joint Center for Regulatory Studies.

Behn, Robert D. 1988. "Management by Groping Along." *Journal of Policy Analysis and Management* 7: 675–92.

Bernier, Luc, and Taïeb Hafsi. 2007. "The Changing Nature of Public Entrepreneurship." *Public Administration Review* 67, no. 3: 488–503.

Birkinshaw, Julian, and Susan A. Hill. 2005. "Corporate Venturing Units: Vehicles for Strategic Success in the New Europe." *Organizational Dynamics* 34: 247–57.

Birkinshaw, Julian, and Michael Mol. 2006. "How Management Innovation Happens." *MIT Sloan Management Review*: 47: 81–88.

Bloom, Paul N., and J. Gregory Dees. 2008. "Cultivate Your Ecosystem." *Stanford Social Innovation Review* 6: 47–53.

Bluedorn, Allen C., and Gwen Martin. 2008. "The Time Frames of Entrepreneurs." *Journal of Business Venturing* 23: 1–20.

Bornstein, David. 2004. *How to Change the World: Social Entrepreneurs and the Power of New Ideas.* Oxford University Press.

Buttel, Frederick H. 1989. "How Epoch Making Are High Technologies? The Case of Biotechnology." *Sociological Forum* 4: 247–61.

Carter, Nancy M., and Candida G. Brush. 2004. "Gender." In *Handbook of Entrepreneurial Dynamics: The Process of Business Creation,* edited by William Gartner and others, chapter 2. Thousand Oaks, Calif.: Russell Sage.

Casson, Mark, and Marina Della Giusta. 2007. "Entrepreneurship and Social Capital: Analysing the Impact of Social Networks on Entrepreneurial Activity from a Rational Action Perspective." *International Small Business Journal* 25, no. 3: 220–44.

Clarysse, Bart, and others. 2005. "Spinning Out New Ventures: A Typology of Incubation Strategies from European Research Institutions." *Journal of Business Venturing* 20: 183–216.

Companys, Yosem E., and Jeffrey S. McMullen. 2007. "Strategic Entrepreneurs at Work: The Nature, Discovery, and Exploitation of Entrepreneurial Opportunities." *Small Business Economics* 28: 301–22.

Corso, Mariano, and Luisa Pellegrini. 2007. "Continuous and Discontinuous Innovation: Overcoming the Innovator Dilemma." *Creativity and Innovation Management* 16: 333–47.

Covin, Jeffrey G., and Morgan P. Miles. 1999. "Corporate Entrepreneurship and the Pursuit of Competitive Advantage." *Entrepreneurship Theory and Practice* 24: 47–63.

Crane, Frederick G., and Erinn C. Crane. 2007. "Dispositional Optimism and Entrepreneurial Success." *Psychologist-Manager Journal* 10: 13–25.

Crutchfield, Leslie, and Heather McLeod Grant. 2007. *Forces for Good: The Six Practices of High-Impact Nonprofits.* San Francisco: Jossey-Bass.

Daft, Richard L. 1978. "A Dual-Core Model of Organizational Innovation." *Academy of Management Journal* 21: 193–210.

Damanpour, Fariborz. 1991. "Organizational Innovation: A Meta-Analysis of Effects of Determinants and Moderators." *Academy of Management Journal* 34: 555–90.

———. 1996. "Organizational Complexity and Innovation: Developing and Testing Multiple Contingency Models." *Management Science* 42: 693–716.

Damanpour, Fariborz, and J. Daniel Wischnevsky. 2006. "Research on Innovations in Organizations: Distinguishing Innovation-Generating from Innovation-Adopting Organizations." *Journal of Engineering and Technology Management* 23: 269–91.

Danneels, Erwin. 2002. "The Dynamics of Product Innovation and Firm Competencies." *Strategic Management Journal* 23, no. 12: 1095–121.

Davis, Susan. 2002. "Social Entrepreneurship: Towards an Entrepreneurial Culture for Social and Economic Development." Paper prepared for the Youth Employment Summit. Alexandria, Egypt, September 7–11 (www.ashoka.org/files/yespaper.pdf).

Dees, J. Gregory. 1998. "Enterprising Nonprofits." *Harvard Business Review* 76 (January–February): 55–67.

———. 2003. "Social Entrepreneurship Is about Innovation and Impact, Not Income" (www.fuqua.duke.edu/centers/case/articles/1004/corner.htm).

Dees, J. Gregory, and Beth Battle Anderson. 2003. "Sector-Bending: Blurring Lines between Nonprofit and For-Profit." *Society* 40, no. 4: 16–27.

———. 2006. "Framing a Theory of Social Entrepreneurship: Building on Two Schools of Practice and Thought." Paper prepared for the 34th annual conference of the Association for Research on Nonprofit Organizations and Voluntary Action. Washington, D.C., November 17–18, 2005. Reprinted in *Research on Social Entrepreneurship: Understanding and Contributing to an Emerging Field*, edited by Rachel Mosher-William. *Occasional Paper Series*, vol 1, no. 3 (Indianapolis: ARNOVA).

Dess, Gregory G., and G. T. Lumpkin. 2005. "The Role of Entrepreneurial Orientation in Stimulating Effective Corporate Entrepreneurship." *Academy of Management Executive* 19: 147–56.

Dess, Gregory G., G. T. Lumpkin, and Jeffrey E. McGee. 1999. "Linking Corporate Entrepreneurship to Strategy, Structure, and Process: Suggested Research Directions." *Entrepreneurship Theory and Practice* 23: 85–102.

Dess, Gregory G., and others. 2003. "Emerging Issues in Corporate Entrepreneurship." *Journal of Management* 29: 351–78.

Di Benedetto, C. Anthony. 1999. "Identifying the Key Success Factors in New Product Launch." *Journal of Product Innovation Management* 16: 530–44.

Downs, George W., and Patrick D. Larkey. 1986. *The Search for Government Efficiency*. Temple University Press.

Drayton, William. 2002. "The Citizen Sector: Becoming as Entrepreneurial and Competitive as Business." *California Management Review* 44: 120–32.

———. 2005. "Everyone a Changemaker." *peerReview* 7 (Spring): 8–11.

———. 2007. "Letter to the Editor." *Stanford Social Innovation Review* 4 (Winter): 5.

Drucker, Peter F. 1985. "Entrepreneurial Strategies." *California Management Review* 27: 9–25.

Druilhe, Céline, and Elizabeth Garnsey. 2004. "Do Academic Spin-Outs Differ and Does It Matter?" *Journal of Technology Transfer* 29: 269–85.

Echoing Green. 2007. *Be Bold*. New York.

Eckhardt, Jonathan T., and Scott A. Shane. 2003. "Opportunities and Entrepreneurship." *Journal of Management* 29: 333–49.

Elkington, John, and Pamela Hartigan. 2008. *The Power of Unreasonable People: How Social Entrepreneurs Create Markets that Change the World*. Harvard Business Press.

Fischer, Eileen, and Rebecca Reuber. 2007. "The Good, the Bad, and the Unfamiliar: The Challenges of Reputation Formation Facing New Firms." *Entrepreneurship Theory and Practice* 32: 53–75.

Fleming, Lee. 2007. "Breakthroughs and the 'Long Tail' of Innovation." *MIT Sloan Management Review* 49: 69–74.

Fleming, Lee, Santiago Mingo, and David Chen. 2007. "Collaborative Broker-
age, Generative Creativity, and Creative Success." *Administrative Science
Quarterly* 52: 443–75.

Forbes, Daniel P. 1999. "Cognitive Approaches to New Venture Creation."
International Journal of Management Reviews 1: 415–39.

Foster, William, and Jeffrey Bradach. 2005. "Should Nonprofits Seek Profits?"
Harvard Business Review 83: 92–100.

Francis, David, John Bessant, and Mike Hobday. 2003. "Managing Radical
Organisational Transformation." *Management Decision* 41, no. 1: 18–31.

Freeman, John, and Jerome S. Engel. 2007. "Models of Innovation: Startups and
Mature Corporations." *California Management Review* 50: 94–119.

Gans, Joshua S., David H. Hsu, and Scott Stern. 2002. "When Does Start-Up
Innovation Spur the Gale of Creative Destruction?" *RAND Journal of Economics* 33: 571–86.

Gartner, William B. 1988. "'Who is an Entrepreneur?' Is the Wrong Question."
American Journal of Small Business 12: 11–32.

Gartner, William B., Terence R. Mitchell, and Karl H. Vesper. 1989. "A Taxonomy of New Business Ventures." *Journal of Business Venturing* 4, no. 3:
169–86.

Gartner, William B., and others. 1994. "Finding the Entrepreneur in Entrepreneurship." *Entrepreneurship Theory and Practice* 18: 5–10.

Garvin, David A., and Lynne C. Levesque. 2006. "Meeting the Challenge of Corporate Entrepreneurship." *Harvard Business Review* 84 (October): 102–12.

Grant, Heather McLeod, and Leslie R. Crutchfield. 2007. "Creating High-
Impact Nonprofits." *Stanford Social Innovation Review* 5: 32–41.

Greene, Patricia G., and Margaret M. Owen. 2004. "Race and Gender." In *Handbook of Entrepreneurial Dynamics: The Process of Business Creation,* edited
by William B. Gartner and others. Thousand Oaks, Calif.: Russell Sage.

Greenhalgh, Trisha, and others. 2004. "Diffusion of Innovations in Service
Organizations: Systematic Review and Recommendations." *Milbank Quarterly* 82: 581–629.

Hargadon, Andrew B., and Douglas Yellowlees. 2001. "When Innovations Meet
Institutions: Edison and the Design of Light." *Administrative Science Quarterly* 46, no. 3: 476–501.

Haveman, Heather A. 1993. "Follow the Leader: Mimetic Isomorphism and
Entry into New Markets." *Administrative Science Quarterly* 38: 593–627.

Hayton, James C., Gerard George, and Shaker A. Zahra. 2002. "National Culture and Entrepreneurship: A Review of Behavioral Research." *Entrepreneurship Theory and Practice* 26, no. 4: 33–52.

Hayward, Mathew L. A., Dean A. Shepherd, and Dale Griffin. 2006. "A Hubris
Theory of Entrepreneurship." *Management Science* 52: 160–72.

Heirman, Ans, and Bart Clarysse. 2007. "Which Tangible and Intangible Assets Matter for Innovation Speed in Start-Ups?" *Journal of Product Innovation Management* 24: 303–15.

Hellman, Thomas. 2007. "When Do Employees Become Entrepreneurs?" *Management Science* 53, no. 6: 919–33.

Henard, David H., and David M. Szymanski. 2001. "Why Some New Products are More Successful than Others." *Journal of Marketing Research* 38: 362–75.

Herrmann, Andreas, Oliver Gassmann, and Ulrich Eisert. 2007. "An Empirical Study of the Antecedents for Radical Product Innovations and Capabilities for Transformation." *Journal of Engineering and Technology Management* 24: 92–120.

Holcombe, Randal G. 2003. "The Origins of Entrepreneurial Opportunities." *Review of Austrian Economics* 16: 25–43.

Hsieh, Chihmao, Jack A. Nickerson, and Todd R. Zenger. 2007. "Opportunity Discovery, Problem Solving and a Theory of the Entrepreneurial Firm." *Journal of Management Studies* 44: 1255–277.

Hunter, Samuel T., Katrina E. Bedell, and Michael D. Mumford. 2007. "Climate for Creativity: A Quantitative Review." *Creativity Research Journal* 19: 69–90.

Husock, Howard. 2007. "Letter to the Editor." *Stanford Social Innovation Review* 4 (Winter): 6.

Husted, Kenneth, and Christian Vintergaard. 2004. "Stimulating Innovation through Corporate Venture Bases." *Journal of World Business* 39: 296–306.

Iyer, Bala, and Thomas H. Davenport. 2008. "Reverse Engineering Google's Innovation Machine." *Harvard Business Review* 86: 59–68.

Jelinek, Mariann, and Joseph A. Litterer. 1995. "Toward Entrepreneurial Organizations: Meeting Ambiguity with Engagement." *Entrepreneurship Theory and Practice* 20: 137–68.

Katz, Jerome A., and Dean A. Shepherd. 2003. "Cognitive Approaches to Entrepreneurship Research." *Advances in Entrepreneurship, Firm Emergence and Growth* 6: 1–10.

Kessler, Alexander. 2007. "Success Factors for New Businesses in Austria and the Czech Republic." *Entrepreneurship and Regional Development* 19: 381–403.

Kingdon, John. 2002. *Agendas, Alternatives, and Public Policies*. New York: Longman.

Kirkwood, Jodyanne. 2007. "Tall Poppy Syndrome: Implications for Entrepreneurship in New Zealand." *Journal of Management and Organization* 13: 366–82.

Kirzner, Israel M. 1997. "Entrepreneurial Discovery and the Competitive Market Process: An Austrian Approach." *Journal of Economic Literature* 35: 60–85.

————. 1999. "Creativity and/or Alertness: A Reconsideration of the Schumpeterian Entrepreneur." *Review of Austrian Economics* 11, nos. 1–2: 5–17.

————. 2005. "Human Attitudes and Economic Growth." *Cato Journal* 25: 465–69.

Koellinger, Philipp, Maria Minniti, and Christian Schade. 2007. "'I Think I Can, I Think I Can': Overconfidence and Entrepreneurial Behavior." *Journal of Economic Psychology* 28: 502–27.

Krueger, Norris F., Jr. 2007. "What Lies Beneath? The Experiential Essence of Entrepreneurial Thinking." *Entrepreneurship Theory and Practice* 31: 123–38.

LaFrance, Steven F., and others. 2006. *Scaling Capacities: Supports for Growing Impact*. San Francisco: LaFrance Associates (July).

Leviner, Noga, Leslie R. Crutchfield, and Diana Wells. 2006. "Understanding the Impact of Social Entrepreneurs: Ashoka's Answer to the Challenge of Measuring Effectiveness." Paper prepared for the 34th annual conference of the Association for Research on Nonprofit Organizations and Voluntary Action, Washington, D.C., November 17–18, 2005. Reprinted in *Research on Social Entrepreneurship: Understanding and Contributing to an Emerging Field*, edited by Rachel Mosher-William, pp. 89–104. *Occasional Paper Series*, vol 1, no. 3 (Indianapolis: ARNOVA).

Light, Paul C. 1998. *Sustaining Innovation: Creating Nonprofit and Government Organizations that Innovate Naturally*. San Francisco: Jossey-Bass.

————. 2003. *Pathways to Nonprofit Excellence*. Brookings.

————. 2006. "Reshaping Social Entrepreneurship." *Stanford Social Innovation Review* 4: 47–51.

Low, Murray B. 2001. "The Adolescence of Entrepreneurship Research: Specification of Purpose." *Entrepreneurship Theory and Practice* 36: 17–25.

Lumpkin, G. T., and Gregory G. Dess. 1996. "Clarifying the Entrepreneurial Orientation Construct and Linking it to Performance." *Academy of Management Review* 21: 135–71.

Mair, Johanna, and Ignasi Martí. 2006. "Social Entrepreneurship Research: A Source of Explanation, Prediction, and Delight." *Journal of World Business* 41: 36–44.

Markman, Gideon D., Robert A. Baron, and David B. Balkin. 2005. "Are Perseverance and Self-Efficacy Costless? Assessing Entrepreneurs' Regretful Thinking." *Journal of Organizational Behavior* 26, no. 1: 1–19.

Martin, Roger L. 2003. "To the Rescue: Beating the Heroic Leadership Trap." *Stanford Social Innovation Review* 1: 36–39.

Martin, Roger L., and Sally Osberg. 2007. "Social Entrepreneurship: The Case for Definition." *Stanford Social Innovation Review* 5 (Spring): 29–39.

McAdam, Maura, and Susan Marlow. 2007. "Building Futures or Stealing Secrets? Entrepreneurial Cooperation and Conflict within Business Incubators." *International Small Business Journal* 25: 361–82.

McGrath, Rita Gunther. 1999. "Falling Forward: Real Options Reasoning and Entrepreneurial Failure." *Academy of Management Review* 24: 13–30.

Miller, Clara. 2004. "The Looking-Glass World of Nonprofit Money: Managing in For-Profit's Shadow Universe." Paper prepared for the Nonprofit Finance Fund. New York.

Mitchell, Ronald K., and others. 2002. "Are Entrepreneurial Cognitions Universal? Assessing Entrepreneurial Cognitions across Cultures." *Entrepreneurship Theory and Practice* 27: 9–31.

Morris, Michael H., and others. 2007. "Antecedents and Outcomes of Entrepreneurial and Market Orientations in a Non-Profit Context: Theoretical and Empirical Insights." *Journal of Leadership and Organizational Studies* 13: 12–36.

O'Reilly, Charles A., III, and Michael L. Tushman. 2004. "The Ambidextrous Organization." *Harvard Business Review* 68: 74–81.

Palich, Leslie E., and D. Ray Bagby. 1995. "Using Cognitive Theory to Explain Entrepreneurial Risk-taking: Challenging Conventional Wisdom." *Journal of Business Venturing* 10: 425–38.

Palinkas, Lawrence A., and Peter Suedfeld. 2008. "Psychological Effects of Polar Expeditions." *Lancet* 371: 153–63.

Peters, Thomas J., and Robert H. Waterman, Jr. 1983. *In Search of Excellence.* New York: Warner Books.

Phills, James A. 2005. "Leadership Matters—Or Does It?" *Leader to Leader* 36: 46–52.

Plummer, Lawrence A., J. Michael Haynie, and Joy Godesiabois. 2007. "An Essay on the Origins of Entrepreneurial Opportunity." *Small Business Economics* 28: 363–79.

Polley, Douglas, and Andrew H. Van de Ven. 1996. "Learning by Discovery during Innovation Development." *International Journal of Technology Management* 11: 871–83.

Puhakka, Vesa. 2007. "Effects of Opportunity Discovery Strategies of Entrepreneurs on Performance of New Ventures." *Journal of Entrepreneurship* 16, no. 1: 19–51.

Quinn, James Brian. 1985. "Managing Innovation: Controlled Chaos." *Harvard Business Review* 63: 73–85.

Rauch, Andreas, and Michael Frese. 2007. "Let's Put the Person Back into Entrepreneurship Research: A Meta-Analysis on the Relationship between Business Owners' Personality Traits, Business Creation, and Success." *European Journal of Work and Organizational Psychology* 16: 353–85.

Robinson, Jeffrey A. 2006. "Navigating Social and Institutional Barriers to Markets: How Social Entrepreneurs Identify and Evaluate Opportunities." In *Social Entrepreneurship,* edited by Johanna Mair, Jeffrey Robinson, and Kai Hockerts. New York: Palgrave Macmillan.

Sambrook, Sally, and Clair Roberts. 2005. "Corporate Entrepreneurship and Organizational Learning: A Review of the Literature and the Development of a Conceptual Framework." *Strategic Change* 14: 141–55.

Sanger, Mary Bryna, and Martin A. Levin. 1992. "Using Old Stuff in New Ways: Innovation as a Case of Evolutionary Tinkering." *Journal of Policy Analysis and Management* 11, no. 1, 88–115.

Schindehutte, Minet, Michael Morris, and Jeffrey Allen. 2006. "Beyond Achievement: Entrepreneurship as Extreme Experience." *Small Business Economics* 27: 349–68.

Schumpeter, Joseph A. 1934. *The Theory of Development*. Harvard University Press.

———. 1939. *Business Cycles: A Theoretical, Historical and Statistical Analysis of the Capitalist Process*. New York: McGraw-Hill.

Seelos, Christian, and Johanna Mair. 2004. "Social Entrepreneurship: The Contribution of Individual Entrepreneurs to Sustainable Development." Working Paper. University of Navarra, IESE (Instituto de Estudios Superiores de la Empresa) Business School (International Graduate School of Management).

Sfeir-Younis, Alfredo. 2002. "The Spiritual Entrepreneur." *Reflections* 3: 43–45.

Shane, Scott A. 2006. "Introduction to the Focused Issue on Entrepreneurship." *Management Science* 52: 155–59.

Shane, Scott, Edwin A. Locke, and Christopher J. Collins. 2003. "Entrepreneurial Motivation." *Human Resource Management Review* 13: 257–79.

Shane, Scott, and S. Venkataraman. 2000. "The Promise of Entrepreneurship as a Field of Research." *Academy of Management Review* 25: 217–26.

Sharir, Moshe, and Miri Lerner. 2006. "Gauging the Success of Social Ventures Initiated by Individual Social Entrepreneurs." *Journal of World Business* 41: 6–20.

Shaw, Eleanor, and Sara Carter. 2007. "Social Entrepreneurship: Theoretical Antecedents and Empirical Analysis of Entrepreneurial Processes and Outcomes." *Journal of Small Business and Enterprise Development* 14: 418–34.

Singh, Robert P. 2001. "A Comment on Developing the Field of Entrepreneurship through the Study of Opportunity Recognition and Exploitation." *Academy of Management Review* 26: 10–12.

Singh, Smita, Patricia Corner, and Kathryn Pavlovich. 2007. "Coping with Entrepreneurial Failure." *Journal of Management and Organization* 13: 331–44.

Song, Michael, Ksenia Podoynitsyna, Hans van der Bij, and Johannes I. M. Halman. 2008. "Success Factors in New Ventures: A Meta-analysis." *Journal of Product Innovation Management* 25: 7–27.

Sørensen, Jesper B. 2007. "Bureaucracy and Entrepreneurship: Workplace Effects on Entrepreneurial Entry." *Administrative Science Quarterly* 52, no. 3: 387–412.

Stam, Erik. 2007. "Why Butterflies Don't Leave: Locational Behavior of Entrepreneurial Firms." *Economic Geography* 83: 27–50.

Steiner, Carol J. 1995. "A Philosophy for Innovation: The Role of Unconventional Individuals in Innovation Success." *Journal of Product Innovation Management* 12: 431–40.

Sternberg, Robert J. 2004. "Successful Intelligence as a Basis for Entrepreneurship." *Journal of Business Venturing* 19: 189–201.

Stevenson, Howard H., and J. Carlos Jarillo. 1990. "A Paradigm of Entrepreneurship: Entrepreneurial Management." *Strategic Management Journal* 11: 17–27.

Sull, Donald N. 2007. "Closing the Gap between Strategy and Execution." *MIT Sloan Management Review* 48: 30–38.

Thompson, John L. 2002. "The World of the Social Entrepreneur." *International Journal of Public Sector Management* 15: 412–31.

Thompson, John, Geoff Alvy, and Ann Lees. 2000. "Social Entrepreneurship—A New Look at the People and the Potential." *Management Decision* 38: 328–38.

Thrash, Todd M., and Andrew J. Elliot. 2003. "Inspiration as a Psychological Concept." *Journal of Personality and Social Psychology* 84: 871–89.

Tierney, Pamela, and Steven M. Farmer. 2002. "Creative Self-Efficacy: Its Potential Antecedents and Relationship to Creative Performance." *Academy of Management Journal* 45: 1137–148.

Tushman, Michael L., and Charles A. O'Reilly, III. 1996. "Ambidextrous Organizations: Managing Evolutionary and Revolutionary Change." *California Management Review* 38, no. 4: 8–29.

Udell, Gerald, and Mike Hignite. 2007. "New Product Commercialization: Needs and Strategies." *Journal of Applied Management and Entrepreneurship* 12: 75–92.

Valliere, David, and Norm O'Reilly. 2007. "Seek the Summit: Exploring the Entrepreneur-Mountaineer Analogy." *International Journal of Entrepreneurship and Innovation* 8: 293–308.

Van de Ven, Andrew H. 1993. "The Development of an Infrastructure for Entrepreneurship." *Journal of Business Venturing* 8, no. 3: 211–30.

Vohora, Ajay, Mike Wright, and Andy Lockett. 2004. "Critical Junctures in the Development of University High-Tech Spinout Companies." *Research Policy* 33: 147–75.

Waddock, Sandra A., and James E. Post. 1991. "Social Entrepreneurs and Catalytic Change." *Public Administration Review* 51: 393–401.

Ward, Thomas B. 2004. "Cognition, Creativity, and Entrepreneurship." *Journal of Business Venturing* 19, no. 2: 173–88.

Wei-Skillern, Jane, and others. 2007. *Entrepreneurship in the Social Sector.* Los Angeles: Russell Sage.

Weerawardena, Jay, and Gillian Sullivan Mort. 2006. "Investigating Social Entrepreneurship: A Multidimensional Model." *Journal of World Business* 41: 21–35.

Westhead, Paul, and Mike Wright. 1998. "Novice, Portfolio, and Serial Founders: Are They Different?" *Journal of Business Venturing* 13, no. 3: 173–204.

Westhead, Paul, Deniz Ucbasaran, and Mike Wright. 2005. "Experience and Cognition: Do Novice, Serial and Portfolio Entrepreneurs Differ?" *International Small Business Journal* 23: 72–98.

Wolcott, Robert C., and Michael J. Lippitz. 2007. "The Four Models of Corporate Entrepreneurship." *Sloan Management Review* 49: 75–82.

Zhang, Marina Y., and Mark Dodgson. 2007. "A Roasted Duck Can Still Fly Away: A Case Study of Technology, Nationality, Culture and the Rapid and Early Internationalization of the Firm." *Journal of World Business* 42: 336–49.

Zhao, Hao, and Scott E. Seibert. 2006. "The Big Five Personality Dimensions and Entrepreneurial Status: A Meta-Analytical Review." *Journal of Applied Psychology* 91, no. 2: 259–71.

Zurick, John. 2007. "Letter to the Editor." *Stanford Social Innovation Review* 4 (Winter): 4.

———. Forthcoming. *The Maverick's Guide to Social Entrepreneurship.*

FURTHER READING

Ajzen, Icek. 1991. "The Theory of Planned Behavior." *Organizational Behavior and Human Decision Processes* 50: 179–211.

Aldrich, Howard E. 1990. "Using an Ecological Perspective to Study Organizational Founding Rates." *Entrepreneurship Theory and Practice* 15: 7–25.

Atherton, Andrew. 2007. "Preparing for Business Startup: 'Pre-Start' Activities in the New Venture Creation Dynamic." *Journal of Small Business and Enterprise Development* 14: 404–17.

Austin, James E., and others. 2007. "Capitalizing on Convergence." *Stanford Social Innovation Review* 5: 24–31.

Baron, David P. 2007. "Corporate Social Responsibility and Social Entrepreneurship." *Journal of Economics and Management Strategy* 16: 683–717.

Baron, Robert A., and Gideon D. Markman. 2003. "Beyond Social Capital: The Role of Entrepreneurs' Social Competence in Their Financial Success." *Journal of Business Venturing* 18: 41–60.

Beckman, Christine M., M. Diane Burton, and Charles O'Reilly. 2007. "Early Teams: The Impact of Team Demography on VC Financing and Going Public." *Journal of Business Venturing* 22: 147–73.

Bird, Barbara. 1988. "Implementing Entrepreneurial Ideas: The Case for Intention." *Academy of Management Review* 13: 442–53.

Boschee, Jerr, and Jim McClurg. 2003. "Toward a Better Understanding of Social Entrepreneurship: Some Important Distinctions." Washington: Social Enterprise Alliance (www.se-alliance.org/better_understanding.pdf).

Brockner, Joel, E. Tory Higgins, and Murray B. Low. 2004. "Regulatory Focus Theory and the Entrepreneurial Process." *Journal of Business Venturing* 19, no. 2: 203–20.

Brugmann, Jeb, and C. K. Prahalad. 2007. "Co-creating Business's New Social Compact." *Harvard Business Review* 85: 80–90.

Busenitz, Lowell W., and Jay B. Barney. 1997. "Differences between Entrepreneurs and Managers in Large Organizations: Biases and Heuristics in Strategic Decision-Making." *Journal of Business Venturing* 12: 9–30.

Busenitz, Lowell W., and others. 2003. "Entrepreneurship Research in Emergence: Past Trends and Future Directions." *Journal of Management* 29: 285–308.

Cheng, Yu-Ting, and Andrew H. Van de Ven. 1996. "Learning the Innovation Journey: Order Out of Chaos." *Organization Science* 7, no. 6: 593–614.

Colvin, Jeffrey G., and Morgan P. Miles. 1999. "Corporate Entrepreneurship and the Pursuit of Competitive Advantage." *Entrepreneurship Theory and Practice* 23: 47–63.

Cooney, Kate. 2006. "The Institutional and Technical Structuring of Nonprofit Ventures: Case Study of a U.S. Hybrid Organization Caught between Two Fields." *Voluntas* 17, no. 2: 137–55.

Cooper, Arnold C., Carolyn Y. Woo, and William C. Dunkelberg. 1988. "Entrepreneurs' Perceived Chances for Success." *Journal of Business Venturing* 3: 97–108.

Cunningham, J. Barton, and Joe Lischeron. 1991. "Defining Entrepreneurship." *Journal of Small Business Management* 29: 45–61.

Dacanay, Marie Lisa M. 2006. "Social Entrepreneurship: An Asian Perspective." Paper prepared for the 2nd International Social Entrepreneurship Research Conference. New York University, Stern School of Business, April 7–9.

Daft, Richard L., and Karl E. Weick. 1984. "Toward a Model of Organizations as Interpretation Systems." *Academy of Management Review* 9: 284–95.

Dart, Raymond. 2004. "The Legitimacy of Social Enterprise." *Nonprofit Management and Leadership* 14: 411–24.

Dearlove, Des. 2004. "Interview: Jeff Skoll." *Business Strategy Review* 15: 51–53.

Dees, J. Gregory. 1996. "The Social Enterprise Spectrum: Philanthropy to Commerce." Case 9-395-116. Harvard Business School Publishing.

———. 2001. "The Meaning of 'Social Entrepreneurship.'" Duke University, Fuqua School of Business, Center for the Advancement of Social Entrepreneurship (www.fuqua.duke.edu/centers/case/documents/dees_sedef.pdf).

Dees, J. Gregory, Beth Battle Anderson, and Jane Wei-Skillern. 2002. "Pathways to Social Impact: Strategies for Scaling Out Successful Social Innovations." Working Paper. Duke University, Fuqua School of Business, Center for the Advancement of Social Entrepreneurship (August).

Dimov, Dimo. 2007. "Beyond the Single-Person, Single-Insight Attribution in Understanding Entrepreneurial Opportunities." *Entrepreneurship Theory and Practice* 32: 713–31.

Gaglio, Connie Marie, and Jerome A. Katz. 2001. "The Psychological Basis of Opportunity Identification: Entrepreneurial Alertness." *Small Business Economics* 16: 95–111.

Gartner, William B. 1989. "Some Suggestions for Research on Entrepreneurial Traits and Characteristics." *Entrepreneurship Theory and Practice* 13: 27–37.

Gartner, William B., and others, eds. 2004. *Handbook of Entrepreneurial Dynamics: The Process of Business Creation*. Thousand Oaks, Calif.: Russell Sage.

Gupta, Vipin, Ian C. MacMillan, and Gita Surie. 2004. "Entrepreneurial Leadership: Developing and Measuring a Cross-Cultural Construct." *Journal of Business Venturing* 19: 241–60.

Harding, Rebecca. 2004. "Social Enterprise: The New Economic Engine." *Business Strategy Review* 15: 44–47.

Hemingway, Christine A. 2005. "Personal Values as a Catalyst for Corporate Social Entrepreneurship." *Journal of Business Ethics* 60: 233–49.

Heirman, Ans, and Bart Clarysse. 2007. "Which Tangible and Intangible Assets Matter for Innovation Speed in Start-Ups?" *Journal of Product Innovation Management* 24: 303–15.

Hill, Robert C., and Michael Levenhagen. 1995. "Metaphors and Mental Models: Sensemaking and Sensegiving in Innovative and Entrepreneurial Activities." *Journal of Management* 21 (November–December): 1057–074.

Hornsby, Jeffrey S., and others. 1993. "An Interactive Model of the Corporate Entrepreneurship Process." *Entrepreneurship Theory and Practice* 18: 29–37.

Humphries, Maria, and Suzanna Grant. 2005. "Social Enterprise and Re-Civilization of Human Endeavors: Re-Socializing the Market Metaphor or Encroaching Colonization of the Lifeworld?" *Current Issues in Comparative Education* 27: 1–17.

Kaish, Stanley, and Benjamin Gilad. 1991. "Characteristics of Opportunities Search of Entrepreneurs versus Executives: Sources, Interests, General Alertness." *Journal of Business Venturing* 6, no. 1: 45–61.

Kerlin, Janelle A. 2006. "Social Enterprise in the United States and Europe: Understanding and Learning from the Differences." *Voluntas* 17: 247–63.

Kirchoff, Bruce A. 1991. "Entrepreneurship's Contribution to Economics. *Entrepreneurship Theory and Practice* 16: 93–112.

Kramer, Mark R. 2005. "Measuring Innovation: Evaluation in the Field of Social Entrepreneurship." Prepared for the Skoll Foundation. Boston: Foundation Strategy Group.

Krueger, Norris. 1993. "The Impact of Prior Entrepreneurial Exposure on Perceptions of New Venture Feasibility and Desirability." *Entrepreneurship Theory and Practice* 18, no. 1: 5–21.

Krueger, Norris F., Jr., Michael D. Reilly, and Alan L. Carsrud. 2000. "Competing Models of Entrepreneurial Intentions." *Journal of Business Venturing* 15: 411–32.

Learned, Kevin E. 1992. "What Happened Before the Organization? A Model of Organization Formation." *Entrepreneurship Theory and Practice* 18: 39–48.

Lee, Lena, Poh-Kam Wong, and Yuen Ping Ho. 2004. "Entrepreneurial Propensities: The Influence of Self-Efficacy, Opportunity, Perception, and Social Network." Working Paper. National University of Singapore Entrepreneurship Centre (January).

Licht, Amir N., and Jordan I. Siegel. 2006. "The Social Dimensions of Entrepreneurship." In *Oxford Handbook of Entrepreneurship*, edited by Mark Casson and Bernard Yeung. Oxford University Press.

Lichtenstein, Benyamin, B., and Nancy M. Carter, Kevin J. Dooley, and William B. Gartner. 2007. "Complexity Dynamics of Nascent Entrepreneurship. *Journal of Business Venturing* 22: 236–61.

Light, Paul C. 2006. "Searching for Social Entrepreneurs: Who They Might Be, Where They Might Be Found, What They Do." Paper prepared for the 34th annual conference of the Association for Research on Nonprofit Organizations and Voluntary Action. Washington, D.C., November 17–18, 2005. Reprinted in *Research on Social Entrepreneurship: Understanding and Contributing to an Emerging Field*, edited by Rachel Mosher-William, pp. 13–37. Occasional Paper Series, vol 1, no. 3 (Indianapolis: ARNOVA).

———. 2008. *A Government Ill Executed: The Decline of the Federal Service and How to Reverse It*. Harvard University Press.

Low, Chris. 2006. "A Framework for the Governance of Social Enterprise." *International Journal of Social Economics* 33: 376–85.

Lumpkin, G. T., and Gregory G. Dess. 2001. "Linking Two Dimensions of Entrepreneurial Orientation to Firm Performance: The Moderating Role of Environment and Industry Life Cycle." *Journal of Business Venturing* 16: 429–51.

Mair, Johanna, and Ignasi Martí. 2004. "Social Entrepreneurship: What Are We Talking About? A Framework for Future Research." Working Paper. University of Navarra, IESE (Instituto de Estudios Superiores de la Empresa) Business School (International Graduate School of Management).

Mair, Johanna, and Ernesto Noboa. 2003. "Social Entrepreneurship: How Intentions to Create a Social Enterprise Get Formed." Working Paper. University of Navarra, IESE Business School.

Mair, Johanna, Jeffrey Robinson, and Kai Hockerts, eds. 2006. *Social Entrepreneurship*. New York: Palgrave Macmillan.

Manfredi, Francesco. 2005. "Social Responsibility in the Concept of the Social Enterprise as a Cognitive System." *International Journal of Public Administration* 28: 835–48.

Manimala, Mathew J. 1992. "Entrepreneurial Heuristics: A Comparison between High PI (Pioneering-Innovative) and Low PI Ventures." *Journal of Business Venturing* 7, no. 6: 477–504.

Mohan-Neill, Sumaria Indra. 1995. "The Influence of Firm's Age and Size on Its Environmental Scanning Activities." *Journal of Small Business Management* 30: 10–21.

Moon, Myung Jae. 1999. "The Pursuit of Managerial Entrepreneurship: Does Organization Matter?" *Public Administration Review* 59: 31–43.

Mort, Gillian Sullivan, Jay Weerawardena, and Kashonia Carnegie. 2003. "Social Entrepreneurship: Towards Conceptualization." *International Journal of Nonprofit and Voluntary Sector Marketing* 8: 76–88.

Nicholls, Alex, ed. 2006. *Social Entrepreneurship: New Models of Sustainable Social Change.* Oxford University Press.

Peredo, Ana Maria, and Murdith McLean. 2006. "Social Entrepreneurship: A Critical Review of the Concept." *Journal of World Business* 41: 56–65.

Porter, Michael. 1980. *Competitive Strategy: Techniques for Analyzing Industries and Competitors.* New York: Free Press.

Prabhu, Ganesh N. 1999. "Social Entrepreneurial Leadership." *Career Development International* 4, no. 3: 14.

Reich, Robert B. 2001. "Entrepreneurship Reconsidered: the Team as Hero." *Harvard Business Review* 65: 77–83.

Reynolds, Paul D. 1991. "Sociology and Entrepreneurship: Concepts and Contributions." *Entrepreneurship Theory and Practice* 16: 47–70.

Roper, Juliet, and George Cheney. 2005. "Leadership, Learning and Human Resource Management: The Meanings of Social Entrepreneurship Today." *Corporate Governance* 5: 95–104.

Schumpeter, Joseph A. 1942. *Capitalism, Socialism, and Democracy.* New York: Harper & Brothers.

Seelos, Christian, and Johanna Mair. 2005. "Social Entrepreneurship: Creating New Business Models to Serve the Poor." *Business Horizons* 48: 241–46.

Sen, Pritha. 2007. "Ashoka's Big Idea: Transforming the World through Social Entrepreneurship." *Futures* 39: 534–53.

Shane, Scott A. 2008. *Illusions of Entrepreneurship: The Costly Myths that Entrepreneurs, Investors, and Policy Makers Live By.* Yale University Press.

Sharir, Moshe, Miri Lerner, and Ronit Yitshaki-Hagai. 2006. "Long Tem Survivability of Social Ventures: Qualitative Analysis of External and Internal Explanations." Paper prepared for the 2nd International Social Entrepreneurship Research Conference. New York University, Stern School of Business, April 7–9.

Shaver, Kelly G., and Linda R. Scott. 1991. "Person, Process, Choice: The Psychology of New Venture Creation." *Entrepreneurship Theory and Practice* 16: 23–45.

Shaw, Eleanor. 2004. "Marketing in the Social Enterprise Context: Is It Entrepreneurial?" *Qualitative Market Research: An International Journal* 7: 194–205.

Sim, Edward W., and others. 2007. "Exploring Difference between Inventors, Champions, Implementers and Innovators in Developing New Products in Large, Mature Firms." *Creativity and Innovation Management* 16: 422–36.

Simms, Shalei V. K., and Jeffrey Robinson. 2005. "Activist or Entrepreneur? An Identity-Based Model of Social Entrepreneurship." Paper prepared for the U.S. Association of Small Business and Entrepreneurship (USASBE) 2006 conference (paper submitted August 15, 2005). Tucson, Arizona, January 12–15, 2006.

Simsek, Zeki, Michael H. Lubatkin, and Steven W. Floyd. 2003. "Inter-Firm Networks and Entrepreneurial Behavior: A Structural Embeddedness Perspective." *Journal of Management* 29: 427–42.

Smith, Ken G., Martin J. Gannon, Curtis Grimm, and Terence R. Mitchell. 1988. "Decision Making Behavior in Smaller Entrepreneurial and Larger Professionally Managed Firms." *Journal of Business Venturing* 3: 223–232.

Solo, Carolyn Shaw. 1951. "Innovation in the Capitalist Process: A Critique of the Schumpeterian Theory. *Quarterly Journal of Economics* 65: 417–28.

Spear, Roger. 2006. "Social Entrepreneurship: A Different Model." *Internal Journal of Social Economics* 33: 399–410.

Stewart, Alex. 1991. "A Prospectus on the Anthropology of Entrepreneurship." *Entrepreneurship Theory and Practice* 16: 71–91.

Stopford, John M., and Charles W. F. Baden-Fuller. 1994. "Creating Corporate Entrepreneurship." *Strategic Management Journal* 15: 521–36.

Thornton, Patricia H. 1999. "The Sociology of Entrepreneurship." *Annual Review of Sociology* 25: 19–46.

Van de Ven, Andrew H., and Rhonda M. Engleman. 2004. "Event- and Outcome-Driven Explanations of Entrepreneurship." *Journal of Business Venturing* 19: 343–58.

Venkataraman, S., and Andrew H. Van de Ven. 1998. "Hostile Environmental Jolts, Transaction Set, and New Business." *Journal of Business Venturing* 13: 231–55.

Wallace, Sherri Leronda. 1999. "Social Entrepreneurship: The Role of Social Purpose Enterprises in Facilitating Community Economic Development." *Journal of Development Entrepreneurship* 4: 153–74.

Weick, Karl. 1995. *Sensemaking in Organizations.* London: Russell Sage.

Whyte, Glen, Alan M. Saks, and Sterling Hook. 1997. "When Success Breeds Failure: The Role of Self-Efficacy in Escalating Commitment to a Losing Course of Action." *Journal of Organizational Behavior* 18: 415–32.

Wickham, Phillip A. 2003. "The Representativeness Heuristic in Judgments Involving Entrepreneurial Success and Failure." *Management Decision* 41: 156–67.

Williams, David R., W. Jack Duncan, and Peter M. Ginter. 2006. "Structuring Deals and Governance after the IPO: Entrepreneurs and Venture Capitalists in High Tech Startups." *Business Horizons* 49: 303–11.

Zacharakis, Andrew L., and Dean A. Shepherd. 2001. "The Nature of Information and Overconfidence on Venture Capitalists' Decision Making." *Journal of Business Venturing* 16: 311–32.

INDEX